Serial Killers

From The Case Files of

and

J F Derry

Contents

PREFACE viii

PAST 1 – 8

Vlad the Impaler (Romania)
Elizabeth Báthory (Hungary)
Gilles de Rais (France)
Gilles Garnier (France)
Peter Stumpp (Germany)
Darya Nikolayevna Saltykova (Russia)
Lewis Hutchinson (Jamaica)
Micajah Harpe (USA)
Wiley Harpe (USA)
William Burke (Scotland)
William Hare (Scotland)
Thug Behram (India)
William Palmer (England)
Mary Ann Cotton (England)
John Flickinger (USA)
The Austin Axe Murderer (USA)
Amelia Dyer (England)
Maria Swanenburg (Netherlands)
Belle Gunness (USA)
William Gohl (USA)
George Joseph Smith (England)
Béla Kiss (Hungary)
Carl Großmann (Germany)
Jack the Ripper (England)

BATTERERS

Yang Xinhai (China) 9
Ramadan Abdel Rehim Mansour (Egypt) 10
Raya and Sakina (Egypt) 12
Abdul Latif Sharif (USA, Mexico) 14
Donald Neilson (England) 16
Levi Bellfield (England) 17
Alexander Pichushkin (Russia) 19
Theodore Robert "Ted" Bundy (USA) 21

Serial Killers

First published in 2012

A catalogue record for this book is available from the British Library

ISBN: 978-0-857331-80-9

Published by Haynes Publishing, Sparkford, Yeovil,
Somerset BA22 7JJ, UK
Tel: 01963 442030 Fax: 01963 440001
Int. tel: +44 1963 442030 Int. fax: +44 1963 440001
E-mail: sales@haynes.co.uk
Website: www.haynes.co.uk

Haynes North America Inc., 861 Lawrence Drive, Newbury Park, California 91320, USA

Images © Mirrorpix

Creative Director: Kevin Gardner
Designed for Haynes by BrainWave

Printed and bound in the US

BEHEADERS

William Lee Cody Neal (USA) 27
Edmund Emil Kemper III (USA) 31
Herbert Mullin (USA) 31

BOMBERS

Glennon Engleman (USA) 44
Theodore Kaczynski (USA) 45

SHOOTERS

Edward Theodore Gein (USA) 54
Robert (Willie) Pickton (Canada) 61
David Berkowitz (USA) 63
John George Haigh (England) 68
Stephen Griffiths (England) 69
Richard Ramirez (USA) 73
Richard Leonard Kuklinski (USA) 76
Giuseppe Greco (Italy) 78

STABBERS

Luis Alfredo Garavito (Columbia) 79
Peter Tobin (England, Scotland) 80
Peter Manuel (Scotland) 82
Henry Lee Lucas (USA) 83
Ottis Toole (USA) 83

POISONERS

Beverley Gail Allitt (England) 86
Waltraud Wagner (Austria) 92
Javed Iqbal Mughal (Pakistan) 93
Georgia Tann (USA) 94
Miyuki Ishikawa (Japan) 94
Júlia Fazekas (Hungary) 96
Vera Renczi (Romania) 96
John Bodkin Adams (England) 97
Graham Frederick Young (England) 100
Arnfinn Nesset (Norway) 101
Edson Izidoro Guimarães (Brazil) 102
Orville Lynn Majors (USA) 102
Harold Frederick Shipman (England) 103

RIPPERS

Peter Sutcliffe (England) 107

Gordon Cummins (England) 111
Anthony John Hardy (England) 112
John Sweeney (England) 116

REAPERS
Henry Howard Holmes (USA) 123
John Wayne Gacy (USA) 126
Gerald Gallego (USA) 133
David Birnie (Australia) 137
Delfina González Valenzuela (Mexico) 140
María de Jesús González Valenzuela (Mexico) 140

KEEPERS
Leonard Lake (USA) 142
Charles Chi-Tat Ng (USA) 142
Gary Heidnik (USA) 146
Marc Dutroux (Belgium) 149
David Parker Ray (USA) 152

CANNIBALS
Andrei Romanovich Chikatilo (Russia) 159
Dean Corll (USA) 162
Leonarda Cianciulli (Italy) 164
Pedro Rodrigues Filho (Brazil) 165
Shen Changping (China) 166
Shen Changyin (China) 166
Nikolai Dzhumagaliev (Uzbekistan) 167
Albert Fish (USA) 167

STRANGLERS
Pedro Alonso López (Columbia) 172
Daniel Camargo Barbosa (Columbia) 177
John Reginald Christie (England) 178
Ahmad Suradji (Indonesia) 178
Jürgen Bartsch (Germany) 179
Kenneth Bianchi (USA) 180
Angelo Buono (USA) 180
Ian Brady (England) 181
Myra Hindley (England) 181
Paul Bernardo (Canada) 184
Karla Homolka (Canada) 185
Robert Black (Scotland) 185

Dennis Rader (USA) 187
Jack Unterweger (Austria) 188
Gary Leon Ridgway (USA) 189
Steven Gerald James Wright (England) 190
Jeffrey Dahmer (USA) 193

SMOTHERERS

Dennis Andrew Nilsen (England) 195
Fritz Haarmann (Germany) 199
Serhiy Tkach (Ukraine) 200
Donald Henry Gaskins, Jr (USA) 200
Frederick West (England) 201
Rosemary West (England) 201

OTHERS 208 – 212

The Lima Ripper (Peru)
The Axeman of New Orleans (USA)
The Cleveland Torso Murderer (USA)
Jack the Stripper (England)
The Zodiac Killer (USA)
The Capital City Murderer (USA)
The Monster of Florence (Italy)
The Highway of Tears Killer (Canada)
The Black Doodler (USA)
The Family Murderers (Australia)
The Original Night Stalker (USA)
The Toronto Hospital Murderer (Canada)
The Tynong Murderer (Australia)
The Frankford Slasher (USA)
The Stoneman (India)
The Hwaseong Murderer (South Korea)
The Beer Man (India)
The Rainbow Maniac (Brazil)
The Long Island Serial Killer (USA)
The Nanjing Killer (China)
The Orange County Killer (USA)
The Hollywood Ripper (USA)
The Dating Game Killer (USA)
The Grim Sleeper (USA)
The Speed Freak Killers (USA)

PREFACE

There's method in his madness
William Shakespeare

Lust, power, madness and money drive our lives, pitching us against others in a daily competition, a daily struggle for survival. But however much these conflicts arouse hostility towards others, we know the difference between right and wrong, and most of us do not act on our impulses. Most of us know when to stop. Most of us.

Serial killers have always been a part of human society. As far back as we can trace, there have been individuals who have killed without justification, not sanctioned by any law, not as part of any war, but murdering for their own means. Their motivations range from simple greed, lust and thrills, through to grand plans for saving the world. They usually revolve around domination and control, and most involve sexual deviance.

Unstable and abusive childhoods are common too, along with poor education but high IQs. The killers may have had strict parents, sometimes devout, sometimes incestuous, or they might have been ridiculed as a child, perhaps emasculated or mocked for bed-wetting. Their frustrations are often expressed through torturing animals – as a forerunner to their human victims – and petty crime. But it's usually not until they become adults that their past fully catches up with them and their childhood games mature into murder. They can often be seen as people obstructed from realizing their full potential, they are frustrated and angered by their past. They are also psychopaths.

There are an alarming number of people, estimated at one in every hundred, that we mix with every day, in the street, at work, even at home, who do not share our moral code. They are certifiable psychopaths who lack empathy and remorse. Mix the psychopath's cold-heartedness and disconnection from the rest of society with the pressures and urges of everyday life, and you have a time bomb primed to go off. You have someone who does not live within the rules. You have the makings of a serial killer.

It was an urge ... A strong urge, and the longer I let it go the stronger it got, to where I was taking risks to go out and kill people risks that normally, according to my little rules of operation, I wouldn't take because they could lead to arrest.

Edmund Kemper

This book takes an original look at serial murder; it is organized by bringing serial killers who used similar methods to murder their victims together, and there are so many ways to kill someone: bloodletting, bludgeoning, burying alive, blowing up, drowning, poisoning, shooting, stabbing, starving, strangling and suffocating. Each chapter begins with a description of the kind of people you will encounter, their crimes, what they did in graphic detail and, where appropriate, their histories and psychology, and motivations. Their despicable acts go far beyond any notion of decency, beyond your worst imaginings and deep into the realm of horror.

Unlike other murderers, many serial killers rape, torture and mutilate their victims, who are often left bitten, burned, cannibalized, castrated, decapitated, disembowelled, dismembered, with eyes and feet and breasts removed, heads crushed, and sometimes skinned. The killers often stalk their victim before attacking, are always in cold-blooded control and know exactly what they want. I make no apology for the goriness in telling you about this. There is no hiding from the revolting state that they left their victims. There is no hiding from them.

PAST

So far as he is able, a prince should stick to the path of good but, if the necessity arises, he should know how to follow evil
Niccolò Machiavelli

The name "serial killer" probably derived from the American term "serial homicide" in the 1970s, itself possibly coined from the British "serial murder" used in the 1960s. But there have always been mass murderers. In medieval times their crimes might have been blamed on werewolves and vampires. In reality, the human perpetrator matched the monster, and was probably more evil.

If ever there was evil personified then it came in the form of Vlad III, Prince of Wallachia, also known as the "son of the Dragon". In his native Romanian tongue, this translated as "Dracula". Thanks to Bram Stoker's classic novel and numerous film adaptations, we have a fixed idea about the vampire count, but this prince earned his reputation for something equally sinister and bloodthirsty during his rule in the mid-fifteenth century. It also earned him the nickname "Vlad the Impaler". A total of 10,000 enemy soldiers and civilians were tortured and executed by his command, but his legacy stems from the estimated 20,000 people he had impaled alive on stakes outside the city walls of his capital. He was assassinated in 1476.

A century later in neighbouring Hungary, Vlad's female counterpart was born. Countess Erzsébet Báthory de Ecsed (also known as Elizabeth Báthory) and her collaborators were said to have abducted or lured over 600 young women to her castle with promises of paid work, before torturing and killing them. Methods of torture were said to include mutilation, beatings, burning and starvation. Legend has it that the countess bathed in the blood of virgins to keep her youth, which led to her nicknames of "The Blood Countess" and "Countess Dracula". She was arrested in 1610 along with four accomplices, and died in her castle under house arrest in 1614.

Contemporaneous with Vlad the Impaler was Gilles de Montmorency-Laval, Baron de Rais, whose daring and often reckless exploits as a young man saw him rise quickly to high rank and gained him an array of honours, not least at the famous Siege of Orléans where he fought alongside Joan of Arc. After retiring from active service, he dabbled in the occult, and discovered a passion for the torture and murder of children, who were abducted from the local area by his henchmen. We know from confessions made at his trial that de Rais would toy with his victims, hanging them with rope from a hook and masturbating over them, then taking them down and pretending to comfort them before maiming and killing them.

> To practise his debauches with the said boys and girls, against the dictation of nature, he first took his rod in his hand and rubbed it so it became erect and sticking out; then placing it between the limbs of the boys or girls, not bothering with the natural female receptacle, and rubbed his rod or virile member on the belly of the said boys and girls with much libidinous excitement until he emitted his sperm on their stomachs.

He used a variety of methods, including decapitation, for which he kept a specific sword, breaking necks or cutting throats. He would often dismember the bodies, and slash the children's abdomens, sodomizing their neck stumps and innards, or, sitting on their dismembered stomachs, would laugh as he watched them die.

> He had considerable pleasure in watching the heads of children separated from their bodies. Sometimes he made an incision behind the neck to make them die slowly, at which he became very excited, and while they were bleeding to death he would sometimes masturbate on them, and sometimes he would do this after they had died and their bodies were still warm.

He burned the bodies piece by piece in the fire in his room, disposing of the ash around his estate. More than 600 children may have met their end this way. He met his end in 1440 along with two of his accomplices, being burned at the stake. Charles Perrault's 1697 fairy tale *Bluebeard* was probably based upon his story.

As well as vampires, serial killers were hailed as real-life werewolves. Gilles Garnier, also known as "The Hermit of St Bonnot" and "The Werewolf of Dole", lived a hermit's existence in the Franche-Comté province of France. Struggling to find food for himself and his wife, he supposedly welcomed a spectre's gift of a magic ointment with supernatural powers that could transform him into a wolf, which he used to prey on children, eating their raw flesh off the bone. He was burned at the stake in 1573.

Peter Stumpp was a German farmer known as the "Werewolf of

Bedburg". Over 25 years, he cannibalized untold numbers of men and women, as well as 14 children. His victims included two pregnant women and their foetuses, and his own son. During his trial, he admitted to an incestuous relationship with his daughter, which automatically condemned her to a death penalty. They were both executed in 1589.

In the mid-eighteenth century, Darya Nikolayevna Saltykova was a wealthy Russian of noble descent who married well but was widowed young, leaving her with a substantial estate, staffed largely by local young women. Early complaints that members of staff had died at the estate were not investigated for some time, leaving her free to continue to beat, torture and murder up to 147 victims with impunity. She was given a life sentence in 1768 and died in 1801.

Lewis Hutchinson was born in Scotland where he studied medicine, but emigrated to Jamaica in the 1760s to run an estate by the name of "Edinburgh Castle". At first, Hutchinson's crimes were to build up his own stock of cattle by stealing from neighbours, but, soon afterwards, travellers in the sparsely populated vicinity of the estate started to disappear. Often he would shoot passers-by with his rifle for sport. Other times he would offer shelter and hospitality, only to murder his guests after he had fed them. He may have killed more than 43 people, dismembering his victims and drinking their blood, before throwing their body parts into a pit for his animals to feed on. He was tried and hanged in 1773.

Micajah "Big" Harpe and Wiley "Little" Harpe were brothers who assaulted, robbed and murdered indiscriminately, earning themselves the nickname "The Bloody Harpes". A favourite method was to slash their victim's body open, fill it with stones and throw it into a river. Micajah allegedly killed his own baby daughter by smashing her head against a tree because her crying irritated him. A posse captured Big Harpe in 1799 and stuck his head on a pole at a crossroads in Webster County, Kentucky, still known as "Harpe's Head". Little Harpe was tried and hanged in 1804. They are regarded as America's first serial killers.

William Burke and William Hare sold the corpses of their murder victims to the Edinburgh medical and anatomy schools purely for profit. There may have been as many as 30 victims between 1827 and 1828, although 16 is the more commonly accepted tally. A body left under a bed led to their downfall. Hare turned King's evidence and fled the country, whereas Burke was hanged in Edinburgh's Lawnmarket in 1829, watched by 25,000 spectators. Ironically, he was then dissected. His skeleton still hangs in the University of Edinburgh's medical school, and his skin was made into various items, including the cover for a pocketbook, currently on display in the Surgeons' Hall Museum, Edinburgh.

Belonging to the Thuggee cult in India, from which English gets the word "thug", which targeted groups of travellers, robbing and murdering them, Thug Behram was one of the world's most prolific serial killers. Some sources suggest he murdered close to 1,000 victims in a 50-year-long murderous career beginning in 1790. All his victims were strangled using his ceremonial cummerbund, which he embellished with a large and heavy medallion, skilfully positioned on the victim's throat to add greater pressure. He was hanged in 1840.

William Palmer, known as "The Rugeley Poisoner" and "The Prince of Poisoners", was an English doctor thought to have murdered his brother, his mother-in-law, and four of his children before they reached their first birthday. In all cases, cause of death was "convulsions" and as it was common for children to die as infants, this didn't arouse suspicion. Palmer was greedy and miserly, running up debts from betting on horses. He murdered his wife and cashed in her life insurance to feed his gambling addiction and service his debts, and then tried the same trick after goading his alcoholic brother into an early death. However, the insurance company refused to pay up and recommended a full investigation into the deaths. When he was convicted of the murder of his friend and associate John Cook by poisoning, questions were asked about the earlier deaths in his family, and it was suggested that he poisoned his children rather than meet the cost of feeding them. Thirty thousand spectators turned out to see his hanging at Stafford Prison in 1856. Stepping up to the trapdoor, Palmer is reported to have asked the executioner, "Are you sure it's safe?" When you are next asked, "What's your poison?" it may be a reference to the not-so-good doctor.

Mary Ann Cotton's father was a devoutly religious and very strict miner. As a consequence she found it difficult to make friends. However, she did manage to marry four times, with three of her husbands and all 12 of her children dying, usually after developing stomach pains. She had administered arsenic in order to collect the life insurance. She was found out on the death of her 12th child but the date of her trial was delayed in order for her to have her 13th child in prison. She was hanged in 1873.

The so-called "Bloody Benders" were a group of murderers posing as a family led by John Flickinger, who ran a small shop and inn from 1872 to 1873, and routinely killed their guests. So many travellers passing through the area went missing that people started to avoid it. Several bodies were found in the creek, with their skulls crushed and throats cut. In a well-practised routine, guests to the inn would be offered a particular seat at the table, above a trapdoor. The unsuspecting guest would be bludgeoned and his throat cut, before the body was dropped through the trapdoor. Eventually, suspicion for the missing people fell on the Bender family, who fled from their home. After an exhaustive search of their property, 19 bodies and a large number of body parts were found buried under the house. In almost all cases, the victims had had their heads smashed with a hammer, and their throats cut. The Benders escaped, but several accomplices in a wide network used to launder the victims' belongings were arrested.

"The Austin Axe Murderer" or "The Servant Girl Annihilator" killed at least seven women and one man, and seriously injured six women and two men, in the city of Austin, Texas, between 1884 and 1885. In all cases, victims were attacked while asleep in their beds, some were dragged outside while unconscious but still alive to meet their death. The victims' bodies were posed, and six of the murdered females were found with sharp objects pushed into their ears.

Amelia Dyer, also known as "The Ogress of Reading", trained as a nurse but soon turned her attention to "baby farming" as a more lucrative career, whereby she accepted money to take care of babies, although in actual fact she allowed them to perish. At first she starved them, administering opiates or alcohol to sedate unsettled babies, which often resulted in an earlier death. But she soon realized it would be easier and more profitable to hasten their deaths, strangling her 400 or so victims with a white tape and disposing of the bodies. She was hanged in 1896.

Maria Swanenburg is thought to have poisoned up to a hundred people with arsenic in Leiden, South Holland. Many of her attempts failed, but left her victims with lasting chronic health problems. She was motivated by greed, ensuring that she benefited financially from many of her victims' deaths, either by claiming their life insurance or inheriting from them. Her first victims were her own parents. She was given a life sentence in 1883, and died in 1915.

A Norwegian who emigrated to America, Belle Gunness, a large and immensely strong woman, was apparently assaulted at a country dance when she was pregnant with her first baby, causing her to miscarry. It is said that her character changed as a result of this incident. Her assailant was never prosecuted but died shortly after the incident, apparently of stomach cancer, although it seems probable that he was Gunness' first victim and gave her a taste for murder. Gunness' first husband also died, apparently on the only day that two life insurance policies overlapped, and although some of her husband's relatives suspected that she had poisoned him, both insurance policies paid out. There are conflicting stories about how many children Gunness went on to have, and what happened to them but the most popular account suggests that she had four children, two of whom died of acute colitis as babies. Both had life insurance, which was paid out. Gunness' second husband also met an early death, apparently due to an unfortunate accident in the house. Over the years that followed, Gunness had a number of suitors, some of whom were attracted by a newspaper advertisement, an early "lonely hearts". Gunness murdered each after cheating them out of their life savings, or collecting their life insurance. She apparently ordered a number of large trunks, presumably for concealing bodies, and was thought to bury others in the hog pit, in which locals observed her digging at night. The precise number of her victims is unknown, but when her home was searched and the grounds excavated, a large number of body parts were found. She is thought to be responsible for at least 40 deaths, but she escaped capture, despite an arson attempt on her life in 1908 by one of her suitors, after which she disappeared.

William "Billy" Gohl murdered dozens of sailors passing through Washington State until his capture in 1910. Involved in a range of criminal activity, he was suspected of the killing of many migrant workers found dead on the shore close to where he worked as a bartender. Sailors returning from time at sea often had money. If Gohl ascertained that a sailor had valuables but no relatives close by who would miss him, that man would become Gohl's next victim. He simply shot his victims in the head, stole their valuables and threw them into the river. Gohl was eventually charged with two counts of murder and died in 1927 while serving a life sentence.

As well as being a serial killer, George Joseph Smith was also a serial bigamist, clocking up seven marriages in six years. Known as the "Brides in the Bath Murderer", he killed his victims by pulling their legs upwards while they were in the bath, causing a sudden flood of water into the nose and throat, leading to instantaneous loss of consciousness. The case was significant in legal terms, being one of the first where forensic pathology was used to solve the case, and where similarities between crimes were used to prove intent on the part of the perpetrator. He was convicted and hanged in 1915.

Béla Kiss, a Hungarian tinsmith who dabbled in both astrology and the occult is rumoured to have killed at least 24 young women. He stored their bodies on his property in huge metal drums, filled with pickling liquid. The search of his house in 1916 also revealed letters from some 74 women, together with photographs, and many books about poison and strangulation. It seems that he was motivated by greed, attempting to swindle money out of the many women he corresponded with, and killing them if they became difficult. Kiss evaded arrest despite many rumours about his whereabouts and some potential sightings, none of which were ever confirmed.

Carl Großmann had sadistic sexual tendencies and had multiple convictions for child molestation. Many young women visited him in his flat and it is thought that at least 50 were murdered there. Großmann traded meat on the black market, and apparently ran a hot dog stand. Rumour has it that, like Fritz Haarmann, the meat he sold and served was the human flesh of his victims. He was arrested in 1921 when screams were heard and the alarm was raised, and a young woman he had just killed was discovered in his apartment. He was given a death sentence but committed suicide in his cell.

"Jack the Ripper", also known as "The Whitechapel Murderer" is considered the forerunner to all modern serial killers. The murders were horrific, the mutilation of victims unparalleled, and even though the victim count wasn't as terrible as the tallies we have seen already, and others that we will meet later, the impact on the media and the public alike was immeasurable. Really, it was in the pages of the daily rags that his fame was immediately sealed. Newspapers strove to outdo each other with their gory reporting and exclusive interviews in a circulation battle. The first policemen to arrive on the scenes were a source of great spectacle:

> *"Well, I can tell you it didn't take me a moment to see that the Whitechapel murderer had been our way. Her head lay here on this coal-hole," said he, throwing the light of his lantern on it, "and her clothes were thrown up breast-high. But the first thing I noticed was that she was ripped up like a pig in the market. There was the big gash up the stomach, the entrails torn out and flung in a heap about her neck; some of them appeared to be lying in the ugly cut at the throat, and the face – well, there was no face. Anyone who knew the woman alive would never recognise her by her face. I have been in the force a long while, but I never saw such a sight."*

Since then, the murders have been immortalized in literature, and on stage and screen, and the wealth of alternative versions of the story in all manner of media has conflated reality and fiction, so creating a super-villain character more suited to the pages of a comic book. And yet, the identity of the killer remains a mystery and will probably do so forever more.

That doesn't stop amateur sleuths proposing their own suspects. This has been going on ever since the first of the Ripper's five murders in August 1888. In total there may have possibly been as many as 11, stretching to February 1891, although these others are often considered to be copycat killings, or unrelated. The names of the known prostitute victims, "the Canonical five", are almost as famous as their killer. They are: Mary Ann Nichols, Annie Chapman, Elizabeth Stride, Catherine Eddowes and Mary

Jane Kelly. But that still leaves the mystery of the Ripper's name.

There have been over 30 suspects in the Ripper case, including Prince Albert Victor, Duke of Clarence and Avondale, and Charles Dodgson, otherwise known as "Lewis Carroll". As a contemporary of Jack the Ripper, it was even suggested that Amelia Dyer herself was the Ripper, but, as in the cases of many of the other suspects, there is no evidence to support these claims.

Recent developments include the diary of the Ripper coming to light in 1992, and purportedly written by Liverpool cotton merchant James Maybrick, who would have been 49 years old at the time of the first Ripper murder. A watch engraved with, "J. Maybrick", the initials of the five victims and "I am Jack" also appeared a year later. Both artefacts appear to match the correct age expected for being over a century old, but experts have found inconsistencies in certain details and consider them a hoax. However, Maybrick has also been suggested as a suspect for "The Austin Axe Murderer" despite little evidence. An anonymous Malay cook has also been suggested to be both of these murderers. Most recently, the great-great-grandson of Henry Howard Holmes has claimed that handwriting by his infamous relative matches that of the Ripper.

A further question surrounding the Ripper case is why did the killings stop abruptly in 1891? One suggestion is that the start of similar murders in New York and other US cities coincided with the Ripper moving there. A letter that appeared to be in the same handwriting as those sent to London police was received by a New York newspaper in 1893, mentioning details of a previous murder that supposedly only the Ripper would know.

If true, then there is good evidence that the identity of the Ripper is known. James Kelly, a skilled furniture upholsterer, stabbed his wife in the neck in 1883 and was incarcerated in Broadmoor, but escaped in 1888 to coincide with the start of the Whitechapel murders. He disappeared until 1927 when he gave himself up to police, but is known to have travelled in the USA between the dates corresponding to the murders there. His profession would have given him the knife skills observed in the disembowelling of the victims – although not necessarily the surgical skills – and he is known to have been vehemently opposed to the immorality of prostitutes. If, on the other hand, this is merely coincidence, we may never know the true identity of this, the most notorious serial killer.

BATTERERS

Genius is always allowed some leeway, once the hammer has been pried from its hands and the blood has been cleaned up
Terry Pratchett

Beating someone to death is one of the most brutal ways to kill. The victim may be knocked unconscious by the first blow, rendering them defenceless against the killer tying them up, gagging them, raping them, killing them by some other means. Sometimes the severity of the blows gives us a measure of the killer's rage, skulls smashed and heads split open. Then, there is never any doubt about the cause of death.

Yang Xinhai
A.K.A. The Monster Killer
COUNTRY China
VICTIMS 67
METHOD bludgeoned

Yang Xinhai was a serial offender, being repeatedly imprisoned for rape and attempted rape, until he modified his criminal behaviour in 2000 to include murder. One possible catalyst for this change was breaking up with his girlfriend because of his previous convictions. Whatever his motivation, Yang displayed typical serial killer psychopathy, "Killing people is very usual, nothing special [...] When I killed people I had a desire. This inspired me to kill more. I don't care whether they deserve to live or not. It is none of my concern [...] I have no desire to be part of society. Society is not my concern."

Anyone in the homes Yang broke into at night, mainly farmsteads, would be killed in their sleep by blows from hammers, axes and shovels. Each time, he dressed in new clothes and outsized shoes, and used a brand new implement, all of which he discarded immediately after.

Because of widespread communal living in rural China, this meant that he would often eradicate whole families. One hammer attack left a father and his 6-year-old daughter dead and the pregnant wife raped and with serious head injuries. In December 2002, Yang killed a farmer and his mother, wife, son and daughter. The farmer's father escaped only because he was staying at a new house that the family were due to move into a few days later. The elderly man recalled, "seeing his granddaughter that fateful morning. She was lying on the ground, with a hole in her head. The room was full of blood."

Yang was apprehended in 2003 because, during a routine police check, he looked suspicious; he was charged with "crimes of intentional homicide, willful and malicious injury, pillage and rape". He quickly confessed to 65 murders and 23 rapes, and was sentenced to death in February 2004. He was executed by a gunshot to the back of the head soon afterwards.

Ramadan Abdel Rehim Mansour
A.K.A. al-Tourbini (The Express Train)
COUNTRY Egypt
VICTIMS 30
METHOD bludgeoned, drowned

The usual response to the capture of a serial killer is astonished silence. Very rarely does their arrest shock the public's social conscience into emphatic consternation, causing an eruption of national fervour and an outpouring of disgust that someone so vile could live amongst them, be free to operate as they want and perpetrate their crimes. A parliamentary investigation resulted from the apprehension of Marc Dutroux because Belgians were so stunned by the failure of their legal system to locate and contain such a monster in their midst. Dutrouxes everywhere applied to change their surname. Recently, Egypt has experienced its own decent into darkness. When the latest serial killer was caught, and his nickname started being used in marketing campaigns for small businesses, some claimed it was "incomprehensible" and that it, "clearly indicates is that something has gone terribly wrong with contemporary Egyptian society".

Ramadan Abdel Rehim Mansour went the way of many youngsters in Cairo. Poverty, abuse, lack of education and caring support made home life an unattractive proposition, so he left the small town of Tanta, the provincial capital of Gharbia, at an early age and joined a street gang in the city. Thousands of children live on the streets of Cairo and other Egyptian cities. There are so many now that passers-by don't notice them anymore. The problem has got out of hand and they are so numerous that no one wants to take responsibility for them. It would be too big an undertaking. Despite this many think the problem is "blown out of proportion" or "exaggerated" and so choose to ignore the children instead.

Mansour was more attentive, noticing these children and seeing a ready supply of anonymous and therefore susceptible victims.

Street gang life hardened Mansour, shaping him into the criminal he became. Gang leaders both taught and tortured him. He learnt how to survive on the streets by doing their bidding. Do something wrong and he would be punished with razors cuts. This was just correctional. The usual route to revenge was rape, and the gangs were abundantly vengeful, knowing they were safe from retribution. The punishment for threatening to go to the police was death. When Mansour tried to sexually assault his fellow gang member, a 12-year-old boy Ahmed Nagui, Nagui sought protection from the police, but Mansour was released for lack of evidence. Mansour immediately raped Nagui in revenge, then murdered him for his disloyalty. It wasn't long before Mansour had risen to the rank of gang leader himself.

As in other Arabic nations, homosexuality in Egypt is a serious taboo. While homosexuality itself is not illegal, a gay man can be convicted for debauchery and defamation of Islam, which are illegal, and carry a sentence of five years' hard labour. It is sufficient for a policeman to see that a man is not wearing traditional baggy white cotton underwear to raise a suspicion of his being gay, and to bring about a conviction. Consequently, gay rights are almost unheard of, and sex between any males can only ever be possible as rape, and, therefore, as a punishment.

It is arguable whether Mansour's motivations were pleasure or punishment, but if he was exacting revenge on wider society that had put him on the streets then his targets were defenceless and pitifully vulnerable. Over the course of a seven-year period, an alarming number of dead and seriously injured street children were found along a certain stretch of railway track running between Cairo and Alexandria. They had all been raped and tortured and then thrown onto the trackside, discarded to die. Mansour and his gang were known to travel this route regularly. They favoured the smaller police presence in Alexandria compared to the large force in the capital, which Mansour moaned, "is swarming with cops".

Ironically, it was a diligent vice squad in Alexandria that started keeping tabs on the gang, but the big break came when they arrested 18-year-old Ahmed Samir Abdel Moneim, nicknamed Boqqo, and Mansour's right-hand man, the 19-year-old Mohammed Abdel Aziz Salama, known as El-Seweisi. Salama had left home at the age of 7, when his father, who worked in the Ministry of Education, kicked him out of the house, for reasons forgotten. The only way to survive on the streets was to be part of a larger group – safety in numbers – so he joined up with other street children who taught him how to steal food and beg.

Moneim and Salama confessed to the murder of 14 victims in Cairo,

Alexandria, El-Behaira, Gharbeyya, Qalyoubeya and Beni Sueif. They admitted that they had lured street children onto the tops of trains en route from Cairo to Alexandria, where they then raped them and tossed the naked bodies onto the opposite tracks. Other victims were drowned in the Nile, stuffed down drains, dumped in sewers or buried alive. It wasn't long before Mansour was arrested and brought in for questioning; he told prosecutors that he was possessed by a female jinn who ordered him to rape 10 to 14-year-old children.

People deal with the shock of serial killers very differently. One way of coping is by using dark humour, a show of bravado and opportunism, often distasteful to others. That was certainly true of the evidently mercenary use of Mansour's capture as a marketing strategy. Nicknamed "al-Tourbini" (The Express Train) for his chosen mode of transport when carrying out his crimes, restaurants in Mansour's hometown, Tanta, started advertising "al-Tourbini sandwiches", tuk-tuk drivers suddenly started calling their vehicles "al-Tourbini", and telecommunications businesses were renamed "al-Tourbini: The Butcher of Gharbia". It's very possible that soon they will have no shortage of serial killer names to choose from. Several street gangs are reported to be kidnapping and raping Egyptian street children.

Raya and Sakina
COUNTRY Egypt
VICTIMS 17+
METHOD suffocated, strangled

Mansour has joined the dubious ranks of Egyptian multiple murderers. Ancient history is littered with mass killings, such as that of 70,000 newborn male infants on the command of Ramses II who feared a prophecy of a future challenger for his throne. But in modern times Raya and Sakina hold the crown for most infamous.

Born around the turn of the century in Upper Egypt (the higher ground in the south), they later moved northwards towards the port city of Alexandria, where Raya met and married Hasaballah, a thief and hashish smuggler, while her young sister Sakina worked in a brothel until Abdel-Aal fell in love with her and they moved to troubled Alexandria. The First World War was over for this pivotal allied port, but ongoing civil unrest throughout the main centres of Egypt kept the security forces busy, giving rise to a crime spree that carried on unchecked and was only questioned by the press, but too late:

Where are the police? Where is the sword of government that
should fall on the necks of bloodthirsty criminals? Where is
the vigilant eye of justice that should never wink? Where is the
mighty hand of authority? Indeed, the government has been
too intent upon training the hordes of its secret political police
to concern itself with training forces necessary to safeguard
our internal security or personal safety. It is time for us to
ask it to address the dangers posed by that negligence. The
recent murders are a great calamity, the horrors of which have
blackened the forehead of the 20th century.

The murders mentioned had begun in 1919. Soon after reaching Alexandria, the entrepreneurial Raya and Sakina opened a chain of brothels, locating them conveniently close to a British soldier camp, mosques and the poorest district of the city, Labban. In no time they were involved in protection rackets, prostitution, alcohol, drugs, theft, racketeering and, ultimately, murder. The papers reported, "Women slaughtered in Labban." While clearing the drainage well beneath his home a man had discovered the skull and remains of a woman. Sakina had been a recent tenant. Nearby, an undercover policeman was suspicious about the strong smell of incense wafting from the house he was passing. A search unearthed three more dead women in various stages of decomposition. It was Raya's house. In total, 17 corpses were found on the brothel sites.

The ensuing investigation and confessions revealed two types of victim and the murder method, incriminating the sisters, their husbands and two male accomplices, Orabi and Abdul Razik, who worked as bouncers at the brothel. Typically, Raya would go to the marketplace...

Where she would single out the woman wearing the most
jewellery. She would strike up a conversation with her about the
wares and prices in the store they happened to be in or standing
in front of. If she found the woman responsive, she would work
the conversation around to saying that she had come into
possession of some wares from the customs zone which she had
for sale for cheap prices. Then she would invite the woman to
her home to see these wares. Sometimes she would use other
pretexts for luring women to her home, holding out the promise
of monetary reward or jewellery.

Once inside, the victim was offered a drink, one laced with sedative, and, when rendered incapable, Hasaballah would clamp a towel over the victim's mouth, Raya and Sakina would hold her down, Orabi and

Abdul Razik would hold her hands behind her back and Abdel-Aal would pin down her feet until she stopped breathing. Stealing from the corpse was then a matter of course. Others died because they "knew too much about their activities". One such unfortunate, "was being paid to keep her mouth shut. Evidently, they feared her gabbing tongue because she would taunt them about what she knew, so they killed her to silence her once and for all."

At the same time as these murders, the papers were also running the headline, "Women disappear in Tanta." In a similar sting Mahmoud Allam, with his wife and a female accomplice, murdered women and prostitutes for their jewellery. Desperately looking for a cause of this criminality, the murders were blamed on the shared depravity of Tanta and Alexandria, "British alcoholic beverages are now being sold in Cairo at lower prices than in London. Hashish and cocaine are available everywhere and easily procured."

There was a public outcry, a united moral outrage and widespread concern for social order in Egypt. Nonetheless, titillated tourists still flocked to the houses where the Raya and Sakina murders had taken place. The story had gripped the nation and their names became household ones, seeping into everyday language. Children were told to return home, "before Raya and Sakina get you". Misdemeanours were described as "doing a Raya and Sakina".

There was only one conclusion possible to this story, one that would challenge social mores almost to the extremes affected by the very murders. Allam had been sentenced to death, and Raya and Sakina would also have to be executed, but no Egyptian women had ever previously received the death penalty. The two sisters and their husbands plus a further two male accomplices, brothel bouncers Orabi and Abdul Razik, were sentenced to death in May 1921, but were not executed until December 1921. Their notoriety lives on to this day.

Abdul Latif Sharif
COUNTRIES USA, Mexico
VICTIMS 500+
METHOD bludgeoned

In contrast, perhaps the least known Egyptian serial killer is Abdul Latif Sharif, largely due to the doubt surrounding his final conviction, despite his track record, and because his crimes were committed on foreign soil. Born in Egypt in 1947, Sharif emigrated to New York in 1970 as a highly paid research chemist, became known for his drunken highly charged sex life, and developed a reputation for an obsessive interest in young girls. Losing his job for embezzlement in 1978, Sharif relocated to Pennsylvania where it was noted that there was a tendency for some of his girlfriends to mysteriously disappear. A couple of years later, while visiting his home an acquaintance noticed various possessions belonging to an ex-girlfriend, along with a muddy shovel in Sharif's porch.

In 1981 Sharif moved to a new job in Palm Beach, Florida; within a few months he had raped two young women but was bailed by his new employer, until the legal bills became too costly, at which point he was fired. Making a new matrimonial home in Gainesville, he beat his wife unconscious, prompting her to divorce him, but no charges were brought. He was only jailed in 1983 when a 23-year-old woman answered his ad for a live-in housekeeper, and was then beat and repeatedly raped by him; he threatened her by saying, "I will bury you out back in the woods. I've done it before, and I'll do it again."

Sharif was released in 1989, before the end of his 12-year sentence, even though he had escaped and had to be recaptured. Now living in Texas, a drink-driving offence in 1991 brought him to the attention of an ex-Florida official who recognized the previous offender. Deportation hearings dragged on, but were interrupted in 1993 when Sharif held a woman captive in his home and repeatedly raped her. A deal was struck with the authorities and he exited the USA, moving to Ciudad Juárez, in the Mexican Chihuahua desert. Very soon he became implicated – through allegations of rape and links to a 17-year-old rape and murder victim, Elizabeth Castro Garcia – to the sudden spate of dead female factory workers (*maquiladoras*) found in specific locations on the borders of the city. Tried and imprisoned for 30 years in 1999, Sharif was sent to the Chihuahua maximum-security jail, and died in 2006.

However, in a twist devastating to the local population, the *maquiladora* murders continued with exactly the same pattern ever since Sharif's incarceration. Nancy Gonzalez, a surviving 14-year-old rape victim identified her attacker as a bus driver for the factory, nicknamed "El Dracula", who confessed to his part in a conspiracy with four other bus drivers. They were paid $1,200 by Sharif for each murder committed and had to show him the victim's undergarments as proof. Demanding a minimum of two murders per month, it seems that Sharif had been able to maintain contact with his henchmen from prison via mobile phone. Every *maquiladora* murder is unlikely to have been committed by Sharif's gang as members of other groups and cartels have been found guilty. Nevertheless, within just the year prior to his arrest, 520 women and girls had been killed, and the toll, still mercilessly growing, is now estimated to be in its thousands. Again there has been a public outcry, a disbelief that this massacre can be allowed to continue, as summed up by Amnesty International:

> An environment has been created that is extremely conducive to committing crime and it allows many of the perpetrators to go free or to avoid being held to account [...] As everything has become dominated by gang-related violence, the limited changes that were made have been exposed, leaving in place the same culture in which misogyny and violence against women can flourish.

Donald Neilson
A.K.A. The Black Panther
COUNTRY England
VICTIMS 5
METHOD shot, bludgeoned

Bullied at school for the similarity of his surname, Nappey, to nappy, Donald Neilson changed his name when his daughter was born to avoid her suffering the same indignation. Neilson started his career in crime in order to supplement his meagre income as a failed builder. He carried out a lengthy string of 400 burglaries for which he was never caught. Neilson became increasingly greedy, graduating on to post office raids. As time went on he became more confident, violent and ruthless and killed three postmasters. The wife of one of his victims told police, "he was so quick he was like a panther", which, together with his characteristic dark clothing, led to his nickname of "The Black Panther".

Neilson's most infamous crime was the daring kidnap of the 17-year-old heiress Lesley Whittle, from her bedroom. Leaving behind a box of Turkish delight and a £50,000 ransom note, Neilson warned that he would kill his victim if her family involved the police – something which they chose to ignore. The operation to capture Neilson went badly wrong due to a series of police blunders, and after extensive media coverage and a full search of the park where the ransom money was to have been dropped, Whittle's body was found at the bottom of an underground ventilation shaft, hanging from the ceiling by a steel cable.

The Black Panther became Britain's most wanted man, but the trail went cold until, almost a year later and quite by chance, Neilson was approached by police, who had observed him behaving suspiciously. Neilson pulled a gun and attempted to abduct the police, forcing them to drive their car at gunpoint, but due to their quick thinking and courage, he was overpowered and his true identity confirmed. A psychologist who assessed Neilson described him as "the classic psychopath of all time". A fifth victim, badly hurt when he disturbed Neilson preparing for the ransom money to be dropped off, died from his injuries more than a year and a day after the crime, meaning Neilson could not be held legally responsible for his murder. Neilson was diagnosed with motor neurone disease in 2008 while serving his whole life tariff at Norwich Prison, and died in December 2011.

Levi Bellfield
A.K.A. The Bus Stop Killer
COUNTRY England
VICTIMS 3
METHOD bludgeoned

A vehicle is an unusual weapon of choice for a serial killer, but Levi Bellfield was an impulsive killer who had an overinflated ego, despised rejection and had a pathological hatred of blond-haired women. The former nightclub bouncer and manager of a car clamping business, was convicted in February 2008 of murdering 19-year-old Marsha McDonnell in 2003 and 22-year-old Amelie Delagrange in 2004, and of the attempted murder of 18-year-old Kate Sheedy, also in 2004.

He drove over me twice … I think that's quite enough

A STUDENT told the bus stop murders trial yesterday how she was run over and left for dead by a stranger in a people carrier.

Former convent school head girl Kate Sheedy, 21, said the vehicle raced towards her after she got off a bus, knocked her face down, then reversed over her before roaring off.

She wept: "He drove over me twice. I think that's quite enough."

Kate – who was only two minutes walk from her home – had a crushed liver, punctured lung, broken ribs and collar bone and lacerated back.

She told the Old Bailey: "I tried to stand up and fell straight back on the ground again. I tried to shout but it was barely a whisper.

"I crawled some distance and collapsed again. I realised I was severely injured and needed help. First, I phoned my mother, then an ambulance."

Ex-nightclub bouncer Levi Bellfield, 39, was allegedly at the wheel of the people carrier, which had blacked-out windows and was filmed on CCTV.

Bellfield, said to have stalked bus stops looking for women victims, denies two murders and two attempted murders.

Kate, then 18, told how she got off a bus near her home in Isleworth, Middlesex, after a night with friends celebrating her last day at school.

She said: "I started to walk and became aware of a parked vehicle. Its engine was running and the lights were off.

"The windows were blacked out. It made me feel very nervous. I don't know what it was, maybe some sixth sense."

Kate said she crossed the road to avoid walking past the people carrier.

She went on: "As I got to the middle of the road, the car's lights flashed on and the engine revved.

"It pulled away and looked like it was driving away from me. But it did a U-turn and came back down the road, drove straight towards me and hit me. I was thrown face down to the ground.

"It drove straight over me. My head was underneath the car and my legs were protruding out. The right hand front wheel went over me.

"Then it braked suddenly and reversed completely over me so that the same wheel went back over me again. [...]

Daily Mirror, 27th November 2007

In this modern day and age of CCTV surveillance, Bellfield was seen slowly driving his vehicles repeatedly past the same bus stops, stalking his victims. He had sexual relationships with underage girls and fitted out the back of his van for impromptu sex. He bludgeoned McDonnell and Delagrange to death with a hammer after he followed them getting off their buses home. Tragically, Delagrange was a visiting French student who was unfamiliar with the area and inadvertently missed her stop, so then had to walk home from the next stop on the bus route. Bellfield was given a life sentence.

When 13-year-old Amanda "Milly" Dowler disappeared in March 2002, it sparked one of the most high-profile searches for a missing person ever witnessed in the UK. She had disembarked from her train home one station early to go to a café with friends. Afterwards, Dowler had phoned home to say that she was on her way. She set off on foot and was seen by a family friend, but a CCTV camera a short distance further on had no record of her making it that far.

In September of the same year, her decomposed remains were discovered in Yateley Heath Woods in Hampshire, about 25 miles away from Dowler's last sighting. Her clothes and possessions were not found. In May 2011, Bellfield was tried for Dowler's abduction and murder, and the attempted abduction of 11-year-old Rachel Cowles the day before, trying to lure her into his car by saying, "Hello, I have just moved in next door to you, would you like a lift home?" The Cowles hearing was abandoned because of prejudiced reporting by the press. However, for Dowler's murder, Bellfield was given a further life sentence in June 2011.

Bellfield has tried to sue the prison service for an attack by fellow inmates at Wakefield Prison in September 2010, which left him with facial cuts and bruising. In November 2011, he changed his name to Mohammed and converted to Islam, supposedly to receive the benefits of better halal food and extra break time during prayers five times a day, and to avoid harassment from Muslim extremists. In February 2012, Bellfield lost an appeal against his sentencing, confirming that he has been given a whole life tariff.

The Dowler case again came to prominence in July 2011, when investigation of phone hacking by the *News of the World* revealed Dowler's mobile phone had been accessed by journalists along with those of celebrities, Members of Parliament and sports stars. The scandal led to several arrests and resignations, and the closure of the paper. Allegations were made that journalists had taken the extreme measure of deleting voicemails on Dowler's phone to free up space for new messages. The consequence was that her family were misled into thinking she was still alive. While unfortunate, and true that her phone had been hacked, the deleting of messages turned out to be an automatic setting on Dowler's phone.

Alexander Pichushkin
A.K.A. The Chessboard Killer, The Bitsa Park Maniac
COUNTRY Russia
VICTIMS 62
METHOD bludgeoned, drowned

Chess is a fine game. A game of cunning and strategy. An intelligent game, that pits foe against foe in a struggle for ultimate survival, but there can be only one victor. Chess is a serial killer's game.

It's not. In fact chess is an ancient and brilliant game, and fun for all the family, and it's all about the taking part. But for some arbitrary reason

Alexander Pichushkin decided to keep a tally of his murders with a chess board. In fact, he set himself the challenge of matching a murder with each of the eight-by-eight squares.

Other than the national obsession for the game in his homeland of Russia, his reasons possibly stemmed from a desire to achieve a personal goal of beating Andrei Chikatilo's total of 52 kills. A short-sighted and modest aim one might think, knowing that Saltykova was held accountable for the death of 138 of her serfs.

A SERIAL killer set himself a target – one murder for all 64 squares on a chess board.

Alexander Pichushkin, 33, has admitted battering 62 people to death – just two short of his aim.

After his arrest he told police: "For me a life without murder is like a life without food for you."

In a confession seen on TV he added: "I felt like the father of all these people since it was I who opened the door for them to another world."

Detectives found his chessboard with numbers up to 62 stuck to the squares – and bottle tops from the vodka he used to get victims too drunk to resist.

He then battered them with a hammer in a Moscow park, dumping some bodies in a well, others in a sewer.

He was arrested after killing a woman who had left a note to her son with the name and address of the man who had asked her on a date.

Pichushkin went on trial in Moscow yesterday charged with 49 killings.

His mother Natalia said: "At our last meeting in prison he told me 'Thank God they caught me otherwise I would never stop'."

Now Pichushkin – judged to be sane by psychiatrists – could face life in a Siberian prison colony.

Daily Mirror, 14th September 2007

Southwestern Siberia is indeed where Pichushkin ended up; as part of his sentence he endured 15 years in solitary confinement in the Omsk maximum-security prison colony. Pichushkin was arrested in June 2006 after a woman he dated failed to return home. Unusually, he had chosen a young female victim; previously, he had mostly murdered elderly homeless men in the popular 22-square kilometre recreation area south of Moscow called Bitsa Park, plying them with vodka in memory of his dead dog, and smashing their skulls in with a hammer. His *coup de grâce* was inserting the empty vodka bottle or a stick into one of the holes punctured in his victim's head.

Pichushkin was spotted with his date on a CCTV recording, and tracked down thanks to a metro ticket stub found on the women's body. Arrest soon followed. Pichushkin did match his hero in one way. Just as Chikatilo had, he relished re-enacting his murders for the police. In October 2007 he was sentenced to hard labour for life, beginning with 15 years in solitary confinement. After the hour-long verdict had been read out, Pichushkin was asked if he understood the ruling. Growling at the judge, he replied, "I'm not deaf."

THE Chessboard Killer said yesterday he is missing his 15-year murder spree.

Alexander Pichushkin, 33 – who kept count of his victims on the squares of a chessboard – said he enjoyed his gruesome slaying of up to 62 people.

Jailed for life by a Moscow court last year, he said in a chilling interview: "I feel no regrets. I got what I wanted."

Repentance was just a "silly formality".

He "enjoyed the process" of killing, adding: "People's lives are not long. And they are cheaper than sausages."

And he claimed the only nightmares he had were about his pet dog dying.

Daily Mirror, 13th March 2008

There is a fable that the inventor of chess was offered any reward for his genius by his grateful emperor. He merely asked for a single grain on the first square and thereafter to double the amount as it accumulated on each successive square. The number of grains soon became fantastic, and the prize was impossible to deliver. The inventor was beheaded as a lesson to other clever clogs.

Theodore Robert "Ted" Bundy
A.K.A. The American Jack the Ripper
COUNTRY USA
VICTIMS 36
METHOD bludgeoned
MUTILATION dismembered, decapitated, bitten

If one buys into the idea that what makes a serial killer is part nature, part nurture, then Ted Bundy's tale doesn't seem to tick many of the usual boxes – some of them, but not all. He was clearly a psychopath, but he didn't come from an abusive background, nor was he a chronic bed-wetter, and he wasn't known to torture animals. But many of these influences were present in his life, via the person he was closest to, and whom he respected above all others, his maternal grandfather, Samuel Cowell, a racist bigot, wife beater, animal torturer and bully.

Bundy was born a bastard: his mother had had several relationships with servicemen towards the end of the war, making identification of his paternity difficult. To avoid the stigma of bearing a child out of wedlock and to protect their daughter from social prejudice, her parents then posed as Bundy's parents. His mother, he was told, was his older sister, and to make matters really confusing, rumours circulated that his grandfather could also have been his biological father. They all lived together in Philadelphia.

When Bundy was 5 years old, his mother fell in love with, and married, a military cook in Tacoma, Washington, who gave the family his Bundy surname. Bundy thought him unintelligent and poor, and withdrew to become introverted and emotionally detached. On discovering the truth about his parentage in 1969, it further alienated him from his mother and her husband.

The news also came at a time when Bundy was susceptible, as it coincided with him being dumped by his long-term girlfriend, and his first "true love". This is probably the catalyst that, like so many other serial killers, suddenly turned him on to murder. However, during his confessions made 20 years later, Bundy, who was known to be manipulative, would blame another source for his homicidal transformation:

> As a young boy of 12 or 13, I encountered, outside the home, in the local grocery and drug stores, softcore pornography. Young boys explore the sideways and byways of their neighborhoods, and in our neighborhood, people would dump the garbage. From time to time, we would come across books of a harder nature – more graphic. [...] The most damaging kind of pornography – and I'm talking from hard, real, personal experience – is that that involves violence and sexual violence. The wedding of those two forces – as I know only too well – brings about behavior that is too terrible to describe. [...] Once you become addicted to it, and I look at this as a kind of addiction, you look for more potent, more explicit, more graphic kinds of material. Like an addiction, you keep craving something which is harder and gives you a greater sense of excitement, until you reach the point where the pornography only goes so far – that jumping off point where you begin to think maybe actually doing it will give you that which is

just beyond reading about it and looking at it. [...] In conjunction
with my exposure to pornography, alcohol reduced my inhibitions
and pornography eroded them further. [...] I can only liken it
to (and I don't want to overdramatize it) being possessed by
something so awful and alien, and the next morning waking up
and remembering what happened and realizing that in the eyes
of the law, and certainly in the eyes of God, you're responsible.
To wake up in the morning and realize what I had done with a
clear mind, with all my essential moral and ethical feelings intact,
absolutely horrified me.

The authorities were not convinced by his alleged contrition. Already an accomplished liar and thief by the time his girlfriend had jilted him, Bundy reinvented himself as an outgoing, confident Washington University graduate of psychology with prospects. His understanding of psychology possibly contributed towards his manipulation and exploitation of others.

Bundy entered a long-term relationship with a loyal but shy secretary, and managed several simultaneous affairs, including keeping in touch with his previous, estranged girlfriend. In 1973, involvement with the Republican Party gave him reason to travel to where she was living. During that trip he seduced her with his new personality and rekindled their relationship, apparently for the sole, vengeful purpose of being able to dump her without explanation a year later, "I just wanted to prove to myself that I could have married her."

Bundy started killing sometime between 1969 and 1971, but nothing would go on record until he was 27 years old, in 1974, about the time he ended the sham relationship. His victims were all similar looking, young, pretty, and dark-haired with a centre parting. But his methods were varied. Stealing into their bedrooms, Bundy would bludgeon some of his victims to death in their sleep. One particular victim survived with brain damage, having been battered and having had a bed rod forced into her vagina. Bundy removed the bloodied nightclothes of another victim and dressed her before carrying her off. Her body was never found.

At other times, Bundy would appear to have a broken arm or leg, and be seen struggling with something, like a briefcase, or a manual task. He would request help from a passing young women who, seeing that Bundy was handsome, intelligent and well-dressed, would accompany him to his light brown Volkswagen Beetle. Others accepted lifts. A swift blow to the head with a crowbar or other blunt instrument, and his victim would be rendered unconscious and at his mercy.

When he had control over his victim, Bundy sodomized and raped them. They were finally killed by strangulation or further blows to the head. His viciousness could be so extreme that skulls were smashed, exposing the victim's brain. He also had a fetish for biting his victim, leaving teeth marks, which were ultimately used as evidence against him, and biting off nipples. In addition to the bed rod, Bundy also used bottles to sexually assault his victims.

Bundy kept some of his victims alive or revisited them after they were dead, shampooing their hair and applying make-up, and lying with them overnight, later saying, "If you've got time, they can be anything you want them to be." He admitted to having sex with the decomposing bodies, until the smell became too bad. Many of the victims were decapitated with a hacksaw. He buried the severed heads separately to the body, or took them back to his apartment. Heads were found with front teeth removed, possibly to facilitate oral sex. He also burned some heads in a girlfriend's fireplace, something he knew was risky because it was too warm to warrant a fire, and there was a good chance he might be interrupted.

In July 1974, police were able to release an artist's composite sketch formed from descriptions provided by people who had witnessed Bundy approaching women. The drawing bore a good enough resemblance for his secretary girlfriend and ex-work colleagues to identify him.

His girlfriend was already suspicious of his strange behaviour, and had reported her concerns to the police more than once. She had noticed that his movements matched some of the disappearances reported in the news. His behaviour was also strange. He was controlling about her appearance, particularly about her maintaining a centre parting in her hair, and she would awake to find him inspecting her body beneath the bed sheets with a torch. She challenged him over how he managed to obtain expensive items despite being permanently skint. He threatened her to keep quiet. She had also confronted him about oddities he would produce, such as surgical gloves, plaster of Paris, crutches, a meat cleaver, a knife he kept in his car and a sack of women's clothes.

Bundy's VW Beetle had also become well known from being spotted at the places he abducted his earlier victims, but it was a routine traffic stop in August 1975 that led to his arrest. Having been pulled over, the equipment he had in his car immediately raised the policeman's suspicions, as did the absence of the front passenger seat. A further search found masks, handcuffs, a crowbar, an ice pick, bags and rope. The policeman thought he had rumbled a burglar.

Although there were suspicions, there wasn't sufficient evidence to link Bundy to any crimes, so he was released and put under surveillance. In September 1975, he sold the VW, which the police impounded. Forensics went to work on the car and found hairs that matched three known murder victims. This was enough to bring him into custody. Bundy was put into a line-up and a witness identified him as the perpetrator of an attempted abduction in November 1974. He spent from October 1975 until February 1976 freed on bail, then stood trial and was found guilty of kidnapping and assault, and sentenced, in June 1976, to a maximum of 15 years in Utah State Prison.

Bundy attempted to escape three times. Twice he was successful. The first time he was caught hiding amongst bushes in the prison yard, carrying personal documents, road maps and airline schedules. The second time he was standing trial for murder in Aspen in June 1977. Bundy used his privileges while defending himself to access the courthouse law library. While there he jumped from a window and went on the run for six days. Again he was apprehended carrying papers showing that the escape had been planned. The final escape, in December 1977, involved accumulating funds, and then using a hacksaw blade to cut a hole in his cell, losing enough weight so that he could crawl through the ceiling into the adjoining home of a prison officer. He stole some civilian clothes and walked out of the jail's front door.

This time Bundy made it to Denver and then took a flight to Chicago. In early January 1978, he was in Florida supporting himself by shoplifting and stealing credit cards. A week later Bundy broke into a Florida State University sorority house to bludgeon, strangle, sexually assault and mutilate the four sleeping female students inside. The attacks took about 15 minutes, were horribly violent, but went unnoticed by 30 people sleeping nearby. Bundy bludgeoned and sexually assaulted another student in a nearby apartment as he made his way off campus. Two of the five women died. The survivors were severely injured.

Bundy's final victim before he was recaptured was a 12-year-old girl he abducted from her school in Lake City, Florida. Bundy raped and beat her inside his newly acquired vehicle, a white van that he used to drive her away. Reaching secluded countryside, she suffocated, her face forced into the mud, as Bundy anally raped her. He then mutilated her body with a knife.

Bundy was arrested when another stolen vehicle was noticed by an attentive policeman who didn't recognize it as being from the area. Bundy tried to flee, was fired at, feigned being hit, tussled with the policeman again, but was overpowered and taken into custody.

Bundy stood trial for the five Florida murders and assaults in June 1979. Again he represented himself in court, playing up to the media circus that had assembled. Three trials were subsequently held for separate crimes, including the murder of his last victim. Witness evidence was overwhelming, along with dental matches, so that each jury took little time in coming to their verdict. By February 1980, Bundy had accumulated three death sentences. He had also accumulated a wife, a co-worker he had met in 1974, whom he managed to get pregnant, paying off guards to look the other way as they slipped behind a vending machine for sex during visiting times.

Bundy confessed to 30 murders, but indicated the FBI estimate of 36 was very close. However, other estimates place the total nearer 100. As his execution drew near, having been delayed and rescheduled several times, Bundy opened up and confessed, describing in detail how he had carried out his killings and why he had revisited the bodies. He was still confessing minutes before he was taken to the execution chamber in January 1989.

MASS killer Ted Bundy died in the electric chair yesterday as mobs toasted his execution at "Bundy barbecues."

Hundreds of onlookers wearing "Burn, Bundy, Burn" T-shirts gathered outside a Florida jail to hear the news that the beast who killed THIRTY-SIX women had died in the arms of "Old Sparky."

As they waited they tuned in to a radio station where a DJ was urging "turn off your coffee pots so Sparky can have more juice."

Others carried sparklers in the pre-dawn darkness and sang "On top of Old Sparky all loaded with juice" to the tune of Old Smokey.

A nearby bar was serving "Bundy fries" and "Bundy toast" and a sign read: "Roast in peace."

Most bizarrely, two policemen in Birmingham, Alabama, hosted a "Bundy barbecue" in support of capital punishment. Then Christmas tree lights were switched on at the exact moment 2,000 volts surged through the killer.

When the news came through that Bundy was dead a roar went up from the waiting crowd outside the jail.

Drivers hooted their horns, a gleeful onlooker waved the American flag and another let off firecrackers [...]

Daily Mirror, 25th January 1989

BEHEADERS

*If you can keep your head when all about you
are losing theirs*
Rudyard Kipling

We have had a long-term relationship with beheading, especially as a form of execution. Our term for "capital punishment" comes from the Latin "caput" for "head". The Egyptians feared being beheaded as it would bar them from the afterlife, whereas Norse myth promised that warriors losing their heads in battle would be reunited with their bodies in Valhalla. During the French Revolution decapitation by Madame Guillotine was considered the noblest way to be put to death, but an unskilled executioner might take three attempts to sever a neck, as was the case in the unfortunate end of Mary, Queen of Scots. For the serial killer decapitation has other meanings. In terms of evidence, separating body and head makes it harder to identify human remains. In terms of gratification, a head can become a plaything or souvenir.

William Lee Cody Neal

A.K.A. Wild Bill Cody
COUNTRY USA
VICTIMS 500
METHOD bludgeoned
MUTILATION decapitated

The case of William Neal occupies that grey area between serial killer and spree murderer. Even though his murders were carried out within a few days of each other, they were premeditated, planned for some time, and the fact that he took time to party between murders probably counts as cooling off. He also showed other tell-tale signs of being a serial killer, such as torturing and killing family pets as a child. Overall, Neal's actions were certainly less like the impulsive actions of spree murderers such as Herbert Mullin, who we will meet a little later.

Neal was a con man and embezzler. Using his fraudulently made money, charm and panache, Neal endeared himself to his female victims, who were vulnerable types looking for happiness, wining and dining them in top restaurants and clubs where he was well known.

Used it for strip clubs and limo rides [...] I think the only month that I ever counted how much money I blew in one month was $22,000 at a strip club. Just like, poof. Now, how many people can live on that and keep throwing it away and just do it?

Impressed and seduced by his ways, four women married him, but Neal was a violently jealous man. Mentally torturing his partners, he would control their every move and attack on any suspicion of infidelity or promiscuity, even in previous relationships, while having affairs and openly exhibiting his own confusing immoral conduct: insisting on sharing porn, forcing them to attend swingers' clubs and strip joints to engage in sexual acts with strangers. When he had extended periods away from home, he would persuade neighbours to spy on his wives to maintain control, which also included selling their possessions and defrauding them of savings.

Anybody stupid enough to believe me deserves to get fucked [...] It's like, man, if I'm going to be a whore, let me get paid for it.

At their most vulnerable, even when pregnant, Neal demanded a divorce, always blaming them for the break-up of the marriage. When slighted and not getting his way, perhaps enraged from losing control, he once threatened, "I'm going to fuck over every women in my path. You ain't nothing but a bunch of whores."

On 30th June 1998, Neal drove to a builder's yard in Jefferson County, Colorado, to buy Lava soap, four eyebolts, nylon rope, duct tape and a seven-and-a-half-pound, long-handled splitting maul (half axe, half sledgehammer). Seating Rebecca Holberton, his current partner and first victim on a chair in the middle of the living room of her townhouse, he made it clear that he was going to repay her for the money he had taken. Payment came in the form of a blow from the blunt side of the maul to the back of the head, "with such force that it completely caved in the back of her skull sending skull fragments into her brain and gouging out a two-inch piece of skull that went flying across the room". Later Neal would describe how with each swing her head got "sloppier and sloppier". Cocooned in plastic, the body was leant against a wall.

The following day he again offered recompense to Candace Walters, his next victim, many times the amount he owed, backed up with fantastic stories of inherited fortunes and photographs of beautiful mansions.

Beguiled, she was taken to the same townhouse, sat in the chair, and received four head blows from the axe-side of the maul. Neal urinated on her head and shoulders, before wrapping the wounds in plastic, moving the body to the side of the room, and covering it with a blanket.

Yes, I did it, twice [...] It was, like I said, the ultimate humiliation [...] I just whipped it out, and it was basically around the shoulders and head. I just urinated on her because, you know, Lady, you're gone. [...] It was like an Oriental martial arts thing, or an Indian thing. I mean, I hope somebody pisses on me when I'm gone, all right?

Using the victims' credit cards he then went out partying with two more female acquaintances, who were flatmates. He slept with one of the women that night at their apartment, and took the other, Suzanne Scott, back to the townhouse the next day, where he blindfolded, gagged and tied her with rope to the eyebolts screwed into the headboard, so that she was spreadeagled on the bed. Cutting her clothes away, he placed a skull fragment on her bare stomach. After sexually assaulting Scott, Neal left to collect the fourth woman, Angela Fite, a mother of two and someone known to his prisoner, bringing her to the townhouse to show off his handiwork, "Welcome to my mortuary."

Taping the most recent arrival to the chair and positioning her facing Scott, who was bound to the bed in a supine position, Neal smashed the sharp side of the maul into the seated Fite's head six times. Blood spurted onto the bare wooden floorboards. Seeing Scott's anguish, he threw a blanket beneath the falling blood, "so you don't have to hear that".

Undressing and joining Scott on the bed, Neal freed some of her ties and forced her at gunpoint to use her hand to work his penis. Freeing her entirely, he then forced her to perform oral sex on him, knelt within inches of the bludgeoned women still taped to the chair. Unsatisfied, Neal forced her back on the bed where he raped her.

Scott survived the night, most probably by overcoming her terror to show some solicitude, asking Neal to sit with her on the bed, and holding his hand. By being friendly she made it harder for Neal to justify killing her, while he saw his mercy as ensuring someone survived to warn off others who might try to cross him, "the one that made it out alive and the one that was going to send me to the chair". In justifying his actions, and the slaughter of the other women, all Neal offered was, "I was involved in illegal activities – theft, extortion, fraud, embezzlement, forgery. I could keep listing them. I knew they'd be potential snitches. I was right – none of them were trustable", and, "that's what happens when you fuck with me".

*I executed them. I wanted them to go as quickly as possible.
It was not a sexual turn-on for me to kill somebody. I was not
thinking of sex in any way when I murdered [...] It had nothing to
do with saying, "Look, bitch, for all you other ones cheating on
me in the past [...]" It was not a vindictive act to get even, you
see what I'm saying? It was not a malicious sexual act. It was to
put them out the best way I knew how as quickly and as silently
and as fairly as I could [...] Always from the back. See, I didn't
want these people to know what was coming, because they were
good people [...] It was a mercy thing. It was, like, not wanting
them to suffer. The paper said I tortured them, okay? I mean, if
I wanted to torture them, I could have sat there and, I mean, I
could have done all kinds of things.*

Neal took Scott back to her apartment in the morning, where she cleaned up, then they went shopping, picking up a video of *The Jackal* because Neal saw himself as the assassin protagonist. They watched the film with Scott's other flatmate back at the women's apartment, Neal having pledged to confess as soon as it had finished. When the film was over, Neal recorded a confession into a tape recorder, witnessed by the two flatmates. He had a gun with him and had considered committing suicide straight afterwards, but instead he held the women and an additional male friend hostage for three days before finally allowing them to make a call to the police. During that time, Neal did not carry out any further assaults, but did force his hostages to accompany him to more strip joints.

Simultaneously, a co-worker of Holberton was concerned about her protracted absence from work, so he went to her townhouse and discovered the murder scene, alerting the authorities before Neal could enact his manufactured surrender. It was probably fortuitous that it had not been left to him.

*There was going to be at least thirty more people I was going to
get within a three-day period. I had them lined up ready to go,
and there was no doubt I could have got them all. And every one
of those people, I knew. [...] It was going to be a wipeout thing
[...] kill every last one of the son-of-a-bitches who was there
[...] Like it comes in Revelations, Revelations 8:6, about this
pale horse, and on it was a rider, and his name was Death, and
Hades followed him. That's me, okay?*

Representing himself at his trial in 1999, Neal pleaded guilty to all 13 counts against him, including three counts of first-degree murder; two counts of second-degree kidnapping; two counts of first-degree sexual assault; two counts of criminal extortion; two violent crime charges related to the kidnapping; and one count of felony theft. He initially claimed 500 victims and sought the death penalty, "I need prosecution, I need justice to be served, because I'm representing three dead people [...] as well as a rape victim. I want justice to be served and the truth to be known so that people can get on with their lives [...] Chances are I'll be executed for this one, because I deserve to be."

He soon changed his mind, reducing his plea to the three known murders, and now claiming he wanted to live because of a rapid and timely conversion, so that he could "serve God in prison". He also stated, "I am not a rapist. I don't believe that I would ever rape another woman after the taste that I got on this issue, all right? It's something that I can never feel like I've washed myself enough, just like them", and that he, "felt remorse the whole way. For all three. For everybody." Due to a technicality, his three death sentences were commuted to life imprisonment without the possibility of parole, when Colorado changed its sentencing laws in 2003.

Edmund Emil Kemper III
A.K.A. The Co-Ed Murderer
COUNTRY USA
VICTIMS 10
METHOD stabbed, strangled, shot, bludgeoned
MUTILATION decapitated, dismembered

Herbert Mullin
COUNTRY USA
VICTIMS 13
METHOD shot, stabbed
MUTILATION dismembered

Is there any single case that has more wrongdoing than that of Ed Kemper? He was the archetypal serial killer.

It was 27th August 1964, and as usual Ed Kemper was not happy. Physically "Big Ed" looked like a dolt, that unfortunate effect of early development in adolescents. He was only 15, but already 6' 4". People might have looked up to him, literally as well as metaphorically, if only he had some social skills and didn't intimidate them so. He might have been a hero, but his upbringing had destroyed any chance of that. Six years previously his parents had divorced and it still weighed heavily on his mind. He missed his father, the towering 6' 8" figure of Edmund Emil

Kemper Jr, and to say his relationship with his mother was estranged, would be an understatement.

Clarnell E. Kemper, née Strandberg, was a violent woman who constantly victimized Kemper, the middle of three siblings. Her own past and her failed marriage may have contributed to a possible borderline personality disorder. In an unusual alliance for family relations, she shared her persecution of Kemper with her mother-in-law. This then was the mother–grandmother team that Kemper grew to despise. His cancerous loathing of their emasculation of him and his grandfather spread until he was harbouring fantasies that not only they but the whole world would die.

Kemper's early outlet was to burn things and torment animals, both common among children who develop into serial killers: stabbing a cat, burying another alive, digging it up, cutting off its head and putting it on a stick. This was a thought that would recur to him in adulthood, "One side of me says, 'Wow, what an attractive chick. I'd like to talk to her, date her.' The other side of me says, 'I wonder how her head would look on a stick?'"

Moreover, the fast-growing child was beginning to target the confusion and angst in his emotional life. He played "execution" and sex games with his sisters' dolls, once telling them he could only love someone if they were dead. Dared to kiss a teacher he had a crush on, he replied, "If I kiss her, I would have to kill her first." Deciding that her son was "a real weirdo", his mother locked Kemper in the basement at night for fear that he would rape his younger sister.

In the summer of 1963 Kemper fled to seek the solace of his father, who had resettled with a new family, so he was dispatched from there on to his father's parents' 17-acre ranch in North Fork, California. Spurned and cut off, Kemper's hate swelled within until he knew he was "a walking time bomb".

Probably unbeknownst to him, stuck on that remote ranch on 27th August 1964, quite a lot was going on in the outside world. Within the year, the seeds had been sewn for the controversial "Subculture of Violence" explanation of African American crime by one of the theorists in *The Psychology of the Criminal Homicide*. Within the previous few weeks, the Vietnam War had taken a new turn with a USA-backed coup in South Vietnam deposing the increasingly unpopular "Big Minh", Duong Van Minh. Only a fortnight before, Peter Allen and Gwynne Evans had been hanged for the murder of John Alan West, marking the end of capital punishment in the UK. On the 27th itself, a Thursday, the Los Angeles Angels baseball team were to clinch an away win against the Kansas City Athletics, while back in Los Angeles, the new Disney film *Mary Poppins* was to premiere at Grauman's Chinese Theater on Hollywood Boulevard. Delegates at the Democratic National Convention being held in Atlantic City were preparing to hear an acceptance speech from their newly nominated leader Lyndon B. Johnson, whose birthday it was, along with jazz musicians Alice Coltrane and Lester Young, guru Sri Chinmoy, photographer Man Ray, cricketer Don Bradman and, coincidentally in name and date, serial killer Ed Gein, finally apprehended the same year as Kemper's parents' divorce. Also, Gracie Allen, comedy and life partner of George Burns, was going to die that day. But she wasn't going to be the only one. Kemper was going to make sure of that.

With just him and Maude Kemper, his 66-year-old grandmother, in the ranch house, an argument with her was never far away, and, as usual, she had infuriated him. Telling him this, telling him that. Telling him not to stare at her so. Returning to the kitchen table to finish proofreading the last few pages of her latest children's book, it was clear she was unfazed, while his blood boiled. He snatched up his .22 calibre rifle, a Christmas present from Edmund Kemper Sr, his 72-year-old grandfather. He was heading out to let off steam by shooting rabbits and gophers, and especially birds. The birds were the best, because he had been explicitly told not to shoot them. This time was no exception. She had to have one last go at him, "Don't shoot at the birds!" Just like his mother, always bossing him about, telling him what to do. He went out of the screen door, turned, had her in his gun sights, and shot her in the head. Something stirred within him. He shot her again, twice more in the back. Then, stepping inside, he picked up the kitchen knife, close at hand, and repeatedly stabbed her in the back, again and again, and again. He was killing his mother, no, his grandmother, and it felt good. He had "just wanted to see what it felt like to kill Grandma", going further than just lining her up in his rifle sights like he had so many times before. And now he knew.

Kemper had acted in the heat of the moment. This would be his only impulse kill, but now he was calming down, and with blood splattered everywhere, he didn't know what to do. First, he had to deal with the body. He wrapped the head in a towel and dragged his grandmother's body into the bedroom, something that was easy for "Big Ed". But by the time he had done that his grandfather was pulling up the front drive, coming home with the grocery shopping. He couldn't let the old man see what he had done to his wife. A heavy drinking and violent man, he'd get mad. How could he both protect himself and save his grandfather from being upset and angry? Kemper went out to meet his grandfather as he got out of the car, raised his rifle once more, and shot him in the back of the head.

After he had hidden the second body in the garage, Kemper did something that was perhaps unexpected. Whether to deliver his vengeance first hand, or because he really didn't have anywhere else to turn, he phoned his mother in Montana; she told him to phone the police. The news must have come as quite a shock, but not a surprise. She claims to have warned her ex-husband that this would happen one day. Kemper calmly sat on the porch, listening to the birds, enjoying the peace and waiting for the police to arrive.

Psychiatric tests revealed Kemper to have an exceptionally high IQ of 136. He was diagnosed as a "near-genius" paranoid schizophrenic and placed in custody at the Atascadero State Hospital for the Criminally Insane. There he familiarized himself with all the assessments used on the inmates, memorizing favourable responses, so that by his 21st birthday on 18th December 1969, he was able to persuade most of the parole board of his recovery. Kemper was released into his mother's care, against the recommendations of some of the psychiatrists, who thought this might cause further problems.

Now an adult, a giant 6' 9" and weighing nearly 300 pounds, Kemper was forced to return to persecution and continue to live at home with his mother. Their choice of hometown was dictated by her job as an administrative assistant at the University of Southern California, Santa Cruz, but it was to prove strangely prophetic.

> With my Atascadero learning, I kept trying to push her toward
> where she would be a nice motherly type and quit being such a
> damned manipulating, controlling, vicious beast. She was Mrs.
> Wonderful up on the campus, had everything under control.
> When she comes home, she lets everything down and she's just
> a pure bitch; bust her butt being super nice at work and come
> home at night and be a shit.

Santa Cruz had retained the hippy vibe, and was still a laid-back, lazy north Pacific seaside town on the northern edge of Monterey Bay. Kemper had just missed being released in time to see nearby Haight-Ashbury at its height, a cornucopia of drugs and free sex. But the tide had turned and hippies were suddenly getting a bad press. The heady days of the 1960s were a memory, when the scene had been swinging with such laid-back go-with-the-flow intensity. Now, a series of shock waves reverberated through hippiedom. In 1969, and the same month as Woodstock, Charles Manson's "Family", under his direction, brought their incendiary programme of murders to a head. The hippy creed of drugs, sex and devotion to a guru were central to their massacring. Only four months after the relatively peaceful and positive symbolism of Woodstock, another Free concert at Altamont, California, ended with repercussions after an armed assailant was stabbed rushing the stage. The new decade would be less peaceful and loving.

Santa Cruz was unlike other parts of the USA. Although the country had been recently shocked by the assassinations of John F. Kennedy, Martin Luther King and Robert Kennedy, and anti-war riots on campuses and at the Democratic Convention, for a couple of years there had been relatively few arrests of serial killers. Jerome Brudos had recently been apprehended in Oregon for murdering up to a dozen women, removing their breasts or feet, and raping their dead bodies. In Michigan, John Norman Collins was caught after the murder and mutilation of up to nine victims. Otherwise, murders elsewhere followed a recognizable pattern, single fatalities with identifiable motivations. But suddenly, a spate of unexplained killings rocked Santa Cruz:

FAMILY DIE IN MASSACRE AT MANSION

FIVE people were massacred in a horrific "execution"... and dumped, shot and bound, in the swimming pool of a luxury hill top mansion.

Each of the victims—a wealthy surgeon, his family and his secretary – had been shot once in the back of the head.

Then the killers set fire to the £125,000 house at Santa Cruz, south of San Francisco, California. Firemen and police who raced to tackle the blaze saw a trail of bloodstains leading to the pool ... and found the bodies.

A policeman said: "It was the most gruesome sight I have ever seen."

After police had talked of "evidence of foulplay," a statement issued yesterday said: "Other factors are under investigation."

But the police declined to say what the factors were.

The bodies were those of Dr. Victor Ohta and his wife Virginia, both aged forty-five, their sons Derek, 12, and Taggart, 11, and the doctor's secretary, 38-year-old Mrs. Dorothy Gadwallader.

Escaped

The Ohtas' two daughters escaped the massacre. Taura, 18, and Elizabeth, 15, were away at school.

The killers struck on Monday night, shortly before the doctor and his wife were due to leave their home in an exclusive suburb for a hospital dinner.

Police Lieutenant Kenneth Pittenger said yesterday: "It was like an execution.

"At this stage we have established no motive, but we are ruling out nothing. It looks as though more than one person was involved."

All five victims had been shot with revolvers. Dr. Ohta had a second wound in his back.

Their hands had been tied in front of them with scarlet scarves.

And three of the victims had their faces covered – also with scarves.

A massive search was launched for Dr. Ohta's estate car, which was missing from the house.

Two other cars, a Rolls Royce and a Lincoln Continental, had been left behind.

It was the second mass murder of wealthy victims to shake California in little more than a year.

Stabbed

In August last year, film star Sharon Tate and four other people were shot, stabbed and clubbed to death at her luxury home in Hollywood.

Hippie Charles Manson and three girl members of his roving "family" are on trial in Los Angeles for the killings.

Daily Mirror, 21st October 1970

Searching for the fire hydrant among the garden bushes, the fire chief scanned the area with his flashlight. The beam arced across the swimming pool and settled on the upturned face of a dead boy. More bodies were quickly found sunk at the opposite end. Each had been shot with a .22 calibre gun through the back of the neck, except one who had received two .38 calibre wounds to the back and one under an arm. The immediate fear was another Manson-like massacre, but there were no scrawled messages. Even so, Haight-Ashbury was still an obvious place to go looking for drug-crazed hippies.

In fact there had been a message left, but the police had kept it from the press. A piece of paper found under the Rolls Royce windscreen wiper, threatened that anyone, "who misuses the natural environment or destroys same will suffer the penalty of death by the people of the free universe". Publishing this note led to three hippies coming forward to identify someone they knew who had spoken of such ideas, and within hours lone gunman and deranged eco-vigilante John Linley Frazier was in police custody.

Within two years the area was again hit with another wave of killings. Again, there seemed no discernible pattern. The victims seemed chosen at random, and died in a variety of ways and settings: in May 1972 two girl hitchhikers disappeared. Another one vanished, three months later. A homeless man beaten to death with a baseball bat a month after that, then just over a week later another hitchhiker disappeared, but this time her mutilated body and intestines hanging from a tree testified to her fate. The final victim of the year was a priest who was murdered in his confessional, beaten, kicked and stabbed to death.

The new year began in the same vein. A hitchhiker disappeared. A couple were shot in the head then repeatedly stabbed in their own home. On the same day, a mother and her two children, aged 9 and 4, were shot. Within a fortnight, two students were missing. The very next day four teenage campers were gunned down. Their bodies were not found for a further 12 days, during which time a man was gunned down in his driveway.

4 MORE DIE IN MURDER ZONE

FOUR more murder victims were found yesterday in a quiet country area held in a grip of terror by a mass killer.

Fifteen people have now been murdered there in the last six weeks.

The bodies of four longhaired young men were found yesterday in a forest shack near Pelton, California.

Police believe the blood-covered bodies had been there about a week.

Charged

Twenty-five-year-old Herbert Mullin was charged last week with six of the recent killings in Santa Cruz County.

He was accused of killing a woman and her two young sons, a 72-year-old gardener and a married couple.

Mullin is also suspected of stabbing to death a priest who was hearing confessions in church.

Daily Mirror, 19th February 1973

A palpable sense of relief, sweeping the Santa Cruz Valley clean, was felt when Herbert Mullin was arrested. Police assured the public that they had caught the person responsible for all the killings, a paranoid psychiatric patient who was convinced that human sacrifice was the only way to save California from an imminent earthquake.

The difficulty that faced investigators was piecing together the puzzle over time, as new bodies were discovered and new evidence came to light. Only when the victim had been found and where the killings showed some similarity could they be factored into a series of murders.

Consequently, Mullin was not charged with the death of the homeless man, the disembowelled hitchhiker and the priest. Even without bodies to account for the other missing persons, the police found it convenient to attribute their disappearance to Mullin. The rediscovered confidence was short-lived. Even as Mullin was spending his first nights in custody, another double murder was being committed.

In fact, none of the disappearances were due to Mullin. The doubting psychiatrists at Atascadero had been correct. Living with his mother had brought all the feelings of loathing and hatred back to the surface for Kemper. Neighbours said that they argued constantly. The only distraction was in finding an enjoyable job. His dream job was becoming a cop. He attended community college as part of the conditions for his parole, and his intelligence helped him excel. Doing well was going to contribute to him getting into a police academy. He was focussed, endearing himself to the police officers in their favourite bar, and rubbing shoulders with his future colleagues.

Then it all fell apart. He was too tall to be a cop; no Hightowers were allowed in real police academies. Kemper still hung out at the bar, listening in on the police stories, but the dream was over. He looked in different directions for gratification. The only benefit from living with his mother was that her affiliation with the university got him a campus pass. A run of menial work preceded a position with the Californian Highway Division, and he soon had enough saved to move out into a shared apartment and buy a motorbike. However, his income was unsteady and he was forced to return to live with his mother. So, when he received a payout resulting from a crash that broke his left arm, he bought a yellow Ford Galaxie, a car that resembled an unmarked police vehicle, installed a radio transmitter and long whip antenna, just like in the films and on TV.

The car became a second home, and he would cruise for hours, noticing all the pretty hitchhikers, and thinking about sex. And violence. He gave many a ride, maybe 150, but didn't do anything about his thoughts, his urges, his "little zapples". "At first I picked up girls just to talk to them, just to try to get acquainted with people my own age and try to strike up a friendship."

First he had to prepare, to be ready for what he knew he wanted to do to them, and not get caught and convicted as a rapist. He had heard the stories from serial rapists locked up alongside him in Atascadero. Their exploits excited his adolescent mind. Violent sex and domination wasn't considered unnatural. In fact, amongst that crowd, it was the norm, but Kemper saw where they had messed up. They had been caught because they had left evidence, and they had left witnesses, "I decided to mix the two and have a situation of rape and murder and no witnesses and no prosecution."

The antenna had to go, too noticeable, and then he fixed the passenger door so it couldn't be opened from inside. Plastic bags, knives, a blanket and handcuffs went into the boot. Now he was ready.

Months before Mullin's first victim, Kemper picked up his first two hitchhiker victims in May 1972. They were 18-year-old college roommates Mary Ann Pesce and Anita Luchese, who were heading to another campus. After an hour of driving, they passed through a secluded, wooded area. At gunpoint he locked Luchese in the boot, leaving Pesce, whom he favoured and intended to kill first, inside the car, "I was really quite struck by her personality and her looks and there was just almost a reverence there."

Handcuffing her, Kemper tried suffocating Pesce with a plastic bag, but she bit through it, so he stabbed her repeatedly instead. Then he cut off her head. Taking Luchese out of the boot, he stabbed her to death. Kemper returned home with the bodies, where he undressed and dissected Pesce's corpse and beheaded Luchese. Taking photographs and keeping the heads as souvenirs, he dismembered the bodies and stuffed the bits into plastic bags, and buried them in the Santa Cruz Mountains. The heads he finally tossed into a roadside ravine but not before he had enjoyed oral sex with one of them. Only Pesce's head was found a couple of months later, but no other remains, "Sometimes, afterward, I visited there [...] to be near her [...] because I loved her and wanted her." With his other victims, he would continue to rape the heads and other body parts, typically taking them into the shower to masturbate with.

Four months later, in September 1972, Kemper gave a lift to 15-year-old Korean dancer Aiko Koo, who was too impatient to wait for the bus to her dance class. At gunpoint he easily taped her mouth shut, pinched her nostrils closed and suffocated her until she was unconscious with his huge hands. He raped her on the ground as she died, then strangled her with her own scarf, before putting the body back in the car.

I achieved orgasm – I guess it was only fifteen to twenty seconds. It was very quick. At that time I noticed her hair falling over her face and nose. She was still breathing, starting to breathe again. I took the muffler that she had around her neck still and just wrapped it very tight and tied a knot in it and [...] I even choked her around the throat for a moment, but by that time I was convinced she was dead.

He then drove to a bar for a few beers and then home, frequently checking the boot to ensure that her corpse was still there. He was the champion enjoying his spoils.

I suppose as I was standing there looking, I was doing one of those triumphant things, too, admiring my work and admiring her beauty, and I might say admiring my catch like a fisherman [...] They were dead and I was alive. That was the victory in my case.

That evening he drove to his mother's house, dissected Koo's body with an ornamental sabre, and experimented with it.

You know the head's where everything is at, the brain, eyes, mouth, that's the person. I remember being told as a kid, you cut off the head and the body dies, the body is nothing after the head is cut off [...] well that's not quite true. With a girl there's a lot left in the girl's body without a head.

He finally decapitated the head, which he put in the boot of his car. It was still there when he drove to an appointment with the state psychiatrist the next morning. On the basis of this consultation, the psychiatrist recommended that Kemper's juvenile records be sealed so as not to impede future employment. After their meeting Kemper buried the girl's remains, disposing of the head and hands at different locations.

By the time of Kemper's next murder, Mullin's killings had started and suddenly the public were all too aware that they were under attack. Mass paranoia was fuelled by sensationalist TV reporting, which fostered a Jack the Ripper-like terror, replete with surgical know-how and black magic cultism. Nothing was pointing towards Kemper, and he knew how much the investigation was lacking in clues as he continued to frequent the bar where off-duty officers would mingle and discuss the case in his company, allowing him to keep tabs on their progress and pick up tips, like not leaving the hands for fingerprinting. Furthermore, his police buddies even gave him the handcuffs he used in his killing. With only some of the remains of the victims being found, the local police were short on evidence. They thought that they could recognize some pattern in the killings, and realized that they were perhaps seeking more than one culprit for the murder spree.

There was a lull in Mullin's killings for a couple of months, while he attemped but failed to enlist for the Coast Guard and Marine Corps, eventually considering the Army. He had bought a new gun, but hadn't used it yet. But Kemper's urges still raged strong. Early in the new year he picked up 19-year-old female student Cindy Schall, drove her to secluded woodland and shot her with a .22 calibre pistol, which was, like Mullin's, also newly purchased. At his mother's house he had sex with the body in his bed and kept it in his room overnight in order to remove the bullet from the head, getting rid of the evidence in preparation for the decapitation, a moment cherished ever since, as a child, he had pulled the heads off his sisters' dolls, "I remember there was actually a sexual thrill [...] you hear that little pop and pull their heads off and hold their heads up by the hair. Whipping their heads off, their body sitting there. That'd get me off."

Kemper dissected the rest of Schall's body in the bathtub the next day while his mother was at work, then dumped the remains over a cliff overlooking the Pacific Ocean. Within two days, dismembered arms and legs were found, then the upper torso washed ashore, then the lower torso. A surfer found a left hand, used for fingerprinting, but the head and right hand remained missing.

The location of Schall's head would eventually be discovered. Kemper had removed the bullet, then buried the head in his mother's garden facing the house, as a joke, because she, "always wanted people to look up to her". "With her face turned toward my bedroom window and, sometimes at night, I talked to her, saying love things, the way you do to a girlfriend or wife."

The day before Mullin gunned down the four camping youths, Kemper had a furious row with his mother. Storming out of the house to see a film, he headed to the campus to kill time, ranting, "the first girl that's halfway decent that I pick up, I'm gonna blow her brains out". He picked up Rosalind Thorpe and Allison Liu, two hitchhikers in their early 20s, drove a short distance off campus, and shot both with his pistol – Liu twice in the head – wrapped their bodies in blankets and put them on the back seat. Back at home, Kemper ate dinner, then sat patiently waiting for his mother to go to bed. When all was quiet he crept back outside, and decapitated both corpses in the boot of the car while it was parked in the street. Carrying Liu's body inside, he lay it on the floor and sexually abused it before returning it to the boot. As a nightcap, Kemper chopped off the hands. The next day, he dismembered the women's bodies and, as before, threw their remains over a cliff, once again taking care to remove the bullets lodged in their heads.

On 20th April 1973, Kemper's mother was picking on him again, emasculating his very existence. Later, she came home after a night out with friends, insincerely offering, "I suppose you'll want to sit up all night and talk" when he approached her reading in bed. He was sick to death of her talking. Instead, he gave her time to fall sleep, sneaked back into her room with a claw hammer early next morning, and, using his full height, smashed it down onto the back of her skull.

After beating her to make sure she was truly dead, he cut off her hands and head with a pocketknife. He then removed her larynx and tried to grind it up in the waste-disposal unit, but the sinewy strands snagged in the mechanism and her voice box was regurgitated, "Even when she was dead, she was still bitching at me. I couldn't get her to shut up!" Stuffing the torso into the wardrobe he took the head and, "put it on a shelf and screamed at it for an hour [...] threw darts at it [and] smashed her face in".

Before it was unusable, he also raped his mother's head. Kemper then went drinking with his police friends at the bar. It would have occurred to him that until he killed his mother he had been careful about his victim choice; he had not left any obvious leads, selecting strangers who might not be missed immediately, making their remains hard to identify, and keeping tabs on the investigation at the police bar. But now he was definitely going to be suspected. After all, he had done something like this before. So, thinking a second murder may make it less obvious that he was the perpetrator, he concocted a ruse of a surprise party to bring Sally Hallett, his mother's best friend and neighbour to the house the next day. There he strangled her using Koo's scarf, stripped her body and unsuccessfully attempted to rape her, then decapitated her, before fleeing across the country.

I came up behind her and crooked my arm around her neck [...] I squeezed and just lifted her off the floor. She just hung there and, for a moment, I didn't realize she was dead. I had broken her neck and her head was just wobbling around with the bones of her neck disconnected in the skin sack of her neck.

Stealing Hallett's car, then renting another to shake the trail, Kemper endured almost three days of sleepless driving before he phoned the Santa Cruz police. He had made it as far as Colorado. They knew who the murderer was from all the times they had socialized with "Big Ed" but they were not prepared for what he had to tell them, "I killed my mother and her friend. And I killed those college girls. I killed six of them and I can show you where I hid the pieces of their bodies."

A full confession detailed all of the killings, mutilations and necrophilia. Kemper accompanied officers to the locations of body parts yet undiscovered. The reason for some parts being permanently irretrievable was, he confessed, due to his cannibalism. Evidently, he had cooked and eaten two of his victims' dismembered flesh, although this could have been part of an insanity plea for his trial. The jury found him sane and guilty of eight counts of first-degree murder, and he was sentenced to life imprisonment, with the possibility of parole. He is being held at California's Folsom maximum-security prison along with Manson and Mullin, with the next parole hearing in 2012.

With Mullin spending some time in the adjoining cell, Kemper and he have had some run-ins:

> I guess you heard me say that I wanted to kill Herbie Mullin, my fellow mass murderer. Well, there was a time when I thought it would be a good solution for everyone. It would be good for society and save everyone a bundle of money. Instead of spending thousands and thousands of dollars to lock the two of us up for life to protect us from people and people from us.

Kemper killed the women his mother mocked him that he would never be able to know. In doing so, she was punishing her son for her own failing, "You're just like your father. You don't deserve to get to know them." But this just rendered Kemper paralysed in social situations and incapable of mixing normally.

> The hassle with my mother made me very inadequate around women, because they posed a threat to me. Inside, I blew them up very large. You know, the little games women play, I couldn't play, meet their demands, so I backslid [...] My frustration. My inability to communicate socially, sexually. I wasn't impotent. I was scared to death of failing in male–female relationships.

In killing these unattainable women, by keeping body parts, by using them for sex, by consuming their flesh, he took control of the situation, possessed them and proved his mother wrong.

> Alive, they were distant, not sharing with me. I was trying to establish a relationship and there was no relationship there [...] When they were being killed, there wasn't anything going on in my mind except that they were going to be mine [...] That was the only way they could be mine [...] They were like spirit wives [...] I still had their spirits. I still have them.

Most serial killers seek revenge and must keep killing until satisfied. Unlike these, it seems Kemper was able to find closure before he gave himself up. After murdering his mother, on his long drive across the country Kemper picked up two more women, considered his urges but just gave them the lift they wanted, and let them go.

BOMBERS

*Is there not some chosen curse, some hidden thunder
in the stores of heaven,
red with uncommon wrath, to blast the man who
owes his greatness to his country's ruin!*
Joseph Addison

Bombing is probably the last answer you'll give when asked about the ways serial killers kill. It doesn't seem to suit what we know about them. Selecting their victims carefully. Watching them die slowly. Being in total control of the situation. Bombs are far more indiscriminate and efficient in meting out death, and are very quick. Hence, they are more useful to terrorists and spree killers, which is why Anders Breivik, David Copeland and Timothy McVeigh don't appear within these pages, other than this cursory mention. But serial killers who do use bombs tend to still be selective in their victim choice.

What distinguishes a serial killing bomber from a terrorist? Well, in the same way that a Mafia hit man can be a serial killer, not much – except for the fact that the psychology of the serial killer is quite the opposite from having a cause to fight, and die, for. Serial killers are selfish and supercilious. They also enjoy their killing, or extract some kind of gratification, sexual or otherwise. This is not necessarily true for the terrorist who often feels a jingoistic duty to act, rather than a personal, self-serving urge. Below are two examples of serial killer bombers. One very much enjoyed his killing, and was specific about his targets. The other displayed less relish for his killing, but this could be explained by his being partly motivated by a political agenda.

Glennon Engleman
A.K.A. The Killing Dentist, Dr Death
COUNTRY USA
VICTIMS 7+
METHOD car bombs, shot, bludgeoned

Glennon Engleman was a St Louis dentist who murdered at least seven people in a variety of ways over the course of 30 years. He enjoyed all his methods, whether it was by shooting or cracking open a skull with a three-pound hammer. He once told an accomplice that he had a special talent, in that he could kill without remorse. He also said that sex was a form of intimacy, but that death was a higher form of intimacy. However, he also employed a rarer technique among serial killers – bombs.

Most of his victims were his own wealthy clients. He wanted their money and accessed it by persuading female accomplices to seduce them into marriage. They would get a share of the money after Engleman had dispatched their new spouse, with gusto.

One accomplice, Barbara Boyle, conspired with Engleman to kill her husband, Ron Gusewelle, to collect on his life insurance and sizeable inheritance. Engleman talked Boyle into marrying Gusewelle as part of the plot. She was convicted of his murder and given 50 years in prison, but acquitted of the murders of his parents. Engleman had shot them in the back of the head in March 1979 and confessed to their murders while in prison. Controversially, Boyle was released from Dwight Correctional Center on parole in October 2009, after serving only half of her sentence.

Two of Engleman's murders are known to have been carried out with bombs. The first was made to look like an accidental dynamite explosion, which killed his business partner Eric Frey in September 1963. Frey is supposed to have accidently slipped down a well before being blown up. The other was a car bomb that killed Sophie Marie Barrera, owner of the St Louis dental laboratory, in January 1980. Engleman had owed her over $14,000. A month later, Engleman was arrested and convicted of two murders, receiving two consecutive 50-year jail terms. He died in prison from diabetes in 1999.

Theodore Kaczynski
A.K.A. The Unabomber
COUNTRY USA
VICTIMS 3
METHOD mail bombs

A bad bout of hives as an infant left Theodore Kaczynski in isolation at hospital and feeling abandoned at a very young age. His mother would identify this moment in his life as permanently affecting their relationship, over time changing the happy child into a solitary boy with poor social skills. This was later exacerbated by his skipping a grade in school and putting him amongst older pupils, by virtue of his IQ testing at the genius level of 167.

In 1952, the family moved to the Chicago suburb of Evergreen Park. It was the archetypal middle-class American family life, focussing on a healthy body and healthy mind, with education a top priority. Kaczynski responded well and as a 12-year-old his favourite book was Raymond Wesley Anderson's text, *Romping Through Mathematics*. He found school maths classes too simple. Unsurprisingly, he joined the maths club at high school, but also played trombone in the band. He became known as one of the "Briefcase Boys", brainy overachievers known for setting off explosions in class as pranks. These, the first of his bombs, were harmless, but he very quickly advanced on to larger explosions that did do damage, once blowing out a classroom's windows.

Completing his education early, Kaczynski won a scholarship to Harvard when still only 16. There he continued to be antisocial. Fellow students even disliked visiting his dorm room, complaining it was two-foot deep in trash, and smelled of rotting food and stale milk. But despite his personal hygiene, he still managed to achieve 98.9 per cent final grade in mathematical logic. It is interesting to note that there was a prevailing intellectual atmosphere at Harvard at this time, deriding technological progress and the evils of society. There was also a programme of extreme and unsettling psychological tests being carried out, and Kaczynski was one of the participants.

Graduating in 1962, Kaczynski moved on to take a PhD in maths at the University of Michigan, winning the annual prize for best mathematics dissertation. Publishing related maths papers and teaching occupied the rest of his time, although students complained that his teaching was incommunicative and useless. Nonetheless, in 1967, Kaczynski became an assistant professor of mathematics at the University of California, Berkeley, the youngest professor ever hired by the university. His teaching did not improve and more complaints were made of his stuttering and mumbling during lectures, and ignoring students at all other times.

To the surprise of everybody who knew Kaczynski as a dedicated academic, quite suddenly, on the day of Nixon's inauguration in January 1969, he resigned and gave up mathematics for good, aged 26. His superiors were bewildered by his change of tack, "He could have advanced up the ranks and been a senior member of the faculty today." However, a psychiatrist report written 30 years later shed some additional light on Kaczynski's reasons:

In the summer after his fourth year, he describes experiencing a period of several weeks where he was sexually excited nearly all the time and was fantasizing himself as a woman and being unable to obtain any sexual relief. He decided to make an effort to have a sex change operation. When he returned to the University of Michigan he made an appointment to see a psychiatrist to be examined to determine if the sex change would be good for him. He claimed that by putting on an act he could con the psychiatrist into thinking him suitable for a feminine role even though his motive was exclusively erotic. As he was sitting in the waiting room, he turned completely against the idea of the operation and thus, when he saw the doctor, instead claimed he was depressed about the possibility of being drafted. He describes the following: As I walked away from the building afterwards, I felt disgusted about what my uncontrolled sexual cravings had almost led me to do and I felt – humiliated, and I violently hated the psychiatrist. Just then there came a major turning point in my life. Like a Phoenix, I burst from the ashes of my despair to a glorious new hope. I thought I wanted to kill that psychiatrist because the future looked utterly empty to me. I felt I wouldn't care if I died. And so I said to myself why not really kill the psychiatrist and anyone else whom I hate. What is important is not the words that ran through my mind but the way I felt about them. What was entirely new was the fact that I really felt I could kill someone. My very hopelessness had liberated me because I no longer cared about death. I no longer cared about consequences and I said to myself that I really could break out of my rut in life and do things that were daring, irresponsible or criminal. He describes his first thought was to kill someone he hated and then kill himself, but decided he could not relinquish his rights so easily. At that point he decided: I will kill but I will make at least some effort to avoid detection so that I can kill again.

Even at this early stage, even before Berkeley, Kaczynski had formulated a plan to complete his degree and to work for two years, so as to save enough money to live in the wilderness, preferably Canada. After a short period back at his parents' home in the Chicago suburb of Lombard, and an unsuccessful attempt to purchase land in British Columbia, he did eventually succeed in buying land near Lincoln, Montana, and inspired by a favourite poet, Henry David Thoreau, he built a remote single room shack, without electricity or running water. Receiving some money from his family towards the initial cost, and periodically thereafter, Kaczynski earned additional money doing menial jobs in Salt Lake City.

Conditions deteriorated in his solitary existence, and feeling the isolation, he found himself desiring a wife and a family of his own. So, returning to Lombard in 1978, he went to work for his brother in a local foam rubber plant. Kaczynski even started dating and seemed happier and more gregarious than ever before, but when he was dumped, it was difficult for him to accept the rejection. His brother was eventually forced to fire him for harassing the ex-girlfriend. Kaczynski was devastated and spent days in his room.

Finding his mountain idyll more and more under threat from development he wrote about his concerns as part of a growing manifesto intended to capture his neo-Luddite philosophy:

> *The technophiles are taking us all on an utterly reckless ride into the unknown. Many people understand something of what technological progress is doing to us yet take a passive attitude toward it because they think it is inevitable. But we don't think it is inevitable. We think it can be stopped, and we will give here some indications of how to go about stopping it.*

When the manifesto was first viewed, prior to Kaczynski's capture, the use of "we" and "FC" as an abbreviation for Freedom Club throughout misled the authorities into thinking they were dealing with a conspiracy. It took some time for them to realize it was probably an author's "we", a common construct in mathematical writing. But we are getting ahead of ourselves. Before any killings, Kaczynski had already decided what he had to do "to go about stopping it":

> *I intend to start killing people. If I am successful at this, it is possible that, when I am caught (not alive, I fervently hope!) there will be some speculation in the news media as to my motives for killing .... If some speculation occurs, they are bound to make me out to be a sickie, and to ascribe to me motives of a sordid or "sick" type. Of course, the term "sick" in such a context represents a value judgment... the news media may have something to say about me when I am killed or caught. And they are bound to try to analyse my psychology and depict me as "sick." This powerful bias should be borne [in mind] in reading any attempts to analyse my psychology.*

The first bombing occurred in May 1978. A primitive, homemade device was sent to a professor of materials engineering at Northwestern University in Evanston, Illinois, but the package looked suspicious so a security guard investigated. The bomb exploded but was only big enough to injure the guard's left hand. A year later, a second bomb was sent to the Technological Institute in Illinois, injuring a graduate student who had joked with his supervisor that it could be a bomb. The small explosion also caused minor cuts and burns.

Six months later a package started smoking in the Boeing 727 cargo hold of American Airlines Flight 444 on the way from Chicago's O'Hare airport to Washington, DC. The device, which had failed to explode, was large enough to have destroyed the plane. In the end, a dozen passengers were treated for smoke inhalation. The FBI recognized a serial bomber was involved, calling the case "UNABOM", in a combination of the locations of universities and the airport. The media were quick to adapt this to dub the mystery criminal "The Unabomber".

The FBI drew up a psychological offender profile of the Unabomber in 1980 to assist them in the case. Profiling had been in use for a couple of decades, and in retrospect it seemed impressively accurate here, describing the culprit as "a man with above-average intelligence with connections to academia", later refined to "a neo-Luddite holding an academic degree in the hard sciences". A subsequent revision based on the bomb fragments tried to take into account the presence of wood shavings. But, not knowing Kaczynski was a proficient carpenter and woodworker, the result was less true to life, imaging the bomber to be "a blue-collar airplane mechanic". A $1 million reward was also offered for anyone who could provide information leading to the Unabomber's capture.

Up in his mountain lair, Kaczynski was refining his bomb making, and even inserting false clues for the FBI, so that in June 1980, a device sent to the president of United Airlines, Percy Wood, severely injured him, causing extensive cuts and burns. The next bomb, sent to the University of Utah in Salt Lake City in October 1981, was diffused before it could go off, but six months later, a secretary working at Vanderbilt University in Nashville was severely burned and injured by shrapnel. Two months later, the same fate befell an engineering professor at Kaczynski's old employer, the University of California, Berkeley. Then, for no apparent reason, the bombings stopped.

Whether Kaczynski felt that he had achieved his mission, or had gone off the idea is unclear, but we do know what contributed to him starting again. On a trek from his cabin, he visited a favoured beauty spot but found it obliterated by a new road being built:

The best place, to me, was the largest remnant of this plateau that dates from the tertiary age. It's kind of rolling country, not flat, and when you get to the edge of it you find these ravines that cut very steeply in to cliff-like drop-offs and there was even a waterfall there. It was about a two days hike from my cabin. That was the best spot until the summer of 1983. That summer there were too many people around my cabin so I decided I needed some peace. I went back to the plateau and when I got there I found they had put a road right through the middle of it [...] You just can't imagine how upset I was. It was from that point on I decided that, rather than trying to acquire further wilderness skills, I would work on getting back at the system. Revenge.

Three bombs followed in quick succession in May, June and November 1985, two of which caused severe wounds. But it was the next bomb that would escalate the severity and vindictiveness of Kaczynski's attacks. Taking a look to check the package left outside his computer store in Sacramento in December 1985, Hugh Scrutton was killed by a booby-trapped nail-and-splinter-loaded bomb. A similar device severely injured another computer store owner, Gary Wright, in Salt Lake City in February 1987. It was on this occasion that Kaczynski was spotted while positioning the bomb. He was described as wearing a hoodie and dark glasses, and the artist's impression would become one of the best-known pictures in America.

However, knowing that his anonymity had been compromised, Kaczynski laid low in his mountain retreat. During this time his family supported him financially, even though he lashed out, blaming everything, from his academic failure as a mathematician to being shorter than his brother, on his parents' expectations of him:

If I experienced any failure or showed any weakness, I found that I couldn't come to you for sympathy. Because rather than giving me moral support you would show your disappointment in me. I was supposed to be your perfect little genius so as to gratify your vanity.

Desperate, his brother wrote to try to heal the rift in their family. The response was not positive:

I get just choked with frustration at my inability to get our stinking family off my back once and for all. And stinking family emphatically includes you! I DON'T EVER WANT TO SEE YOU OR HEAR FROM YOU OR ANY OTHER MEMBER OF OUR FAMILY AGAIN.

This continuing aggression and indifference to his father's long illness and consequential suicide concerned his family to the point of considering having him committed.

After another hiatus, this time of six years, the attacks were resumed in June 1993. Two bombs in as many days deafened a geneticist from Tiburon, California, also blowing off parts of three fingers, and severely damaged the right hand and eye of a computer science professor at Yale University.

In December 1994, advertising executive Thomas Mosser from New Jersey was killed by a mail bomb sent to his home. Kaczynski would later reason that Mosser's company had, "helped Exxon clean up its public image after the Exxon Valdez incident" and, "its business is the development of techniques for manipulating people's attitudes".

The next of Kaczynski's bombs would perhaps strike the greatest fear into the American public – the same fear of being under siege experienced on 9/11. Only five days after the Oklahoma bombing by Timothy McVeigh in April 1995, in what could almost be seen as an attempt to reclaim the bombing crown, Kaczynski targeted timber industry lobbyist and president of the California Forestry Association Gilbert Murray, by sending a mail bomb to the CFA headquarters in Sacramento. Tragically for Murray, Kaczynski's package was addressed to the previous president William Dennison, who had retired.

Also thinking of retiring, Kaczynski demanded that his 50-plus page, 35,000-word essay "Industrial Society and Its Future", called the "Unabomber Manifesto" by the FBI, be published verbatim. The *New York Times* and the *Washington Post* agreed and the manifesto was published in September 1995, and caused a media storm. Kaczynski's brother and wife followed the news of the Unabomber and had increasing suspicions. They knew of Kaczynski's attitude towards technology, something he had expounded upon in an early essay, and which he had made known to them was destroying his wilderness home.

The Kaczynski family hired a private investigator, who then approached a lawyer, Anthony Bisceglie. Bisceglie was struck by the similarity between Kaczynski's essay and the Unabomber's manifesto. Furthermore, the investigator found a pattern match between Kaczynski's known movements and the Unabomber's targets. It wasn't long before the FBI had been informed and they suddenly had a new prime suspect. Disguised as lumberjacks, the FBI finally set up surveillance of Kaczynski's cabin.

They began a lengthy surveillance on Kaczynski's Montana shack near Stemple Pass – a home without lighting, heating or electricity, in-line with his back-to-basics philosophy. Ironically, the FBI used orbiting satellites to bug his home – a high-tech touch he would have despised.

On Wednesday the agents knocked on his door. "Ted, we'd like to have a talk," said one. Kaczynski struggled to escape through a back door. He was hurled to the floor, handcuffed and led away.

Daily Mirror, 5th April 1996

In April 1996, Kaczynski was apprehended and taken off, but the FBI's first priority was to clean him up, as he was in such a wretched and filthy state.

Vicki Morris, a waitress at a local restaurant, said: "He was very dirty and he smelled. But he had no one to impress.

"What's he going to get spruced up for – a tree?"

Daily Mirror, 5th April 1996

Meanwhile, Kaczynski's cabin was searched for evidence. It was a very small building, but held a wealth of clues and was a living museum of his lonely existence, 25 years on and off spent as a hermit in the wilderness, replete with a plentiful stash of tinned and dried supplies. Dirty handprints marked posts and doorways, and an area of grime stretched along a wall, which he'd lean against when sitting on his bed. Opposite, a typed quote was pasted above the door, "Taking a bath in winter breaks an Indiana law."

The investigators found diagrams of explosives, two live bombs and a roster of potential targets, including the names of 25 Berkeley professors of mathematics, and some of Kaczynski's previous classmates. There were also diaries recording several of the bombings, plus the original copy of the Unabomber's manifesto. Links could also be made between his influences and motivations. Prominent among the few dozen books he kept was a copy of Joseph Conrad's 1907 novel, *The Secret Agent*, which features "The Professor", an anarchic explosives expert. It came to light that Kaczynski would sometimes travel under the name "Conrad".

The only find that seemed particularly out of place with the other accessories, for a mountain man existence, was a notebook written entirely in numerical code. The cypher couldn't be cracked until a decade later when it was eventually unscrambled using his own key involving six steps, which he termed "phases", to translate it by addition, subtraction and conjoining numbers, and reading the rows of numbers in specific directions, diagonally across the page, in columns running down the page and so on.

In total, Kaczynski made and dispatched 16 bombs over 18 years, injuring 23 people and killing three. Prior to his trial, court psychiatrists diagnosed Kaczynski as a paranoid schizophrenic, a condition he shared with fellow mathematician and Nobel laureate John Nash who had struggled through the 1950s and 1960s convinced he was the target of a communist conspiracy. Kaczynski's diagnosis was challenged, but in any case he rejected the plea of insanity posted in his defence in an attempt to avoid the death penalty. In April 1996 he was formally charged with 10 counts of illegally transporting, mailing and using bombs, and the murders of Scrutton, Mosser and Murray. He was convicted and received four life sentences without possibility of parole. In January 1998 he attempted, and failed, to hang himself, using shredded underpants.

While serving his sentence, Kaczynski continues to write, although never in reply to his brother. Instead he has corresponded with 400 others, and has also had a collection of essays and a revised version of the Unabomber manifesto published in 2010 as a single volume called *Technological Slavery*. He has unsuccessfully contested confiscation of all his other writing, which he claims forced him to publish the book prematurely. Those other works and his possessions are being sold off to raise compensation for the families of his victims. Even his cabin has been moved in its entirety and now features in a crime museum. Kaczynski is currently being held at the supermax prison in Florence, Colorado, where he still thinks about the mountains:

> *What worries me is that I might in a sense adapt to this environment and come to be comfortable here and not resent it anymore. And I am afraid that as the years go by that I may forget, I may begin to lose my memories of the mountains and the woods and that's what really worries me, that I might lose those memories, and lose that sense of contact with wild nature in general. But I am not afraid they are going to break my spirit.*

SHOOTERS

Well, don't you know that happiness is a warm gun, Mamma
John Lennon

Serial killers don't tend to kill by shooting their victims. It's certainly an effective way, but too quick for some multiple murderers who like to toy with their prey. A gun is a more powerful threat than most weapons, but unwieldy compared to a knife held to the throat, or bare hands, for that hands-on experience. Plus, there may be reasons why a serial killer can't get hold of a gun, or doesn't want to obtain one legally because of the paper trail it may leave. Guns are also noisy, which will give the game away, unless you're in a remote location. Regardless of these negatives, there are always exceptions, often in regions where guns are commonplace and where using them won't attract undue attention, or where the killer can make a quick getaway, or where the victim might be taken somewhere isolated, before their brains are blown out.

Edward Theodore Gein
A.K.A. American Psycho
COUNTRY USA
VICTIMS 5+
METHOD shot
MUTILATION dismembered, decapitated, disembowelled, cannibalism, skinned

Edward Theodore Gein is one of the most famous serial killers of all time, albeit better known in other guises. Immortalized as Norman Bates in Robert Bloch's 1959 novel *Psycho* and the subsequent Hitchcock classic, Leatherface in *The Texas Chainsaw Massacre*, and Buffalo Bill in *The Silence of the Lambs*, Ed Gein was about as distasteful as they come, and all for the love of a mother.

Augusta Gein was a dominating and deeply devout woman of German descent, who usurped her alcoholic husband George as head of the family, and, every day, taught her two sons, eldest Henry and Edward, who was seven years younger, the chaste lessons of the Old Testament, warning them of immoral women. In fact, of all women, except herself. She dissuaded them of sexual thoughts with threats of fire and brimstone, dousing Gein in scalding water after she caught him masturbating in the bathtub, grabbing his genitals and calling them, "the curse of man".

Demoting her husband from owner–manager to clerk, she ran the family grocery business in La Crosse, until they had enough savings to move, in 1913, to a remote 195-acre farm in Plainfield. Although they were still in Wisconsin, they had escaped what she thought were the corrupting influences of the city. Gein's mother continued to exert her control in their new home. She emasculated her sons, chiding them that they were as useless as their father, setting chilling parallels with the early life of Edmund Kemper, which was not the only coincidence between the two Eds.

Gein was discouraged from making friends, which made him even more shy and effeminate than he already was, but his mother's word was gospel, and he was devoted to her. He was bullied at school because of his small stature, and a tic that caused him to laugh impulsively. His only escape was into the pages of magazines and adventure books. He started to dwell on unhealthy fascinations and experienced an orgasm while watching his parents slaughtering a hog.

When his father died from a heart attack in 1940, Gein earned money doing odd jobs and babysitting. Lacking social skills he felt more comfortable in the company of children. The brothers also took on handyman jobs to subsidize the farm, working well together, but Henry started criticizing their mother, rebelling against her rule and wanting to meet women and not to be always a bachelor. He was found dead in suspicious circumstances in 1944 aged 43, while tackling a runaway fire on their land. He had not been burned, but showed signs of having been hit over the head. It is notable that Gein knew exactly where to find the body. However, a ruling of accidental death by asphyxiation was passed and no charges were brought.

Gein now had his mother all to himself, until December 1945 when she died from a stroke, aged 67. It was her second in a short time, and in the interim Gein had waited on her hand and foot, and she had shown promising signs that she was making a recovery. Instead, Gein was suddenly bereft and utterly alone. Staying at the farm he boarded off most of the house, preserving it as a shrine to her memory, living in just the kitchen and the small next-door living-room-cum-bedroom. He continued to do odd jobs and babysit. He was the local handyman, shy, a little odd, didn't hunt like the rest of the menfolk, didn't like blood, but harmless enough.

When not carrying out his menial work, Gein was an avid reader, although his choice of reading matter was considered unsavoury by some, particularly the parents of the children he continued to babysit, and whom he regaled with morbid tales. His favourites were magazines about true crime, lust killings, death and exhumation, and he also enjoyed books on anatomy and the Nazis, disasters, and exotic tales of headhunting and cannibalism. His favourite part of the newspaper was the obituary column. And he also paid regular visits to graveyards.

One of the boys he babysat told of being shown shrunken heads at the Gein farm. The boy's claims were questionable, and in any case Gein simply fobbed off any follow-up enquiries, claiming them to be souvenirs from the South Pacific, sent by a cousin who had served in the Second World War. Had the boy's claims been followed up, Gein might have been caught much sooner, whereas he was eventually arrested in November 1957 following the robbery of a local hardware store, for which he was the prime suspect. Fifty-year-old Bernice Worden, the store owner, was nowhere to be found, but a bloody trail led to the car park.

Deputy Sheriff Frank Worden had returned from a deer hunt and tried calling in at his mother's store, but the front of the shop was locked up. Fetching the spare keys from his house, the first thing he noticed on entering was that the cash register had been taken. The next was a pool of blood. He also noted that half a gallon of antifreeze was the last entry in her sales record. He knew instantly that Gein had to be involved. He had been hanging around the shop a lot recently, vaguely asking about item prices, about the hunting trip, sounding the guys out about how many were going, and for how long. Worden had always found Gein shifty, and had sometimes seen him parked opposite the store, as if staking it out. Furthermore, Gein had said he would be back to pick up some antifreeze.

Police went out to the Gein farm, initially to make enquiries, but it became immediately obvious that they needed to initiate a search. The stench was unbearable but the place too dark to see why, other than there was a thick layer of rotting garbage covering the farmhouse floors, except for where they could see into the pristine, sealed-off rooms. They'd have to get some light in there. Meanwhile, picking his way through the junk in an adjoining shed by the light of his torch, Sheriff Arthur Schley bumped into something. Recoiling he saw it was a decapitated and gutted deer carcass that was starting to go off, adding to the nauseous smell. Staring at the upturned carcass for a moment, picking out features on the freakish form with his flashlight, he was unable to reconcile something niggling at the recesses of his mind. Unable to come to terms with the onslaught on his senses, he couldn't even think straight. Then it hit him, like a head-on collision with a truck. It wasn't a deer.

What the investigators found when they searched the farmhouse was, to say the least, traumatic: four noses; human bones and fragments; human skull bowls; human skull bedpost tops; 10 female heads with sawn-off crowns; more heads in bags; four chairs covered with human skin; bracelets of human skin; a purse with a human skin handle; a knife sheath of human skin; nine vulvae, salted and in a shoe box; a human nipple belt; a pair of lips decorating a window-blind draw-string; and a human bone and skin lampshade, drum and wastepaper basket. The shrunken heads seen by the boy turned out to be masks. Gein had made nine in total, by carefully skinning skulls. They were eyeless, but the scalps still had hair and some of the lips still wore lipstick, and some had been treated with oil, just as one feeds leather. Four he had stuffed with newspaper and nailed to his bedroom wall. But, perhaps more horrifying, they also found a life-size suit, made entirely of human skin, with arms, leggings, socks, vest, shirt – and breasts.

Gein had never come to terms with his mother's death. He wanted to resurrect her, so he exhumed her, and others that looked like her. But he needed to fill her with life. He had to become her. In effect, he craved a sex change and dreamed of being a woman, his mother in particular, because of the power she had over men, as had been convincingly demonstrated to him. Simply dressing up in women's clothing wasn't going to be enough for him. Sex reassignment surgery was by then a couple of decades old, and so feasibly possible, but Gein had his own surgical solution. He would recreate the image of his mother, for which he would need a working knowledge of anatomy, hence the books, and plenty of raw materials. Then, wearing his creation, he would fill the house once more with her presence, acting as she did, looking like she did. His transvestism was going to be more than just skin-deep.

Under interrogation, Gein told police that he had robbed graves about 10 out of the 40 times he had made nocturnal excursions to cemeteries between 1947 and 1952. He had used the obituary column to keep himself well informed of recent deaths, and had specifically selected large, stocky deceased women who physically resembled his mother. The times he came home empty-handed had been when he had come out of a daze-like state that always overtook him. The other times, he had loaded each body into his car, taken it home, decapitated it, then hung it upside down, suspending it by ropes from the wrists and with a crossbar piercing the ankles. This would facilitate disembowelment. Slicing deeply from the genitals to the throat, the guts would simply drop clear to the floor. In other words, being practical, he just employed the standard way of "dressing" an animal in preparation for skinning which, of course, was his next step, before tanning.

He would also cut away the anus and vagina, but claimed to have never indulged in necrophilia with the cadavers, complaining, "They smelled too bad." However, it is probable that he obtained sexual release by fondling the disembodied genitalia. Importantly, for his role play, he needed breasts and a vagina. His mother's vagina was especially important to him. He had kept her vulva too. It was in the box with the others, but hers ... hers needed to stand out. Hers should shine. Hers, he had painted silver.

His statement so infuriated Schley that he smashed Gein's head and face into the wall, but that had the unfortunate effect of nullifying his testimony. The stress of dealing with Gein, searching the house and providing his own testimony in the trial, probably contributed to Schley's premature death in December 1957, only a month after the court ruled Gein insane and therefore not culpable of his actions. Schley had taken it badly. The deer carcass he had discovered had turned out to be Worden. Her head had turned up in a sack in the house. It had a .32 calibre bullet wound and a nail in each ear connected by a wire, ready to be hung on a wall. Her still-warm entrails were wrapped in newspaper and a man's suit, and dumped in the corner. Her heart had been found in a plastic bag in front of the pot-bellied stove. Perhaps waiting?

FARMER AND THE 5 DEAD WOMEN

"Looks like cannibalism" says District Attorney

A DRAMATIC question was put to Farmer Edward Gein today. It was: "Did you eat five women?"

Hollow-eyed, round-shouldered Gein, fifty-year-old bachelor, was facing District Attorney Earl Kileen.

Police had called at Gein's lonely farm in Wisconsin in their search for Mrs. Bernice Worden, 58 – missing from her hardware store at Plainfield since Saturday.

They found her – headless and hanging by the heels from the kitchen ceiling at the farm.

Gein is said, to have told the police: "I've been killing for seven years." Then – according to Mr. Kileen – Gein opened a box and produced five women's skulls.

Mr. Kileen asked him: "Did you eat the five women? Did you intend to eat Mrs. Worden?"

Gein is alleged to have replied: "I can't remember."

According to B.U.P. (American), the skulls and bones of five more people were found in the house of horror.

"It looks like cannibalism," said the District Attorney.

In three hours of questioning today, Gein told the police that he robbed graves to get the skulls and bones.

Under a heavy guard, Gein was taken to the county gaol for further questioning. Wearing faded green trousers, a cap and a jacket, he plodded through heavy snow to the police car.

Police say that he will be taken to a place where – he claims – he dug up the skulls from graves.

Skin Tests

Lamps and chairs have been taken from the farm for tests – to see if their coverings consist of human skin.

Police first went to see Farmer Gein because he had been heard to say that he intended buying antifreeze mixture at Mrs. Worden's shop.

On the counter there they found a copy of a bill for the last item she had sold before closing her shop.

It was for one gallon of antifreeze.

The cash register was missing.

It is said to have been found in Farmer Gein's bedroom and tonight he was charged with stealing the register.

The search of his nine-roomed house goes on.

All police dossiers on unsolved murders and missing people in Wisconsin are being searched, too.

Daily Mirror, 19th November 1957

Gein always denied any accusations of cannibalism. The rumours may have started when his reading preferences were reported in the media. In addition, the refrigerator was full of human organs, some relatively fresh, so it wasn't long before people were speculating about the fact that Gein gave his neighbours presents of venison, although he never went hunting.

Ignoring the hype, the police had a difficult job to do. Over the years there had been a noticeable rise in the number of missing persons reported in Wisconsin and the authorities wanted to know why. Understandably, the prosecution were keen to pin as many of these on Gein as possible, but the incriminating evidence was weak. Eight-year-old Georgia Weckler had disappeared on her way home from school in May 1947. The only clue was tyre tracks left in the snow. Fifteen-year-old Evelyn Hartley had been snatched from a home while babysitting in 1953, a trail of clothing and bloodstains led away from the house. Deer hunters Victor Travis and Ray Burgess simply vanished in 1952. No sign of any of them has ever been found.

Plainfield pub landlady Mary Hogan went missing in 1954, with only a spent .32 pistol cartridge and a pool of blood found, suggesting that she had been shot. Shortly afterwards, a local sawmill operator happened to be chatting with Gein about Hogan's disappearance. Gein was later reported to have joked, "She isn't missing, she's at the farm right now", but the comment slipped by. Her fate was only learnt on discovery of her skinned skull in Gein's house. Her facial skin had been made into one of the masks, softened with oil and put in a paper sack, to be pulled out by an unsuspecting policeman.

Faced with irrefutable evidence during interrogation, Gein had confessed to killing Hogan and Worden. While most of the body parts found in his house could be traced to individual graves, many were not identified and didn't belong to the two murder victims. The question of how many Gein killed remains unsolved, adding to his unsavoury mystique.

While he was being held in the maximum-security Central State Hospital for the Criminally Insane in Waupun, Wisconsin, Gein's house and belongings were put up for auction. A fee was proposed for viewing the property, but locals objected at turning the place into a "museum for the morbid" and the fee idea was dropped. That wasn't enough to save the farm and it mysteriously burned down in March 1958. On being told, Gein shrugged and said, "Just as well." On the other hand, his 1949 Ford sedan was sold and over 2,000 punters queued round the block and paid a quarter each to see the "ghoul car", at the Outagamie County Fair, until showing it was banned.

> *SEE THE CAR THAT HAULED THE DEAD FROM*
> *THEIR GRAVES!*
> *ED GEIN'S CRIME CAR!*
> *$1,000 REWARD IF IT'S NOT TRUE!*

Still desperate to clear up the missing persons list, police brought Gein in to sit a polygraph test a few years later, in 1960. That same year, the police also wanted to dispose of all the evidence collected from the farm, which they had been storing. Most of it was incinerated, but some remains from Catholic graves were put together in a box and received a common burial.

In January 1968, Gein was re-examined and this time found to be sufficiently sane to stand trial for his crimes. The proceedings went ahead in November 1968 and it took only a week for him to be found guilty of the first-degree murder of Worden. But, because he had been officially proclaimed insane when Worden had died, he was found not guilty by reason of insanity, and acquitted. He was returned to the mental institution, was later transferred to Madison's Mendota State Hospital, where he read copiously, took part in occupational therapy and enjoyed listening to the radio, until he died there from respiratory and heart failure due to cancer, in July 1984, aged 77 and senile. The warden described him as a model patient, saying, "If all our patients were like him, we'd have no trouble at all." Gein was buried in Plainfield cemetery, among graves he had robbed, and alongside his mother.

Conversely, the case will not die and won't until there is a definitive answer to how many people he killed, how many graves he dug up, and what motivated such depravity. The community had to come to terms with how they had failed to notice his criminal activities. Gein vehemently blamed the town and his neighbours for not paying him any attention when he was all alone, other than to take advantage, which may have angered him, but undeniably, and prior to that, his mother had instilled a perverse and confusing attitude towards women. Women were harlots, and to be avoided. Her sons were to dedicate themselves to her alone, at the cost to their own chances of having families, seeking happiness and having sex. Yet, this dedication was not rewarded, and they had to remain loyal despite her abuse. Nonetheless, when she died, Gein was left without a guiding light, a moral compass, and the only source of affection that he had received, or was even allowed. The resultant conflicting effect on Gein's psyche was catastrophic.

In 1995, 10 female skeletons, and that of Gein's postman who had gone missing in 1956, were retrieved from a well near the old farm site. Gein never seemed to appreciate the seriousness of his crimes, or that they were crimes at all. Getting an answer to "Why?" from him was never going to be satisfactory. When asked, he replied, "I had a compulsion to do it." Other than that, he kept mum.

Robert (Willie) Pickton
COUNTRY Canada
VICTIMS 49
METHOD shot
MUTILATION dismembered

With echoes of Ed Gein, Robert Pickton lured prostitutes to his pig farm in Port Coquitlam, British Columbia, offering them paid sex and drug-fuelled parties. There, they were handcuffed, raped, strangled or shot, bled and gutted, and their remains fed to his pigs. It is also possible that the victims' meat was ground, mixed with pork mince and given to friends and family. Raiding the farm for illegal firearms in 2002, Canadian police also found possessions belonging to a known missing woman, including an asthma inhaler.

Apprehending Pickton, they carried out a search of the farm, as part of an investigation to locate up to 60 women missing from Vancouver's Downtown Eastside from the 1980s onwards. An undercover policeman planted in Pickton's cell would hear him boasting of 49 murders, and saying he felt disappointed he didn't have the opportunity to, "do one more, make it an even 50. That's why I was sloppy, I wanted one more. Make … make the big five-O."

I KILLED 49 WOMEN AND FED THEM TO MY PIGS

Farmer's confession to undercover cop on murders

Pickton, 56, is said to have picked up the women, mostly prostitutes and drug addicts, from Vancouver's red light district.

He is alleged to have taken them back to his remote 17-acre farm, where he butchered them.

He is then said to have put their bodies through an industrial woodchipper and fed their mince to his pigs, some of which were later slaughtered and sold into the human food chain. Jurors were warned that details of the crimes would be "like a horror movie" and relatives of the victims began to cry as the case was opened.

The court heard that a police interviewer had suggested he was caught because he hadn't cleaned up blood properly. He is said to have replied: "I was going to shut it down. That's when I was just sloppy. Just the last one." […]

The court heard that the heads, hands and feet of two women were found in a freezer at the farm in Port Coquitlam, outside Vancouver.

The heads had been cut in half vertically using a power saw and matched DNA samples from two missing women. Forensic evidence, including partial jaw bones, hand bones and teeth belonging to another four women, was also found there.

Daily Mirror, 23rd January 2007

Other than skulls cut in half, stuffed with human hands and feet, forensics also discovered DNA from 33 women, bloody clothing belonging to a victim, and a jawbone and teeth belonging to another. They also found a .22 revolver with a dildo attached to its barrel, .357 Magnum rounds, two pairs of faux fur-lined handcuffs, a pair of night-vision goggles, and photos of a garbage can containing the remains of a victim. The dildo carried both the victim's and Pickton's DNA.

In December 2007 Pickton was convicted of six murders, commuted from first-degree to second, and sentenced to life in prison with no possibility of parole for 25 years. A further 20 charges were dropped in August 2010. He is currently being held in Kent Institution in British Columbia.

David Berkowitz
A.K.A. Son of Sam, The .44 Caliber Killer
COUNTRY USA
VICTIMS 6
METHOD shot, stabbed

David Berkowitz was the Devil. Inasmuch as that is what he claimed happened to him from a very early age – that he was taken over by demons:

> Around the age of five, I began to experience a lot of emotional problems and inner struggles, various emotional and psychological problems. I was not behaving, not growing up as a normal child. There was this dark, evil, satanic pull in my life [...] As I got older, I began to run the streets, hanging out with some of the older teenagers. I felt these urges to jump in front of cars, to jump off of a walk-bridge. Now, what normal child would have these kind of desires and these self-destructive things? And now, I learned this was demonic. I was demon possessed, and I believe that with all my heart.

Satanism featured significantly throughout Berkowitz's life. He was an unwanted child from an extramarital affair and had been immediately put up for adoption. Shortly after being taken on by his new family, his adoptive mother died from breast cancer in 1967. He was devastated and imagined a plot against him. His childhood fits and misbehaviour soon escalated into theft and pyromania. By the time he was a young man, he had set 1,488 fires in New York City, each documented to show how he revelled in the control he had over the flames themselves, the response of the fire service and the impact on people and places.

Things only got worse when his adoptive father remarried, to a woman Berkowitz despised. It was during his early teens that he was first introduced to the occult, by his new stepsister who was interested in witchcraft. Soon, the rest of the family had moved to Florida, and 18-year-old Berkowitz was left alone in the Big Apple.

After a three-year spell in the Army during which he excelled as a marksman, he was honorably discharged in 1974. He became a postal worker and within the year had joined a spiritualist cult. Initially they only dabbled in seances and fortune-telling, but they were soon involved with drugs, sadistic pornography and violent crime.

Berkowitz suffered periods of psychosis and paranoia around this time, putting a cryptic suggestion of what he was about to do in a letter to his adoptive father:

> It's cold and gloomy here in New York, but that's okay because the weather fits my mood – gloomy. Dad, the world is getting dark now. I can feel it more and more. The people, they are developing a hatred for me. You wouldn't believe how much some people hate me. Many of them want to kill me. I don't even know these people, but still they hate me. Most of them are young. I walk down the street and they spit and kick at me. The girls call me ugly and they bother me the most. The guys just laugh. Anyhow, things will soon change for the better.

Beginning with a knife attack on two women – both of whom survived – in late 1975, Berkowitz then bought a .44 Special Charter Arms Bulldog Pug revolver and between July 1976 and July 1977, used it to shoot 13 people, killing six. There was no rape nor torture, theft nor destruction of property. In each instance, he might rapidly approach a parked vehicle on foot, crouch as he aimed, then discharge the gun's five rounds. Other victims were attacked while actually driving, Berkowitz simply firing indiscriminately through the car windows as he drove alongside in his yellow Ford Galaxie, or, if they were on foot, he might walk towards them them as if to ask directions. Several of the survivors received serious injuries from the attacks, including head injuries, paralysis and blindness. Berkowitz commented, "I didn't want to hurt them, I only wanted to kill them."

How Son of Sam celebrated twelve months of terror on the streets of New York

THE BLOODY BIRTHDAY

THE crazy killer who calls himself "Son of Sam" struck again yesterday.

His latest attack had all the hallmarks of his eleven previous shootings.

This time his victims were two 20-year-olds on their first date – Stacy Moskowitz and Robert Violante.

They were sitting quietly in a car parked in Brooklyn when Son of Sam stepped boldly into the glare of a street light.

Quickly he dropped into his police-style marksman's crouch and fired four shots at the heads of the young couple.

Robert took three of the .44 bullets in his head. One entered his left temple and ploughed through the skull, destroying one eye and damaging the other. If he survives, he will be blind.

Stacy was hit in the back of the head. Surgeons worked for nine hours to remove a bone fragment from her brain.

[… The police] had expected a shooting on Friday night – the first anniversary of Son of Sam's first killing.

One hundred detectives, many of them volunteers, patrolled the city streets on Friday night … but the killer did not appear.

He waited until the exhausted policemen had called off the big stakeout before he took to the streets in search of his next victims.

Daily Mirror, 1ˢᵗ August 1977

Maintaining his occultism, Berkowitz would later claim that he had carried out all his attacks at the whim of a demon, who had possessed his neighbour's dog. The howling dogs in his apartment block told him to kill. They demanded the blood of young, pretty girls:

> *I'd come home [...] like at six-thirty in the morning. It would begin then, the howling. On my days, off, I heard it all night, too. It made me scream. I used to scream out begging for the noise to stop. It never did. [...] The demons never stopped. I couldn't sleep. I had no strength to fight. I could barely drive. Coming home from work one night, I almost killed myself in the car. I needed to sleep [...] The demons wouldn't give me any peace.*

It was by seeking some peace by attacking the neighbours' dogs that Berkowitz drew unwanted attention to himself. He had previously courted infamy, getting the idea of sending letters to the police from reading a book about Jack the Ripper. In his first letter, left with the bodies of a couple he had just murdered as they smooched in their car, he introduced himself as the "Son of Sam", resulting in the press latching onto the pseudonym, something he very much enjoyed. Subsequent letters taunted his hunters, naming the police captain and an investigative journalist, but they were mainly scatty and puzzling. His third letter displayed an attempt to phrase his frustrations, almost poetically, but the rest of it was contemptuous:

> *Hello from the gutters of N.Y.C., which are filled with dog manure, vomit, stale wine, urine, and blood. Hello from the*

sewers of N.Y.C. which swallow up these delicacies when they are
washed away by the sweeper trucks. Hello from the cracks in the
sidewalks of N.Y.C. and from the ants that dwell in these cracks
and feed on the dried blood of the dead that has seeped into
these cracks [...] please inform all the detectives working the
case that I wish them the best of luck. Keep 'em digging, drive
on, think positive, get off your butts, knock on coffins, etc. Upon
my capture I promise to buy all the guys working on the case a
new pair of shoes if I can get up the money.

Unbeknownst to him, his crowing was providing the police with a lot of useful information that they could use to construct a psychological profile, in which he was described as, "neurotic and probably suffering from paranoid schizophrenia and believed himself to be a victim of demonic possession".

Spreading the idea of devil worship, Berkowitz wrote strange, threatening letters to his two most recent landlords. Both had owned noisy dogs, and Berkowitz had shot them. He also wrote to a deputy sheriff who happened to be a neighbour, tipping him off that the landlords were in fact part of a demon coven run by General Jack Cosmo. The potential connections were there, but the city was in panic and every police resource was already dedicated to trying to keep the streets safe.

What ultimately proved to be his downfall though was suspiciously loitering on the pavement outside his apartment block for several hours, afraid to approach his car having received a parking ticket for blocking a fire hydrant. This got him noticed by a local resident, who then made the connection between Berkowitz and the Son of Sam killer after he attacked a couple in the same area. The police followed the lead and traced the parking ticket to Berkowitz. He was arrested in August 1977, as he emerged from his apartment into the corridor, where police were waiting for him. He said, "You got me. What took you so long?"

Berkowitz's plan to plead insanity failed him and he was found fit to stand trial. Pleading guilty to six murder charges, he was sentenced to 365 years in jail. He later amended this confession to accept responsibility for only three of the murders. The remainder, he alleged, were carried out by the "twenty-two disciples of hell", other members of the satanic cult, as set out in a letter he had arranged to be found if he was captured:

This is a warning to all police agencies in the tri-state area:
For your information, a satanic cult (devil worshippers and
practitioners of witchcraft) that has been established for quite
some time has been instructed by their high command (Satan)

to begin to systematically kill and slaughter young girls or people of good health and clean blood. "They plan to kill at least 100 young wemon [sic] and men, but mostly wemon [sic], as part of a satanic ritual which involves the shedding of the victim's blood ... Warning: the streets shall be run with blood. I, David Berkowitz, have been chosen since birth, to be one of the executioners for the cult.

While this account has some credibility, and the case was reopened to consider the claims, Berkowitz never testified in court about the cult, and the official police line has always been that there was a lone gunman. Interviewed in prison in 1979, Berkowitz himself admitted the demon dogs were really a bluff, in case he was caught, so he could plead insanity. The name "Sam" was his landlord neighbour, and the "son" bit was supposed to be the dog, actually called "Harvey". General Jack Cosmo turned out to be the previous landlord.

His real reason for shooting women stemmed from his resentment of his mother, and because of his failings with women, despite what he had written in his first letter, "I am deeply hurt by your calling me a wemon [sic] hater. I am not. But I am a monster." He got off on stalking and shooting women, and he would masturbate as soon as possible afterwards. He would return to his crime scenes and be further turned on by bloodstains, perimeter tapes and police chalk marks, and he also attempted unsuccessfully to locate the graves of his victims.

I was literally singing to myself on my way home, after the killing. The tension, the desire to kill a woman had built up in such explosive proportions that when I finally pulled the trigger, all the pressures, all the tensions, all the hatred, had just vanished, dissipated, but only for a short time.

In spite of this confession, conspiracy theorists have continued to seek a satanic aspect, even proposing a devilish pact between Charles Manson and Berkowitz. Such speculation about the case generated even more publicity for the already notorious serial killer who had exacted a reign of terror over the city for a whole year. As a consequence of Berkowitz's relationship with the press, there was a concern that he would be approached by publishers seeking an exclusive book deal. This was deemed immoral, as he would be profiting from his crimes. The Son of Sam Law now authorizes the state to hold all proceeds from such a venture and pay the money to the victim's families as compensation.

In 1979, Berkowitz was attacked in prison, resulting in him having to have 52 stitches; however, he refused to identify the knife-wielding attacker. He did claim it was a revenge attack by his old cult. Since then Berkowitz seems to be a reformed character, becoming a born-again Christian in 1987. He has consistently declined attending his parole hearings:

> *In all honesty, I believe that I deserve to be in prison for the rest of my life. I have, with God's help, long ago come to terms with my situation and I have accepted my punishment [...] As I have communicated many times throughout the years, I am deeply sorry for the pain, suffering and sorrow I have brought upon the victims of my crimes. I grieve for those who are wounded, and for the family members of those who lost a loved one because of my selfish actions. I regret what I've done and I'm haunted by it.*

He is currently being held at Sullivan Correctional Facility in Fallsburg, New York, from where he sued his former attorney in 2005, for stealing letters and personal belongings. Berkowitz only agreed to drop the case if money from publishing the material was sent to the families of victims. An out-of-court settlement made a deal and the case was closed. Now he's working on his autobiography, and again the proceeds will be sent to the families of his murder victims, proving that however demonic, every dog has its day.

John George Haigh
A.K.A. The Acid Bath Murderer
COUNTRY England
VICTIMS 9
METHOD bludgeoned, shot

A gambler motivated by greed, John Haigh stole from his victims and swindled money from their families. He famously disposed of six of his victims' bodies in an acid bath. His last victim was a wealthy 69-year-old widow, who had approached him about a business idea she had for creating artificial nails. He lured her to his workshop where he shot her in the back of the head, hid her fur coat, cash and jewellery, and put the body in a tank full of acid. He revisited the tank regularly to check on the state of the body, and when he was confident that it had fully decomposed, he disposed of the sludge in his backyard.

Haigh confessed to the murder, telling police how he had destroyed the body, boasting, "How can you prove there's a murder if there's no body?" This was a misunderstanding of *corpus delicti*, which requires a crime is proven to have occurred before anyone can be charged. In the case of murder, Haigh assumed a body would be needed. He was wrong and there was plenty of forensic evidence to make up for the lack of a corpse. On searching the backyard, police discovered three human gallstones and a set of dentures in the sludge, the latter identified by the women's dentist. Haigh confessed to nine murders. The press named him "the vampire killer" when during his trial he claimed to have drunk the blood of his victims, but this was probably a ruse to appear insane and be given a more lenient custodial sentence than the death sentence he did receive.

Stephen Griffiths
A.K.A. The Crossbow Cannibal
COUNTRY England
VICTIMS 14+
METHOD crossbow shooting, stabbed, bludgeoned, strangled
MUTILATION dismembered, cannibalism, burned

Compared to David Berkowitz's .44 Special Charter Arms Bulldog Pug revolver, which could deliver a bullet at speeds of around 300 metres per second, a commando-style recurve crossbow could be considered a poor alternative, especially with a bolt velocity of only 60 metres per second, and an accuracy of only 50 metres. Okay, so the crossbow is perhaps four times cheaper, but it's also four times heavier, and you need to draw the string back with the same energy as that needed to lift a six-foot man. All a bit of an effort, except, of course, if your prey is nearby, a sitting duck, and you get a thrill from seeing one of your bolts sticking out of someone's head. Exactly why the crossbow was Stephen Griffiths' particular weapon of choice we may never know, but in using it, and declaring himself during his court hearing "The Crossbow Cannibal", he certainly carved himself a unique niche.

Criminology student Griffiths, 40, appeared in court on Friday charged with murdering Susan [Rushworth], 43, Shelley [Armitage], 31, and Suzanne [Blamires], 36.

He told a district judge he was "the Crossbow Cannibal" – a reference to the weapon suspected of having been used to kill Suzanne and to a newspaper report that police fear body parts may have been eaten.

Suzanne's remains were found last week in black bin liners

floating in the River Aire – four miles from Griffiths' city centre flat. Her head was discovered in a rucksack on the riverbank.

The prostitute, who once trained to be a nurse, is said to have been murdered last weekend when a crossbow bolt was fired into her head.

Daily Mirror, 31 May 2010

Daily Mirror, 31st May 2010

Griffiths was studying towards a PhD in psychology, specializing in a comparative study of serial killers in the nineteenth century and their modern-day counterparts. He was a model student, attending all his lectures, and the subject clearly fascinated him – to the point where he felt compelled to join their ranks, in particular aspiring to reach the notoriety of local killer Peter Sutcliffe, "The Yorkshire Ripper". Sutcliffe preyed on prostitutes, and so would he. He also coincidentally attended the same grammar school as 1940s serial killer John George Haigh, "The Acid Bath Murderer".

Griffiths was committed to murder. He was in no doubt that was where his future lay and he executed his victims ruthlessly. The details of his first two murders are not known, but modern technology and an Orwellian society captured his last killing, that of Suzanne Blamires, on CCTV, which was what then led to his arrest:

Armed police arrested Griffiths on Monday after a caretaker at his Bradford block of flats reviewed CCTV footage. The accused man's solicitor Phillip Ainge works for a law firm whose founder Kerry Macgill represented Yorkshire Ripper Peter Sutcliffe in 1981.

Daily Mirror, 29th May 2010

Blamires had tried to flee Griffiths' flat but he was too quick, and knocked her unconscious. Disappearing from the camera frame momentarily he returned carrying a recurve-style crossbow, where the tips curve away from the archer. He shot a bolt into her head then dragged the lifeless body away, quickly dumping it in the nearby river. A delay in apprehending Griffiths might have been avoided if the caretaker had rung the police immediately, instead of first selling his story to the *Sun* newspaper!

Throughout his detention, Griffiths has been quietly belligerent, not offering much information to his interrogators other than a minimal confession. He was not forthcoming about what he had done with the other bodies, nor the extent of his murders.

"What sort of location have you put them in?"
"Can't know. Where a robot ... where a computer would put it.
Yeah, you know, a rational, emotionless aberration would put it."
"Why did you feel the need to kill her?"
"I don't know. I don't know if I was ... Like I say, you just ...
sometimes you kill someone to kill yourself, or kill part of you. I
don't know. I don't know. It's like deep issues inside me."
"So, why did you feel the need to kill any of the girls?"
[Mumbles] *"I don't know."*
"Pardon?"
"I DON'T KNOW! I don't know. Well, I'm misanthropic, I don't
have much time for the Human race."

However, this apparent disconnection from his circumstances soon changed. While in custody, Griffiths unsuccessfully attempted suicide thrice, once by tying a sock around his neck and putting a plastic bag over his head, another time by slashing his arm with a glass. The third time he swallowed batteries and pills.

The overdose had been witnessed by prison officers. The source added: "He took the pills at tea time and was also seen swallowing the batteries."

[An] insider added: "He tried to kill himself just weeks ago, too, by cutting his throat. He has told inmates that he doesn't want to stand trial and has been causing a lot of trouble."

Daily Mirror, 20th November 2010

It was as if Griffiths had awakened from a dazed stupor, and the situation he had suddenly found himself in must have struck him as being more serious than he could ever have imagined. Gone was the fantasy of the prostitute killer, the second Yorkshire Ripper, and here was an assured future of all too real punishment for his crimes. In December 2010, he received three life sentences, without the possibility of parole.

But Griffiths hadn't finished being troublesome. He still hadn't told police where the other bodies had been disposed, nor had he helped in other investigations, for at least seven possible murders, and probably more, that he was suspected of carrying out. While being held in the Category A Wakefield Jail, he tried to starve himself to death, only accepting liquids, and creating a costly burden for the prison system who have to keep him under constant surveillance. He eventually broke his fast, only to claim a failing in the prison service for their lack of provision!

KILLER Stephen Griffiths has given up his hunger strike after 120 days. And the warped Crossbow Cannibal now plans to sue prison bosses for "failing" to look after him. He told guards he gave up eating to see how his victims felt just before death. A source said: "Griffiths thinks he can sue the prison service for failure in their duty of care. You could not make it up."

Daily Mirror, 28th March 2011

It recently transpired that the authorities had been keeping their eye on Griffiths for a long time before his arrest and imprisonment. He was diagnosed a schizoid psychopath in 1991 after attacking a supermarket manager with a knife, and was sentenced to three years. At the time he told psychiatrists that he could see himself becoming a serial killer in the future. In 1992 he was in prison again for a further two years for another knife attack. Then while a part-time student at the University of Bradford, police had been watching him since 2009 for a whole two years prior to his killings, confiscating hunting weapons and noting things like his taste in books, for example about dismemberment.

The police also confiscated his hunting weapons during this period, but implements such as Bowie knives and Commando crossbows are readily available, and easily replaced. As a further precaution and a security intervention for the block of flats as a whole, which was known to be frequented by prostitutes and drug addicts, the housing association owning the building, in response to the police contacting them, upgraded the CCTV system – the one that finally caught him red-handed. But, apparently aware he was being filmed, Griffiths showed his defiance by sticking his middle finger up at the camera, moments after firing his bolt into the unconscious Blamires.

If Griffiths knew that the camera footage would lead to his capture, then perhaps he had resigned himself to his downfall. Perhaps with each victim he was killing a part of himself. His continued suicide attempts would suggest that he feels the job remains unfinished:

"Crossbow Cannibal" Stephen Griffiths has tried to kill himself in jail for a SIXTH time … and he did it with a razor handed to him by a fellow inmate.

The serial killer, 42, who is on permanent suicide watch, slashed his wrists in his cell in the middle of the night.

Prison officers saw what Griffiths was doing and rushed in, grabbing the razor and pinning him down to stop him.

The killer was examined by a doctor who said his wrist wound should be treated with stitches.

But Griffiths, serving life for murdering three women, refused so nurses wrapped his arms in bandages to stop the bleeding.

Daily Mirror, 22nd January 2012

Richard Ramirez
A.K.A. The Night Stalker/Prowler
COUNTRY USA
VICTIMS 14
METHOD shot, bludgeoned
MUTILATION ritually dismembered, eyes removed

It took some time for me to find what I wanted. The first killings were bullshit. An unsatisfactory waste of my time. Fucking round with that woman in the garage was lame. Killing her friend in the house was just a fucking mess. The 8-year-old girl was bullshit, man. But, I got my stride on with the Zazzara house. Yeah, got it good. Just had to get him out of the way. Single shot to the head. Bam! Gone, and she was mine. Just didn't know it. Kept looking for her man. Stupid bitch. Told her not to. Told her not to look at me neither. Kept looking too. So, I took her eyes, stupid bitch. Fucking cow. Now she ain't looking at nothing. Yeah, I killed her.

So what. Killing is killing whether done for duty, profit or fun. We've all got the power in our hands to kill, but most people are afraid to use it. The ones who aren't afraid control life itself. I am in control. I am the servant of Satan.

I don't believe in the hypocritical, moralistic dogma of this so-called civilized society. I need not look beyond this room to see all the liars, hater, the killers, the crooks, the paranoid cowards – truly trematodes of the Earth, each one in his own legal profession. You maggots make me sick – hypocrites one and all. And no one knows that better than those who kill for policy, clandestinely or openly, as do the governments of the world, which kill in the name of God and country or for whatever reason they deem appropriate. I don't need to hear all of society's rationalizations, I've heard them all before and the fact remains that what is, is. You don't understand me. You are not expected to. You are not capable of it. I am beyond your experience. I am beyond good and evil. Legions of the night – night breed – repeat

not the errors of the Night Prowler and show no mercy. I will be
avenged. Lucifer dwells within us all.

Ricardo "Richard" Leyva Ramirez was a burglar with a bent for rape and murder. Probably influenced at an early age by a cousin who had served in the Special Forces in Vietnam, Ramirez had been told tales of killing and torturing prisoners, and shown photographs of the severed heads of Vietnamese women, decapitated after they had been forced to perform oral sex. Ramirez was also present when the same cousin shot his wife dead, the gunshots splattering the 11-year-old boy with blood.

In March 1985 Ramirez attempted his first homicidal burglary. He shot 22-year-old María Hernández outside her house in Los Angeles; he failed to kill her thanks to the bullet ricocheting off her keys, but entered the property and shot and killed 34-year-old Dayle Okazaki, who was inside. Minutes later he assaulted and shot 30-year-old Tsai-Lian Yu, a passing female motorist, who died before reaching hospital.

Ten days later, Ramirez shot 64-year-old Vincent Zazzara through the left temple, killing him instantly. His wife was found, face up and naked; she had been stabbed repeatedly in the face, neck, abdomen and groin, and had a large T-shaped cut in her left breast. Her eyes had been gouged out.

I love to kill people. I love watching them die. I would shoot them
in the head and they would wiggle and squirm all over the place,
and then just stop. Or I would cut them with a knife and watch
their faces turn real white. I love all that blood. I told one lady to
give me all her money. She said no. So I cut her and pulled her
eyes out.

In May 1985, Ramirez attacked another elderly couple, octogenarian sisters, one disabled, and a 41-year-old mother and her son, all in their own homes, and all within the same month. The next three months were equally terrifying, causing widespread panic, and stretching the Night Prowler's trail of breaking and entering people's homes from Los Angeles to San Francisco. In Los Angeles, two women had their throats slit and another was seriously injured by being beaten with a metal bar. A 63-year-old woman was attacked and rape was attempted, but was unsuccessful. A 32-year-old man was shot, and his 29-year-old wife was forced to perform oral sex at gunpoint. A 66-year-old couple were murdered and mutilated. Another younger couple were both shot in the head but survived, while yet another couple were also attacked, the 35-year-old man shot, and his 28-year-old wife forced to have anal and oral sex.

In San Francisco, Ramirez shot to death a 66-year-old man, before shooting and beating his wife, who survived to help identify her attacker from police sketches. Ramirez's final attack came in August 1985 when he broke into the apartment of 29-year-old Bill Carns and his fiancée, 27-year-old Inez Erickson. Dispatching Carns with a single shot to the head as he had done with his previous male victims, he then forced Erickson to give him oral sex, but didn't kill her. As he drove off, she was able to partially identify the car, which led to a positive fingerprint match, plus publication of Ramirez's mugshot, obtained from previous arrests. Ramirez dumped the car he had been using in his recent heists. It had been stolen anyway. Now he needed new wheels, but the public had been made aware of him. Other than dark Hispanic looks, he had other outstanding characteristics, like gappy teeth and foul breath.

Seduced by a red Mustang in the predominantly Hispanic 3700 block of East Hubbard Street of Los Angeles, where he hoped to blend in, Ramirez climbed in and fired up the engine. He had missed the fact that Faustino Pinon, the proud owner, was working on the undercarriage. Pinon leapt up and seized the car thief, clinging on as he drove off, despite threats of being shot. The car ploughed into a fence. Ramirez fled, targeting another car nearby, but again the owners were fiercely protective of their property, and he was chased off by a muscular pursuer and his brothers, enthusiastically wielding a metal fence post. He had been recognized, was suddenly prey, and police had to intervene to save his life.

In September 1988, after several legal delays, Ramirez was found guilty of 13 counts of murder, five attempted murders, 11 sexual assaults and 14 burglaries. The trial was overcast with paranoia, fuelled by Ramirez claiming demonic allegiance:

> What Satan means to me ... Satan is a stabilizing force in my life. It gives me a reason to be; it gives me ... an excuse to rationalize. There is a part of me that believes he really does exist. I have my doubts, but we all do, about many things.

He appeared in court shouting "Hail Satan!" while displaying a pentagram drawn on his palm, a symbol he had left at one of his crime scenes. He would later explain, "it was a statement that I was in alliance with ... the evil that is inherent in human nature. And ... that was who I was." When one of the jurors was found shot at her home, the other members of the jury thought Ramirez had solicited an evil intervention, even though the shooting was proven to be due to a domestic dispute. Ramirez received 19 death sentences in November 1989 and was subsequently convicted of a 14th murder. He remains on death row at San Quentin State Prison, but that didn't stop him marrying a fan in October 1996, who pledges her suicide upon his execution.

Los Angeles police have recently announced that they are still on the trail of a serial rapist and killer they had called the Night Stalker, long before Ramirez was given the same name. They have been chasing the original Night Stalker for decades. He is believed to be responsible for at least 52 rapes and 10 murders, and is still active. Like Ramirez, his method is to enter people's homes in affluent areas through a window or door, wearing a ski mask and carrying a knife or gun. Taking pre-prepared ligatures brought for the purpose, he forces the women at gunpoint to tie up their male partners, then ties up any children in the house, or locks them in a bathroom. Placing a porcelain plate on the man's back, he threatens them that the woman will be killed first, then everyone else, if the plate falls. The woman is then taken to another room and repeatedly raped. No one is spared. Usually a metal object found in the house is used to bludgeon the victims to death.

Richard Leonard Kuklinski

A.K.A. The Iceman
COUNTRY USA
VICTIMS 250+
METHOD shot, poisoned, strangled, bludgeoned
MUTILATION dismembered

Richard Kuklinski prided himself on his killing. He wanted to make murder into an exact science, and revelled in the number and diversity of ways he knew of to end someone's life. He also developed a unique way to hide their time of death – freeze them. Hence his nickname, "The Iceman", although this could have been as much for his cold countenance. During interviews, Kuklinski was only ever matter-of-fact, hardly ever showing emotion or remorse or questioning his actions. Other than the method of his murders, Kuklinski might confirm deaths with little more than a wry smile, a customary click of his tongue against his teeth, and a cursory, "He died."

Kuklinski was surrounded by violence and death for most of his life. His mother and his abusive, alcoholic father beat the family. One of his brothers died from his beating, while another raped and murdered a 12-year-old girl. Tired of being bullied, Kuklinski himself killed for the first time when he was 14. He realized that, "People left you alone if you hurt them."

By the mid-1950s Kuklinski had built up a reputation for vengeful violence, and the DeCavalcante crime family in Newark, New Jersey, hired him as a hit man during turbulent times, as control passed over from Stefano "Steve" Badami to Filippo "Phil" Amari. Kuklinski went to work to hone his skills, "to practise and perfect murder", killing for the slightest insult or provocation. He frequented Manhattan, using it as a murder lab, executing scores of victims, and leaving them where they lay. He killed so many homeless men that the police thought there was a civil war on the streets.

The Gambinos, one of the main five American Mafia families, were next to take Kuklinski on as an "Associate". He could never be a fully fledged Mafia member because he wasn't of Italian descent, but mixed Polish and Irish–American. One of his jobs was pirating pornographic tapes, until he was challenged to kill a random passer-by, a dog walker. Kuklinski shot the man in the back of the head and earned respect as an enforcer.

Kuklinski would kill on demand, any time of the day, and any day of the year. "I've had requests where the guy wanted the guy's tongue cut out, and he also wanted his tongue put in his rear end. There was a definite point he wanted to get across." Kuklinski's wife and three children learned not to inquire where he was going in the middle of the night, or even in the middle of dinner. Kuklinski had introduced his father's domestic violence into his own home and they were all too familiar with his short temper.

Kuklinski employed such a range of weaponry that the police never knew the murders were all carried out by the same person. His victims were shot, stabbed, blown up, bludgeoned, burned, asphyxiated or strangled. He also had a penchant for cyanide, administered as an injection, added to food – say, in a restaurant – or spilt from a drink in a bar, which could be framed to look like a drunken accident, but would in actuality be administering the poison to slowly absorb through the victim's skin. Bodies were variously deposited around the city, buried or dumped, sometimes in oil drums in open view, or crushed in the boot of a vehicle in the jaws of a car crusher.

If a new weapon was required, Kuklinski would carry out a trial test beforehand. He needed to use a crossbow on one occasion, so stopped on the way to his marked man, pretending to ask a random stranger for directions. Kuklinski was satisfied that the crossbow bolt, "went half-way into his [the stranger's] head". He also experimented in concealing the time of death by freezing the bodies in an industrial freezer while still fresh. The Iceman's trick was only discovered when a chunk of ice was unexpectedly found inside a victim's heart.

Kuklinski was arrested after a six-year investigation, supported by the testimony of an undercover agent who had managed to win Kuklinski's trust when approached about being hired for a hit. Kuklinski was only too pleased to divulge his plans for carrying out the murder. He was arrested in December 1986, and convicted of five murders and sentenced to five life terms in 1988. He subsequently pleaded guilty to murdering an NYPD detective and received a further 30 years.

Kuklinski died, aged 70, in the secure wing of the St Francis Medical Center in Trenton, New Jersey. He had been in apparent good health, although he had claimed that someone was trying to poison him. He had been due to testify against a member of the Gambino family, and following Kuklinski's death, which was attributed to natural causes, all charges were dropped.

Giuseppe Greco
A.K.A. Scarpuzzedda (Little Shoe)
COUNTRY Italy
VICTIMS 300
METHOD shot, strangled, poisoned
MUTILATION dismembered

Unlike Kuklinski, Giuseppe Greco was born into the Sicilian Italian Mafia. His family was closely associated with the Corleonesi, who instigated the bloody Second Mafia War that ran between 1981 and 1983. Greco was responsible for the execution of a minimum of 58 rival family members, but the true total could be closer to 300. His preferred weapon was the AK-47 Kalashnikov assault rifle, capable of 600 rounds per minute.

Greco's victims were often tortured by him and his henchmen – for example, the 15-year-old son of a rival had an arm cut off while still conscious – before finally being shot. Their bodies were often dismembered and dissolved in acid, or dumped in the sea. Car bombs as well as strangulation and asphyxiation, through either being hanged or throttled, were also common killing methods. On one occasion Greco invited an ally family to a barbecue. The large party of guests were all killed, and the boss personally strangled by Greco, because the relationship had soured. The bodies were probably fed to the pigs.

After years of killing their enemies, the Corleonesi were getting nervous of their partner family's rise to power, and especially Greco's megalomania. To weaken them, several of their clan were massacred, before Greco himself was shot at his home in September 1985, by supposed friends, and his body dissolved in acid. In 1987, Italian law was still able to convict Greco of 58 counts of murder.

STABBERS

It is no coincidence that the verbs "stab", "slice" and "cut" all come from harsh-sounding Germanic precursors that hint at their violent meaning. The knife is part of our daily lives but is easily transformed from useful implement to murder weapon in the wrong hands. A knife blade penetrates and violates the human body, something Sigmund Freud didn't fail to recognize had sexual symbolism, which might tell us why some of the most horrifying reports of serial killings mention a staggering number of knife wounds inflicted "… in the frenzied attack". It is unnecessary to stab anyone more than once or twice, as this is usually enough to prove fatal, so maybe this is an alternative interpretation.

Luis Alfredo Garavito

A.K.A. The Beast, Tribilín (Goofy)
COUNTRY Columbia
VICTIMS 300+
METHOD stabbed
MUTILATION decapitated, dismembered

Child killer "tortured"

A DRIFTER who admits murdering 140 children said he became an uncontrolled "monster".

Handyman Luis Garavito, 42, known as Goofy, told prison psychologists he had been raped and tortured as a child.

In a video shown on Colombian television, he said: "I became a monster. I was tied up and obliged to do things at 12."

Garavito confessed last week to murdering 140 children in a seven-year spree across Colombia.

Daily Mirror, 6th November 1999

Luis Garavito preyed on poor, often homeless, children. His victims were boys aged between 8 and 13 years old, who were often left to play in parks while their parents hawked their wares on the streets and to motorists waiting at traffic lights. Garavito, often dressed as a monk or priest, enticed young boys with promises of sweets or drugs, or money for odd jobs. He also posed as an education official to gain access to schools. When he had won the child's trust, he would lead him onto an overgrown, secluded hillside that afforded a view if anyone was approaching. He then tied up and violently tortured and raped each boy, killing them by slicing the back of their necks, often decapitating them.

Between 1992 and 1998, Garavito is suspected of having raped, tortured, killed and mutilated over 300 boys throughout central Columbia. He would lubricate himself, then anally rape the boy, biting them as well. After killing them, he would stab the torso and slice at their genitals, sometimes sticking their penis into their own mouth. He reused the same killing site several times, but never buried the bodies, leaving them to scavengers and decay. In rare cases, where the murder had occurred in a house, Garavito dismembered the body and disposed of the parts in water, inside weighted-down sacks.

In 1999, having confessed to murdering 140 children, Garavito was found guilty of all except two of these murders and was sentenced to more than 1,853 years in prison. A further 172 cases are still under investigation, but their outcome will make little difference to Garavito's jail term. His sentence was capped at the maximum limit for Columbia of 30 years, then commuted to 22 years for his co-operation in locating the grave sites. He was able to draw detailed maps of the murder sites from memory.

As with Pedro López, "The Monster of the Andes", there has been a recent public outcry in Columbia, and a call for revision of limited sentences as Garavito's possible release draws near. While he has announced a wish to enter politics to help victims of child abuse, the authorities are working hard to find ways of extending his sentence, by bringing about charges for murders in Columbia to which Garavito has not yet confessed, as well as reviewing even more murders he is suspected of committing in Ecuador.

Peter Tobin
A.K.A. Bible John (claimed)
COUNTRIES England, Scotland
VICTIMS 48
METHOD stabbed, bludgeoned

Initially imprisoned in 1993 for a 14-year term that ended early in 2004, for the double rape and attempted murder of two 14-year-old girls, Peter Tobin was again found guilty in 2007 for the rape and murder in Glasgow of 23-year-old Polish student, Angelika Kluk in 2006. Kluk cleaned part-time at the Catholic church where Tobin worked as a handyman. She had been stabbed, bound, raped and bludgeoned with a table leg. Police described the attack as, "horrific and very, very violent". Kluk had been hidden beneath the floor near the church's confessional box, probably still alive. Tobin was identified as the last person to see her alive, but the situation wasn't as simple as all that.

During the trial it came to light that, not for the first time, the Catholic Church wasn't meeting its own proclaimed morality. Kluk was having an affair with a 40-year-old married man who professed his love for her. The incumbent parish priest and self-confessed alcoholic, Father Gerry Nugent, also admitted to having had sex several times with Kluk. When the complexities had been resolved and found peripheral to the case, Tobin was given a life sentence, with a minimum of 21 years.

Suspicious that Tobin may be responsible for more murders, police established Operation Anagram in 2006, to trace his movements across the UK, between Scotland and England, and across the southeast. This led to excavations of the garden at 50 Irvine Drive, a former home of his in Margate, in which was found the skeletons of 15-year-old Vicky Hamilton and 18-year-old Dinah McNicol, who had both disappeared in 1991.

Referring to Angelika's killing, a police source disclosed: "It's extremely unusual for a man of Tobin's age to carry out such a vicious stranger murder where there has been no previous history. It's feared this was not the first time he had struck."

Yesterday's investigation centred on a house in Margate, Kent, where Tobin moved in 1991. Neighbour Doris O'Donnell, 53, told how he dug a huge trench in the 30ftx20ft back garden.

Mrs O'Donnell said: "It must have been about six feet deep. He told everyone it was going to be a sandpit for his two-year-old son, who lived there with him. But social services told him to fill it in.

"The lad used to play in the pit while his dad watched. When I think about it, it sends shivers down my spine."

Daily Mirror, 12th November 2007

Tobin had abducted Hamilton while she had been waiting for a bus home near Falkirk. A month later he moved her body with him to Margate. He cut her in half for convenience, her wrists were bound together behind her back, her ankles tied together and a knotted gag had been forced into her mouth. He left her purse in Edinburgh, near the railway and bus stations, to make it appear as if she had run away. However, police were able to identify Hamilton's remains by matching DNA with a blood sample taken from her as a baby. Additionally, Tobin's fingerprints were on the plastic sheeting wrapped around her skeleton, and his 2-year-old son's DNA was found on the purse, conclusively linking Tobin to the murder.

Tobin was convicted and received two more life sentences, one in December 2008 for the murder of Hamilton, which increased his minimum sentence to 30 years, and the other in December 2009 for the murder of Dinah McNicol, with the recommendation that his "life sentence should mean life". Throughout his incarceration, Tobin has been exploitative, avoiding work duties with excuses of ill health, and even demanding sick pay. Some fellow inmates have found this behaviour irksome, resulting in a vicious attack on him that put him in hospital. Tobin's latest coup at Saughton Prison was negotiating for an orthopaedic toilet seat worth hundreds of pounds.

Tobin's boasts of 48 murders have had the police looking back through their records of cold, or unsolved, murders. There is a good case to be made that he was responsible for the three "Bible John" murders in the Barrowlands of Glasgow during the late 1960s. Some incidental evidence does support the suggestion: Tobin's whereabouts at the time, a religious background also apparent in the murderer, his resemblance as a young man to a police photofit of the culprit, and a missing tooth in his dental records that matches one noticed missing for Bible John. But no hard evidence yet exists.

Peter Manuel
A.K.A. The Beast of Birkenshaw, Bible John (claimed)
COUNTRY Scotland
VICTIMS 18
METHOD bludgeoned, shot

Another potential candidate for Bible John was Peter Manuel. An offender from an early age, Manuel spent nine years in HMP Peterhead for several sexual assaults, and was returned to prison for committing a rape before his first known murder in 1956. He then claimed to have killed 18 people in the next two years, but was charged with eight murders and sentenced to death at Glasgow High Court, and hanged in July 1958. Hannibal Lecter in *Manhunter*, the prequel to *Silence of the Lambs*, is based on Manuel, and Ian Rankin's eighth Inspector Rebus novel *Black and Blue* pits Bible John against a young pretender, "Johnny Bible".

Henry Lee Lucas
COUNTRY USA
VICTIMS 600
METHOD stabbed, bludgeoned, strangled
MUTILATION dismembered

Ottis Toole
COUNTRY USA
VICTIMS 200+
METHOD bludgeoned, burned, shot
MUTILATION decapitated, cannibalism

It's difficult to know what to believe about Henry Lee Lucas. He is known to have killed at least three women, including his mother, and admitted to bestiality, necrophilia and cannibalism. He was also the inspiration for the 1986 film, *Henry: Portrait of a Serial Killer*, and was the only prisoner on death row to have his execution commuted by George W. Bush, the then governor of Texas, who otherwise set a record for ordering the execution of 152 prisoners, more than any other governor in modern American history.

Lucas' parents were both alcoholics, his father an out-of-work double-amputee, and his mother an abusive and violent prostitute, who would beat her nine children and force them to watch her having sex with her clients. She would also dress Lucas as a girl and beat him for accepting gifts, a teddy bear from a sympathetic teacher, and a mule from an uncle. She shot the mule, and on one occasion beat Lucas with a wooden plank, putting him into a coma for three days.

Her neglect led to Lucas losing his left eye when he was 10 years old, after a stabbing accident while fighting with his brother. He ran away from home to wander Virginia, aged 13, and spent half of the next decade in prison for multiple burglaries. Lucas killed his mother when he was 23 years old, rebelling against her wishes that he return home to care for her, but according to him she was not his first victim:

> Lucas told police that he first killed a woman schoolteacher who refused to have sex with him when he was a 13-year-old schoolboy in Clerksburg, Virginia.
>
> Later, he says, he took to the road and began killing girls and women whose ages ranged from 13 to 80.
>
> He served five years in jail in the early 1960s after being convicted of murdering his mother.
>
> The one-eyed killer now loves to brag that detectives

and prosecutors mistook that for a heat-of-the-moment domestic tragedy.

Boasts Lucas: "They never suspected I'd already killed a lot of other women ... and when I came out of jail I killed a whole lot more."

Daily Mirror, 17th October 1983

Returning to his life as a drifter upon release, Lucas eventually met Ottis Toole in 1976 and they began a homosexual relationship. Lucas was also having sex with Toole's 12-year-old niece, Becky Powell. Two years later the three of them set off across country. Lucas later claimed to have murdered hundreds of people as they went. Toole was drinking heavily and taking drugs following the death of his mother, so Lucas and Powell eloped in 1982, leaving an incensed Toole to go on a 13-month killing spree of his own across six states.

Toole's and Lucas' backgrounds were similarly unstable and abusive. Toole was molested and sexually abused by several relatives and family friends while growing up. His mother dressed him as a girl, naming him "Susan", and his grandmother was a satanist. Like Lucas, Toole ran away from home and claimed he committed his first murder as a young teenager. He became obsessed by gay pornography and also became sexually aroused by arson.

Escaping from Toole, Lucas and Powell took refuge in a Pentecostal commune in Stoneburg, Texas, called the House of Prayer. They busied themselves with odd jobs, but Powell was soon homesick and wanted to leave. Lucas resisted, they got into an argument, and he killed her with a carving knife. He then raped, decapitated and dismembered her, scattering the body parts in a field.

In April 1983, Toole was arrested for burning down a church in Jacksonville. He was sentenced to 15 years. Lucas was arrested in June 1983 for illegal possession of a firearm, and later charged with killing Powell and an 82-year-old Texan woman. To improve his prison conditions he confessed to being involved in about 600 murders, naming Toole as his accomplice in over 100.

Toole starting corroborating Lucas' claims, and was tried and sentenced to six life sentences. However, Lucas' claims became increasingly unlikely, including having been a member of a cult of satanic cannibals, making snuff films, killing labour union president Jimmy Hoffa, and providing cult leader Jim Jones with poison for the Jonestown Massacre. He was eventually convicted of 11 murders in all, and sentenced to death, which was commuted to life imprisonment by Governor Bush.

Toole died in prison from liver failure in September 1996, aged 49 years old. He had finally confessed to the unsolved murder of a 6-year-old boy, whom he had decapitated but forgotten about, driving around with the head in his car for several days before discarding it in a canal. Lucas died in prison from heart failure in March 2001, aged 64.

POISONERS

Better murder an infant in its cradle than nurse an unacted desire
William Blake

Poisoners are cowards. They secrete their agents of death into the food and drink of their victims, and wait, knowing all the time the inevitability of their victim's destiny, brought ever closer with every agonising rasp, every poker-like sting. But, ultimate evil must be the health professional serial killer, a vile contradiction. Duty-bound to save lives, even swearing a 1500-year allegiance to Hippocrates, the "father of Western medicine", they abuse and use their position and proximity, turning their training from healing into Hell. Money. Sex. Egomania. Angels and Doctors of Death display all the hallmarks of other types of psychopath serial killers, but rarely have the opportunity or motivation to molest or mutilate their victims. They are content to simply play God, and stack up often terrifying numbers of victims, as they leave no trace of their copious killing.

Beverley Gail Allitt

A.K.A. Angel of Death
COUNTRY England
VICTIMS 4
METHOD poisoned, suffocated

The quiet market town of Grantham sprawls beneath the southeastern slope of the Lincoln Ridge, a range of limestone hills which run almost continuously across England from the Bristol Channel to the Humber, and which once provided a medieval route above the marshlands of the Lower Trent Valley to the west, and the Fen country to the east. It would be inconsequential in most other landscapes, but here it stands proud, surrounded as far as the eye can see by tediously uninterrupted plateau.

The Lincolnshire plain is one place in the UK that most resembles the sprawling nothingness of the US central belt. You might even have called Grantham a hick town. Nothing happened there. National radio had gone so far as to declare it the "Most Boring Town in Britain". The most famous people to be produced thereabouts, in the hundreds of years since Isaac Newton, were Margaret Thatcher, Nicholas Parsons and Doris Stokes. That is, until Granthamians got their very own "Angel of Death", and then everything changed. Such is the impact of the serial killer.

News of a flurry of suspicious deaths at the local Grantham and Kesteven Hospital made front pages across the UK:

FOUR BABIES DIE AT DRUGS PROBE HOSPITAL

FOUR babies all under a year old may have been killed with drug overdoses in a hospital children's ward.

And detectives fear ten other babies and youngsters, who survived heart attacks and breathing difficulties, may also have been poisoned with the same drug.

A 22-year-old nurse from the ward has been given extended leave, it was revealed last night.

The children all fell ill between January and May this year. The hospital called in detectives after tests on one boy who survived revealed an unusual amount of insulin in his bloodstream.

Insulin is quickly absorbed by the body and leaves no trace.

Leave

The children were patients in Ward Four at Grantham's District General Hospital in Lincolnshire.

Every member of the nursing staff in the ward has been questioned.

The father of the nurse: given extended leave said last night. "I know nothing about her being questioned by police.

She is a dedicated nurse. It is her whole life." Medical experts are now examining the records of every patient in the ward in recent months.

They are also talking to older children who were patients in the ward and their parents.

Detective Superintendent Stuart Clifton, said yesterday: "I can't say yet if there is anything sinister."

One problem for police is that the babies who died were cremated.

Staff at Grantham Hospital became concerned earlier this year at the high number of toddlers having cardiac or respiratory arrests.

They expected a normal explanation.

But when insulin traces were found during a blood test on one boy, hospital chiefs called in police.

Ward Four at the hospital has 20 beds and treats children aged from a few weeks up to 11 years.

A senior hospital official said last night: "It may well be that the inquiry will reveal nothing untoward.

"This is a traumatic situation and particularly dreadful for those involved in the inquiry.

"Our nursing staff on the ward are dedicated and we feel for them."

He added: "We want to assure parents their children will receive a high standard of care here."

One child who survived after collapsing in Ward Four was five-year-old Brad Gibson. He suffered a heart attack a day after being admitted with pneumonia.

Doctors and nurses in the ward fought for 32 minutes to revive him.

His mother, Judith, 36, who lives near Grantham, said: "Police told me they are investigating the possible misuse of drugs.

"We couldn't understand why Brad collapsed. He was not seriously ill. But suddenly his heart gave out."

Daily Mirror, 17th June 1991

Beverley Allitt was always an attention seeker. As a child she started wearing bandages and casts to get noticed, but refused to allow examination of her supposed injuries. As she grew into adolescence, her ailments escalated so much that she ended up spending a lot of time in hospital, even having her perfectly healthy appendix removed. She required further medical attention when her surgical scar took longer to heal than usual, because of her interfering with it. Alongside her medical obsessing, Allitt also became overweight and began to self-harm.

People with Munchausen's syndrome knowingly fabricate symptoms in order to receive sympathetic attention, but also sometimes to feel power over bewildered medical specialists. Individual doctors may become inured to a patient's continuous problems. So, to maintain the level of attention, as well as avoid being found out, there is a tendency to hop from one doctor to the next.

As the sufferers are habitual liars, the syndrome was named after Baron Karl Friedrich Hieronymus, Freiherr von Münchhausen, an eighteenth-century German nobleman who was renowned for being more than liberal with the truth, spinning his improvised tales of exotic adventures: on one particular occasion he famously claimed that he caught and hurled back cannonballs, hitching a ride into the fray aboard one. His exploits were spectacularly made into a fantasy film by Terry Gilliam.

While training as a nurse, Allitt's Munchausen's meant that she failed to attend a lot of her course. But her condition extended beyond attention seeking. In addition, she was also proving antisocial, and was suspected of smearing faeces on walls in the nursing home. Her boyfriend would later report that she was aggressive, manipulative and deceitful, falsely telling him she was pregnant, as well claiming to have been raped by him.

When attention seeking by feigning ailments didn't elicit the desired amount of attention, the next step was to harm others, whom she could then appear to care for, and even snatch from the jaws of death. This is known as Munchausen's syndrome by proxy.

The understaffing at Grantham Hospital was so bad that Allitt was taken on a six-month contract in early 1991, as a state enrolled nurse on a maternity ward, despite her poor training record. Staff shortages had left only two trained nurses on the day shift and only one at night. This gave Allitt every opportunity to generate emergencies for her charges, either by injecting medicines at lethal concentrations, suffocation, or by causing asphyxiation by tampering with oxygen supplies. This would position her at the centre of events as often she was the only nurse in attendance of the children; it also maximized the kudos that she imagined due her for summoning the resuscitation team in the nick of time.

Her first victim was 7-week-old Liam Taylor, who was admitted to the ward for a chest infection. Allitt was sympathetic and supportive, persuading his parents to go home to rest. They returned to discover that their son had only just survived a respiratory failure, but the kindly nurse was there on hand. Allitt further endeared herself by volunteering for night duty to keep vigil.

During the night, and despite the parents remaining nearby in the hospital, Taylor lost his healthy colour and quickly developed red blotchiness on his face. The resuscitation team saved him from what would otherwise have been a fatal heart attack, but the damage had been done to his oxygen-starved brain, and his parents would accept the medical advice to switch off the life-support machines. Eleven-year-old Timothy Hardwick suffered from cerebral palsy, and was admitted after an epileptic seizure. While Allitt was on duty, the resuscitation team was summoned to find him turning blue and without a pulse. They were unable to save him.

One-year-old Kayley Desmond was also admitted for a chest infection. Allitt attempted her murder, but Desmond was resuscitated and recovered after transfer to a nearby Nottingham hospital. There, an examination discovered a puncture wound under her armpit, but this wasn't pursued. Five-month-old Paul Crampton, suffering from a chest infection, was administered three insulin overdoses, which sent him into a comatose state, the day before he was transferred to Nottingham. Allitt rode with him in the ambulance unaccompanied, and the boy arrived with higher insulin levels than at the beginning of his trip, but eventually recovered. Five-year-old Bradley Gibson was admitted to the ward for pneumonia, but unexpectedly suffered two cardiac arrests, and only recovered when transferred to Nottingham. Two-year-old Yik Hung Chan had a fall and was kept in overnight, but suddenly turned blue. He responded well when fed oxygen, and was also transferred and recovered at Nottingham.

Two-month-old Becky Phillips was suffering from gastroenteritis. Allitt gave her an insulin overdose which killed her two days later, after she had returned home. Colic was ostensibly diagnosed, so, erring on the side of caution, Becky's twin sister Katie was admitted to the hospital as a precaution. Phillips survived two subsequent attacks, from which Allitt appeared to be her saviour. The parents were so grateful, she was later asked to be their daughter's godmother. When Phillips was transferred to Nottingham, it was discovered she had mysteriously broken five ribs. More critical is the fact that she had suffered permanent brain damage, partial paralysis and partial blindness due to oxygen deprivation. She is now 20 years old, and was awarded £2.125 million in compensation by Lincolnshire Health Authority in 1999.

The last child Allitt attacked was 15-month-old Claire Peck, who was brought into the hospital following an asthma attack. She was left alone with Allitt on two separate occasions, and had a heart attack shortly after each. The final one was fatal. Allitt had injected her with potassium and lignocaine, used after cardiac arrests to subdue abnormal heart rhythms in adults, but lethal at low concentrations in infants.

In all, Allitt murdered four children, and attempted to kill a further nine, over 59 days between February and April 1991. Because of the surreptitious methods involved in administering the drugs, she was confident her crimes would not be detected. The only potential risk, other than getting caught red-handed actually carrying out injections, which was unlikely with so few colleagues on duty, was obtaining the infusions. This she covered up by reporting the refrigerated drug store key missing. What she had failed to consider was that her name would appear on the nurses' rota, showing that she was the only one present at all the deaths. Pages from these records were retrieved while searching her home following her arrest.

Allitt was charged with four murders and taken into custody in November 1991. She was charged with a further three counts of attempted murder in March 1992, but actually getting her to attend trial proved difficult as she had a string of claimed illnesses. During her time in prison she had developed anorexia nervosa.

In February 1993, amongst highly charged scenes at Nottingham Crown Court, Allitt, now 32 kilograms lighter, emerged to hear her charges. The trial lasted until May, when she was sentenced to 13 life sentences. She is currently being held at Rampton Secure Hospital where she is reported to have regained weight and was due to marry a male inmate. She also caused a further outcry from her victim's families when it transpired she is receiving £150 in allowances per month.

In December 2007, the High Court decided upon a minimum prison term of 30 years, meaning that Allitt will be 54 before being considered for parole. The presiding judge said, "I have found that there is an element of sadism in Ms Allitt's conduct and her offending. But that sadism is itself, if not the result, certainly a manifestation of her mental disorder, and it would be unduly simplistic to treat it in the same way as one would if the offender were mentally well. By her actions, what should have been a place of safety for its patients became not just a place of danger, but if not a killing field something close to it."

Allitt won't be the last Angel of Death in Britain. There is a currently open case in England that has been likened to Allitt's killing, but has already claimed more victims:

Fears grow that serial killer is on loose in hospital after deaths of three patients linked to poisoned jabs

HOSPITAL staff fear a Beverley Allitt-style killer is in their midst after the mystery deaths of three patients linked to poisoned drips. [...]

The latest suspected killer struck at Stepping Hill Hospital in Stockport, Greater Manchester.

It is believed dozens of deaths there will now be investigated. [...]

Detectives have already found insulin was injected into saline ampoules on the hospital premises.

A batch of 36 kept in a storeroom between two wards had been contaminated. The vials have a small seal on the top where a needle can be inserted. Detectives say 12 of the vials of saline, usually injected into drip needles to flush them through, have been used on patients.

Daily Mirror, 16th July 2011

Victorino Chua, a 46-year-old male nurse, and Rebecca Leighton, aged 28, have both been held in custody, but released for lack of evidence. Neither work at the hospital any longer, but there have still been six suspicious deaths there as of January 2012, all occurring on the acute care wards, and all involving critically ill patients.

Waltraud Wagner
A.K.A. The Lainz Angels of Death
COUNTRY Austria
VICTIMS 200+
METHOD poisoned, drowned

The elderly patient couldn't understand what was happening. The four friendly nurses had been working the night shift as she had often seen them doing. They had visited each of the beds on the ward like those other times. These four always managed to "do the rounds" together, unlike the other nursing staff, who always seemed to be too busy to loiter at your bedside. She had followed them with her gaze all along the opposite rank of cubicles, tracking their progression towards her.

There had been smiles and nods to start with, but now their faces had changed. Taut lips were now stretched into steely grimaces. A hidden weight was melting her into the mattress. It was frightening, inexplicable, and she wanted to call out, to ask them for help, but tiredness was enveloping her. Darkness was descending, pricked only by bared teeth and the flash of four pairs of darting eyes.

Breath caught in the back of her throat, each shorter than the rest. The panic made her pant. Unable to draw deeply, her lungs heaved for more air. It was as if she was sucking in the whole night, cramming her mouth with the nocturnal void. Wet skin shimmered in the low light and the melody of a long-forgotten song drifted with her into the shadows, "Oh, the shark, babe, has such teeth, dear, And it shows them pearly white."

What had started off with 23-year-old Waltraud Wagner acting alone, injecting a terminal patient with a lethal overdose of morphine, soon developed into a synchronized four-strong team of nurses who went on to inject insulin and tranquillisers, and would come to develop a technique that effectively waterboarded their patients, restraining them and blocking their nose while pouring water into their mouth. Their victims drowned where they lay, in their hospital beds. Post-mortems would only reveal the deceased would have pulmonary oedemas or fluid in their lungs, a common complaint in the elderly.

Originally the nurses had seen themselves as mercy killers, driven by Christian compassion, but soon they were just ridding themselves of difficult and needy charges. They all worked in Pavilion 5 at Lainz General Hospital in Vienna, dedicated to caring for elderly patients, many of whom were terminally ill. Deaths were everyday occurrences.

Wagner and her accomplices, 21-year-old Irene Leidolf, 19-year-old Maria Gruber and 43-year-old Stephanija Meyer, may never have been caught had it not been for their boastful chat being overheard in a bar, where they were revelling in their latest victim's suffering. The eavesdropping doctor who sat nearby went straight to the police, and the arrests were made in April 1989.

Wagner received life imprisonment for 15 murders and 17 attempted murders. Leidolf was also given a life sentence for her part in five murders, and the others received 15 years each for manslaughter and attempted murder. The group confessed to 49 murders carried out over six years; however, one of them estimated Wagner alone was responsible for 200 deaths in just two years, putting the total nearer to 300 murders. Wagner and Leidolf were due for early release for good behaviour in August 2008 but were detained following a public outcry. Gruber and Meyer had already been released with new identities.

Javed Iqbal Mughal
COUNTRY Pakistan
VICTIMS 100
METHOD poisoned, strangled
MUTILATION dismembered

Javed Iqbal felt abused and insulted after his treatment by the police. He was a wealthy, self-made man who expected respect from others. All he had done was report an assault by two young servant boys, but the police hadn't believed his story. In fact, worse than that, he had received a further beating, plus accusations of sodomy. His pride hurt, he vowed to have his revenge on a world he hated.

Iqbal did not deal in half measures and the revenge he exacted was brutal. Over the course of six months, during 1999, he would go on to kill 100 boys:

I could have killed five hundred, this was not a problem. But the pledge I had taken was one hundred children, and I did not want to violate this. My mother had cried for me. I wanted one hundred mothers to cry for their children.

The victims were all aged between 6 and 16 years of age and were mostly runaway orphans living on the streets of Lahore. Iqbal sexually abused them, then poisoned them with cyanide or strangled them, before dismembering the bodies. He dissolved the body parts in vats of hydrochloric acid and discarded the remains in the sewer or the local river.

Iqbal was very methodical in his killing, keeping his victim's clothing and shoes, as well as a log detailing each victim's name, age and date of death. He also kept a photographic record of the body parts, neatly labelled and packed in plastic bags, and recorded his costs, "In terms of expense, including the acid, it cost me 120 rupees ($2.40) to erase each victim."

Iqbal sent his announcement letter to the police in December 1999, telling them what had led him to serial murder. It was also a suicide note, saying that he was going to drown himself in the river. His house was an exhibition of proof. Partially dissolved human remains were labelled, "the bodies in the house have deliberately not been disposed of so that authorities will find them".

Following Pakistan's largest ever manhunt Iqbal's four teenage boy accomplices were arrested, one dying in custody after apparently jumping from a window. Iqbal soon gave himself up by walking into a Lahore newspaper office, afraid that the police might also kill him. Despite the written confession, the matching handwriting and the precise records, plus the overwhelming evidence left at his house, Iqbal pleaded not guilty, claiming to have only witnessed the killings.

Iqbal was sentenced to death by hanging. The presiding judge told him, "You will be strangled to death in front of the parents whose children you killed. Your body will then be cut into one hundred pieces and put in acid, the same way you killed the children"; however, such a death would have countered Islam. Instead, Iqbal and one of his accomplices committed suicide by ingesting poison whilst in their cell in the Central Jail Lahore at Kot Lakhpat in October 2001. Iqbal will never know he failed in his mission. Twenty-six of his supposed murder victims were found alive after his death.

Georgia Tann
COUNTRY USA
VICTIMS 5,000+
METHOD starved, bludgeoned, strangled

Miyuki Ishikawa
A.K.A. Oni-Sanba (The Demon Midwife)
COUNTRY Japan
VICTIMS 169
METHOD starved

"Baby Farms" and "Angel-making" were rife at the turn of the last century. Rather than providing the care they were paid for, orphanages would dispose of babies at alarming rates, naturally pocketing the money anyway. Suspicious, but not uncommon, was the fact that only 88 babies survived out of an annual intake of 719 at the Grey Nun Hospital in Montreal, Canada, built in 1765.

Meanwhile, Amelia Dyer, "The Ogress of Reading", was plying her murderous trade in England up until 1896, while at the Stockholm National Children's Sanatorium, a minister and his wife going by the alias Mr and Mrs Gustav Holmen had probably killed over a thousand children in three years. In the first two or three years of the new century, Madame Guzovska was found to have murdered over 500 babies in Poland, charging from a few to a hundred pounds to dispose of unwanted births, depending on the mother's wealth. Similarly, 300 children were killed in just 1902 alone by a Japanese family running a baby farm in Osaka.

Belle Gunness was famously busy in the United States in the decades to follow, and 1913 witnessed the trial of Madame Kusnezowa in Russia, who was charged with poisoning 1,012 victims in the five years since her baby farm had opened for illegitimate children.

However, the most famous case, immortalized in two made-for-TV films and responsible for the most babies murdered by any single baby farm outfit, was that of Georgia Tann. Advisor to First Lady Eleanor Roosevelt, and considered an expert on child care, Tann, along with her accomplices, was in reality a mass kidnapper, child molester, torturer and murderer.

Assisted by a corrupt partner, a woman Memphis Family Court Judge called Camille Kelly, Tann would legally confiscate children then arrange for their adoption, for a price. Parents might kiss their children goodbye as they delivered them to school, to be told at picking up time that they had been taken away by social services because they were unfit parents. Children who were considered unfit for sale were weeded out and disposed of in various ways: left out in the sun until baked to death, beaten about the scalp to conceal bruising, or hung from the wrists on a coat rack or down a laundry chute.

In the quarter of a century Tann was operating through the Memphis Tennessee Children's Home Society, more than 5,000 babies and young children were killed, their records destroyed to cover tracks. Those that survived often went to abusive homes or were sold into slavery. The most famous case was that of Christina Crawford who was sold by Tann to actress Joan Crawford. She wrote a book about the mental and physical abuse she received from her adoptive mother, which was subsequently made into a film. The accusations polarized the Hollywood clique, with stars such as Bette Davis coming forward to testify to the abuse.

Tann died in 1950, before her atrocities could come to light. About the same time, on the other side of the world, the bodies of 70 babies were found. The Japanese midwife Miyuki Ishikawa was convicted of their deaths, although many more were suspected, but sentenced to only eight years in prison. Her husband Takeshi and Shiro Nakayama, a doctor who had assisted the couple, were given four years each, and a few years later all of the sentences were halved. The case would create such uproar in Japan that laws banning abortion would be revoked as a consequence.

Júlia Fazekas
A.K.A. The Angel Makers of Nagyrév
COUNTRY Hungary
VICTIMS 300
METHOD poisoned

Money is the usual motivator in all these cases but Júlia Fazekas had ulterior motives. Working as a midwife in Nagyrév in central Hungary during the First World War, she advised use of arsenic, extracted by boiling flypapers, for removing any unwanted individual, regardless of financial reward. The victims were often husbands returning home from serving in the Army, who were not willing to accept their wives continuing the affairs that had begun in their absence, often with several POWs at a time. Other victims were family members and children.

An estimated 300 murders took place over 18 years in what came to be known as the "Murder District", each easily covered up because Fazekas and her accomplice were in charge of issuing the death certificates. Thirty-eight people were jailed for the murders, eight of whom were hanged, perhaps including Fazekas, although an alternative account suggests she may have committed suicide, by taking some of her own arsenic.

Vera Renczi
A.K.A. The Black Widow
COUNTRY Romania
VICTIMS 35
METHOD poisoned

Like Júlia Fazekas, Vera Renczi's killings were carried out to facilitate sex. Well, sex and devotion. Spoiled as a child Renczi grew up to be a beautiful and wealthy, but acutely insecure and jealous, adult. She could not tolerate any sign of infidelity in her male partners, and could kill for a mere glance at another woman. Arsenic in wine was a favoured tipple that would topple the victims, sometimes being administered only days into a new relationship. A woman trying to trace her estranged husband finally brought an end to this particular femme fatale, calling the police when he failed to emerge from Renczi's ancient chateau. Forcing their way through three iron doors into the vaulted wine cellar, the police found stacks of coffins, each containing a preserved body. Renczi was arrested for the murder of two husbands, her 10-year-old son who had attempted to blackmail her on discovering her murderous ways, and 32 of her lovers, and spent the rest of her life in prison.

Except, she didn't. That is, Renczi never existed, nor did the Serbian town of Berkereckul where the murders are supposed to have taken place. There are stories of Renczi, the "Mysterious Huntress", frequenting local cafés and bars in the search for new prey. There are even quotes supposedly taken directly from interviews with her:

> I had the power to tantalize them. They would follow me. Then, perhaps a week after they had remained with me at my house, I would notice that they grew either distracted or would say something about having to return home. I would consider these first signs the beginning of the end. And, consequently, my first burst of passion for them would be followed by jealousy, and I would poison them without waiting any further.

But this misinformation can mostly be traced to two articles, one in *The Bee* magazine from May 1925 and the other appearing in the *San Antonio Light* Sunday magazine in August 1925. The latter was owned by William Randolph Hearst who introduced "yellow journalism", a name coined to refer to newspaper stories that were invented or exaggerated to be sensational and sell papers. Since then the myth of the "Black Widow" has been thought to be true, and was given a new lease of life when the story inspired American playwright Joseph Kesselring's *Arsenic and Old Lace*, which was shortly afterwards adapted into a Frank Capra film starring Cary Grant.

John Bodkin Adams
COUNTRY England
VICTIMS 160+
METHOD poisoned

Things started going wrong for Dr John Bodkin Adams in August 1956 after suspicions were raised over the death of one of his patients, a healthy widow who although depressed and on medication following the death of her husband, had not expressed a wish to commit suicide. Therefore, when high levels of barbiturates were found during the post-mortem, questions had to be asked.

DETECTIVE Superintendent Herbert Hannam, of Scotland Yard's murder squad, was called as a surprise witness yesterday at an inquest on a wealthy widow [...] The coroner said that Mrs. Hullett complained of a headache on July 19 and went to bed at 10 p.m. at her home, Holywell Mount, Eastbourne.

Next morning she was found, apparently asleep, and later that day she was found unconscious. She stayed unconscious until she died on July 23.

A police scientist, Mr. Michael Stephen Moss, said he found 112 grains of barbiturate in Mrs. Hullett's body. [...]

Dr. F. E. Camps, pathologist, said 112 grains – or twenty tablets – would be a fatal dose. Most of it was taken after July 19. [...]

Mrs. Hullett had been taking sleeping tablets, which had been left for her by her physician, Dr. John Bodkin Adams. [...]

A Lloyd's underwriter, Mr. Percy Robert Handscomb, said he was a great friend of Mrs. Hullett. [...]

Mrs. Hullett had implicit faith in Dr. Adams and he (Mr. Handscomb) did not think it necessary to advise her to ask for a second medical opinion.

The coroner: Here we have a fit woman, well off, with a daughter to look after. She is having tablets every night and is obviously under the influence of tablets part of the day and you still say you did not think it necessary to have another opinion to try and get her better?

Mr. Handscomb: I am afraid it never entered my head.

Have you ever heard her say she would take her own life? – Not in so many words.

Daily Mirror, 22nd August 1956

With suspicions raised, police conducted an investigation of Adams' former patients, finding out that he had been administering secretive injections and medication, withholding information from nurses and family. In addition to Hullett, the death of Edith Morrell had come to their attention. Morrell had suffered a stroke in June 1948 for which Adams had prescribed varying doses of morphine and heroin until her death in November 1950.

The police first charged Adams with Morrell's murder, and later with the murder of Hullett.

AFTER being arrested on a charge of murdering an Eastbourne widow, Dr. John Bodkin Adams said to his receptionist, "I will see you in Heaven," a court was told yesterday.

The alleged remark was quoted by Detective Superintendent Herbert Hannam, of Scotland Yard, when the fifty-seven-year-old bachelor doctor faced Eastbourne magistrates.

Dr. Adams was accused of murdering eighty-one-year-old Mrs. Edith Alice Morrell, of Beachy Headroad, Eastbourne, in November, 1950.

There were sixteen other charges against the doctor under the Cremation Act, the Forgery Act, the Dangerous Drugs Act and the Larceny Act.

Daily Mirror, 21st December 1956

During interview, Adams revealed his supercilious attitude towards his patients and the police, "Easing the passing of a dying person isn't all that wicked. She [Morrell] wanted to die. That can't be murder. It is impossible to accuse a doctor."

It certainly proved impossible to convict Adams. A cover-up was suspected because of his social position and wealth, with evidence suddenly disappearing, or new exhibits with confusing evidence magically produced, such as records of smaller quantities of drugs having been prescribed. Key witnesses for the prosecution either changed their minds or were less accusatory than before the trial. Furthermore, the police had chosen to proceed on the case of a woman who had been cremated, thereby evidence had already been destroyed. The trial also set two precedents. It became the longest murder trial in Britain, lasting 17 days, and, following his acquittal for murder, Adams was the first person to be bailed before returning for a second murder trial.

If there was a cover-up it was probably because of Adams' homosexuality, which was illegal in those days. He was implicated with two other men, the deputy chief constable of Eastbourne, Alexander Seekings, who had selected which case to take to court, and the magistrate Sir Roland Gwynne, mayor of Eastbourne, who saw Adams daily and took holidays with him, and was brother to Rupert Gwynne, MP for Eastbourne.

Adams was also cleared of the second murder, but despite this it was clear he was an incompetent physician. The search of his house had discovered food and medications being stored together, and he kept no register of the dangerous drugs in his keeping, a professional and legal requirement under the Dangerous Drugs Act of 1951. He had also tried to hide morphine from the investigating officers.

Adams was found guilty in a subsequent trial in July 1957 of 13 offences involving prescription fraud, falsifying cremation forms, obstructing the police and lacking a dangerous drugs register. He was struck off the medical register and was only reinstated in 1961 on his third attempt. In the interim, Adams ran a private practice even though it was widely considered he was guilty of the Hullett and Morrell murders, and more.

Only in retrospect can we see from recently opened police archives that in actual fact Adams was wantonly administering overdoses, probably causing the deaths of at least 160 of his elderly patients over a 30-year period. The Home Office Pathologist Francis Camps, who had given evidence as an expert witness in the inquest into Hullett's death, estimated the death toll to be 163.

Having gained their trust and friendship, Adams had benefited from 132 of his patients' wills, probably making him the wealthiest general practitioner in England. Adams died in June 1983 from a chest infection after a fall while out on a shooting expedition. But his criminal influence succeeded him when it was suggested that Dr Harold Shipman considered Adams a role model for his own killing career.

Graham Frederick Young
A.K.A. The Teacup Poisoner
COUNTRY England
VICTIMS 3
METHOD poisoned

Aged 14, Graham Young murdered his stepmother and became the youngest person to be committed to Broadmoor. Fascinated by Nazism and the occult, at school he took little interest in anything other than chemistry, and developed an obsessive interest in toxicology. Even in those early days, he practised using poison on others, first fellow students, then family members, and, accidently, himself, because he couldn't remember which foods he had laced with poison. Eventually, his family reluctantly began to suspect what he was doing, although his father didn't want to believe his son was deliberately setting out to harm them. It was Young's chemistry teacher who alerted the police when he reported the dubious solutions and literature he found in the schoolboy's desk.

Young admitted his guilt and he was detained under the Mental Health Act in Broadmoor Hospital, where his obsession with poisoning progressed. He continued his study of toxicology and experimented on staff and fellow patients. On his release, his human guinea pigs became the fellow residents of a hostel, and colleagues at the photographic laboratory where he worked. He laced cups of tea with thallium, killing two and making more than 70 unwell.

Young allowed his enthusiasm to run away when the company doctor was sent to reassure the staff. His questions for the doctor were too well-informed – he enquired whether thallium poisoning had been considered – and the police were summoned. His diary provided an accurate and damning record of his experiments, noting doses, observations of symptoms, and a judgement on the future fate of each candidate, mercy or death. The jury did not believe his defence that it was the draft of a novel.

Young was sentenced to life in Parkhurst Prison, where he formed a friendship with Ian Brady through their shared interest in Nazism. He died from a heart attack at the age of 42. An alternative and popular explanation is that he was poisoned by his fellow inmates.

Arnfinn Nesset
COUNTRY Norway
VICTIMS 138
METHOD poisoned

When Norwegian journalists got wind of a bald, mild-mannered, local nursing home manager buying large amounts of a derivative of curare, their curiosity was piqued. Following their lead, police uncovered a series of murders carried out by Arnfinn Nesset at three different institutions where he had worked since 1962. He was tried in October 1982 for 25 murders and five counts of forgery and embezzlement. Even though Nesset had confessed to 72 victims, proof would be hard to come by as the South American poison quickly degrades in the body. In March 1983 Nesset was convicted of 22 counts of murder, one attempted murder, and five counts of forgery and embezzlement. He received the maximum penalty of 21 years in jail; however, he was released in 2004, after serving only 12 years, for good behaviour. Nesset may have killed up to 138 elderly people during his 20-year nursing career – some out of sympathy but many just for enjoyment.

Edson Izidoro Guimarães

A.K.A. Angel of Death, Nurse of Death
COUNTRY Brazil
VICTIMS 131
METHOD poisoned

Edson Izidoro Guimarães worked as a nurse in the emergency department of Salgado Filho Hospital in the Méier district of Rio de Janeiro, Brazil. Guimarães admitted to removing the oxygen masks of terminally ill patients, "The oxygen mask was taken away, yes. There were five patients that this happened to [...] I chose the patients I saw suffering, generally patients with AIDS, patients who were almost terminal. I am in peace because the patients were in a coma and had no way of recovering." However, this did not account for another 126 suspicious deaths, nor the probable motivation of him receiving a 60-dollar payoff for informing funeral homes when a patient died. Furthermore, Guimarães had been seen by a colleague injecting a comatose patient with potassium chloride. In February 2000, Guimarães received a 76-year sentence for four murders, which was commuted to 31 years and eight months in March 2001. He is currently being held in Polinter Prison in Rio de Janeiro where he nurses his fellow prisoners.

Orville Lynn Majors

COUNTRY USA
VICTIMS 130
METHOD poisoned

As with the Lainz Angels of Death, licensed nurse Orville Lynn Majors was also intolerant of demanding and whining patients. Working at Vermillion County Hospital, Majors, if he thought a patient was adding to his workload, would soon inject them with potassium chloride and adrenaline, causing a dramatic rise in blood pressure before cardiac arrest. Following his move to the small, 56-bed hospital, their death rate rocketed from an average 26 per year to over 100, a third of the intake. During his 22 months serving at the hospital, 147 people died, many while Majors was on shift. He was arrested in December 1997, tried and convicted of six murders. Seventy-nine witnesses stepped forward to testify against him, many having seen him administer injections, something for which he was not qualified. Amazingly, none had reported his activities beforehand. His nursing colleagues even ran a sweepstake on which patient would be next to die while Majors was on duty.

360 YEARS FOR "ANGEL OF DEATH"

A FORMER nurse who was jailed for 360 years yesterday is believed to be America's worst serial killer.

Orville Lynn Majors is linked to the deaths of 130 old people over two years at a hospital where he worked.

The man nicknamed the Angel of Death was convicted of six murders and sentenced at Brazil, Indiana, to 60 years for each.

The victims were four women and two men aged between 56 and 89.

Prosecutors said Majors, 38, injected them with fatal overdoses of potassium chloride, which stopped their hearts.

Vials of the substance were found in his home and in his car.

A former roommate testified that Majors said he hated old people and told him: "They should all be gassed."

A friend said the nurse confessed to him, a year after he was fired from the hospital in Indiana, that he had murdered patients.

At least 15 bodies were exhumed during the police investigation.

Daily Mirror, 16th November 1999

Harold Frederick Shipman
A.K.A. Dr Death
COUNTRY England
VICTIMS 352
METHOD poisoned

Harold Shipman is Britain's worst serial killer – Dr Death indeed. When his case came to light there was a horrid realization that someone in one of our most trusted professions, someone we rely on for our health, could actually be killing us off in our dotage, one by one. This was made even worse by the painfully slow and gradual way that the total possible number of his murders was discovered:

137 MORE

Shipman may have killed patients in hospital before he became a GP

SERIAL killer Dr Harold Shipman, who murdered 215 patients, could have claimed ANOTHER 137 victims, including four babies.

Lawyers are investigating deaths he certified when he was a junior hospital doctor, before his days as a notorious GP in Hyde, Greater Manchester.

A further 45 deaths in Hyde were logged as "highly suspicious".

Shipman Inquiry chairman Dame Janet Smith will rule on the deaths at Pontefract General Hospital, West Yorks, when she publishes her final report on the serial killer next week.

Shipman worked at the hospital between 1970 and 1974 and lived in the grounds with his wife and two children.

The inquiry originally concluded that there had been no suspicious deaths at Pontefract.

But an unnamed health professional last year voiced suspicions about Shipman.

Lawyers from the Manchester-based inquiry have since spent months tracking down relatives of patients who had their death certificates signed by Shipman while he was in Pontefract.

A spokesman for the Shipman Inquiry said: "The inquiry looked at 137 deaths because that's the number of deaths he certified during his time there.

"It remains to be seen how many are deemed suspicious. Just because he certified that number doesn't mean they are all suspicious."

Shipman was given 15 life sentences after he was convicted at Preston Crown Court in January 2000 of killing elderly patients by lethal injection.

He was found hanged in his prison cell at Wakefield Jail last January.

Daily Mirror, 20th January 2005

Shipman had the ultimate God complex, taking it upon himself to decide when someone's life was over, convincing himself that he was acting out of sympathy, but never bothering to check with his patients that prescribing euthanasia was okay by them, and clearly being motivated through his feeling of superiority, and, occasionally, greed for their wealth.

Shipman was born in Nottingham, the second child of Vera and his lorry-driving father, also named Harold. At only 17 years of age, he was to witness early on the beneficial effects of administering analgesic pain relief when his mother was given morphine during the latter stages of cancer. The lesson would stay with him into his own professional career.

Shipman won a scholarship to attend Leeds School of Medicine, graduating in 1970 to start a placement at the Pontefract Infirmary in the West Riding of Yorkshire. In 1974, he was fully qualified and started in general practice at the Abraham Ormerod Medical Centre in Todmorden, West Yorkshire, but was disciplined in 1975 for forging prescriptions. He was self-medicating opium-like painkiller pethidine.

Fined and passed through drug rehabilitation, but banned from working with drugs, Shipman served as medical officer for Hatfield College in Durham, and worked for a short time for the National Coal Board. He returned to general practice in 1977, joining the Donneybrook Medical Centre in Hyde, Greater Manchester.

Over the course of the next two decades, Shipman became a respected member of the community, supporting local schools and the St John's Ambulance Brigade, founding his own surgery in 1993, and even being interviewed on medical matters for national TV. Amongst his colleagues he was considered sometimes arrogant and patronizing towards his patients, but the latter loved him for his kindly bedside manner.

Everything started to change in March 1998 when Deborah Massey from Frank Massey & Son's funeral parlour approached Dr Linda Reynolds at the Brooke Surgery, which was in a partnership with Shipman's surgery and was located just across the road. The employee had become concerned by the number of official cremation forms that Shipman was bringing to them, needing countersigned, for his recently deceased elderly patients. John Pollard, the coroner for the South Manchester district was informed and police investigators called in, but they were unable to collect sufficient evidence to bring about a prosecution. It wasn't until September 1998 that Shipman was eventually arrested. In the meantime, he had killed three more people.

It was the suspicious death of his last victim, 81-year-old Kathleen Grundy, a former Lady Mayor of Hyde, and the persistent pursuit of the truth by her daughter, lawyer Angela Woodruff, that proved to be Shipman's downfall.

A DOCTOR is being investigated over the deaths of up to 20 patients.

The inquiry was launched after relatives of widow Kathleen Grundy, 81, said she had changed her will to make GP Harold Shipman her main beneficiary.

Mrs Grundy's body was exhumed earlier this month. Detectives are awaiting the results of tests. Police said yesterday: "The investigation may involve looking at the deaths of up to 19 other people. There is nothing to indicate anything sinister at this stage."

Married Dr Shipman, 52, of Hyde, Greater Manchester, refused to comment. He said: "I'll give you five seconds of my time for a picture. But I have nothing to say."

It is believed police were contacted after Mrs Grundy's relatives found her will had been changed so nothing was left to her solicitor daughter Angela Woodruff, 53, or adored grandsons Richard, 24, and Matthew, 23.

Charity worker Mrs Grundy, of Hyde, died suddenly in June. Dr Shipman signed her death certificate giving the cause of death as "old age." He is thought to have taken advice from the Medical Defence Union.

Daily Mirror, 20th August 1998

Shipman was charged with defrauding Grundy's will, which led to a more in-depth investigation and exhumation of bodies. Shipman was convicted of 15 murders in January 2000 and sentenced to a life jail term. The 215 deaths directly attributable to him were mostly elderly female patients of his whom he injected with lethal doses of diamorphine, a medical preparation of heroin. He then forged medical records to exaggerate or invent their medical conditions, sometimes reporting a fictitious drug addiction to cover up the high levels of heroin in their systems. While he also stole jewellery, forging Grundy's will had been an unusual move, and may have been down to greed as he neared retirement.

RIPPERS

Disarm, disarm
The sword of murder is not the balance of justice
Blood does not wipe out dishonor
nor violence indicate possession
Julia Ward Howe

Most people outside the surgical and forensic professions are unprepared to witness the human body laid open, like an animal carcass in a butcher's shop. This is something that is deep-rooted in our psyche, a barrier from nature that is partly cultural, taught in the churches, temples and sacred texts of global religions, and partly a survival mechanism, a reminder that in reality we are just skin, flesh and bone. The standard for all modern serial killers was clearly set by the infamous Whitechapel Murderer, who broke through that barrier, and celebrated the internal workings of the human body. Such post-mortem-like displays of the victims' innards were sickening because the killers' atrocities forced us to take a good look at ourselves, in more ways than one.

Peter Sutcliffe
A.K.A. The Yorkshire Ripper
COUNTRY England
VICTIMS 13
METHOD bludgeoned
MUTILATION dismembered

The case of the Yorkshire "Ripper" is almost as infamous as his notorious Whitechapel namesake. In 1981, after a five-year reign of terror that crippled West Yorkshire between October 1975 and November 1980, Peter Sutcliffe was found guilty of murdering 13 women and attacking seven others. Sutcliffe had actually first assaulted a prostitute in 1969, bludgeoning her with a stone in a sock. He had hit her with such force that the stone had ripped through the toe of the sock, but she had survived and, even though Sutcliffe was identified as the attacker, she didn't bring charges against him.

Sutcliffe's favoured method from then on was using a machinist's hammer, which wouldn't let him down so easily. He also slashed and stabbed his victim's stomachs or backs. He stabbed one woman 51 times with a sharpened screwdriver. Another he struck twice on the back of the head, then stabbed her in the neck, chest and abdomen 15 times. He then masturbated onto the back of her trousers and underpants. For comfort while kneeling, Sutcliffe would wear a V-necked sweater under his trousers, the padded elbows pulled over his knees. This positioned the neck of the sweater over his crotch, allowing quick access to his genitals. However, he didn't have sex with the women, nor sexually assault them beyond removing their underwear. Another victim, who survived to tell the tale, saw him masturbate as he watched her sprawled on the ground, bleeding from her head wounds. When he had finished, Sutcliffe gave the women a five pound note to buy her silence.

Both Sutcliffe and the police recognized the significance of another five pound note that he had used to pay for sex. The police found the mint banknote in a victim's handbag and were able to trace it as having come from one of 8,000 local pay packets. Sutcliffe had been included in the interviews of 5,000 men, that spanned three months, to follow up the lead, but no further clues came of it. Sutcliffe had also realized the potential giveaway of the note, and had returned to the crime scene in an attempt to retrieve it from the victim's possessions. Frustrated at not finding it, he stripped her corpse and stabbed her 18 times, in her breasts, chest, stomach and vagina. One slash extended from her left shoulder to her right knee. He finally tried to decapitate the body but was not adequately prepared.

The five pound note would eventually lead the police to whittle their list down to only 300 suspects. Sutcliffe was one of them, as well as being on several other lists, such as car sightings, general witness descriptions and names suggested by the public. His car and only two others were on their sightings list three times, more than the rest. But the police were inundated with leads and suggestions, especially after the Wearside Jack audiotape was sent to them, and mistakenly turned their attention towards Sunderland and men with a Geordie accent. Through one reason or another, Sutcliffe was eliminated from enquiries a dozen times.

It wasn't until 2006 that Wearside Jack was identified from a DNA sample found on the envelope of one of his letters to be ex-labourer and window cleaner John Humble. In sending the tape, and three letters in total, one to taunt the detective in charge of the case, and two to a newspaper, Humble had massively impacted the investigation. He was sentenced to eight years on four counts of perverting the course of justice. It transpired from identifying the hoaxer that he himself had phoned the incident room to tell them that the tape was a hoax, but it was just another of the many calls the police thought to be a hoax.

One of Humble's letters from 1978 made mention of a murder in Lancashire, taunting the police, "How many is it now? Four or five? What about Preston in 1975. I think you will find it's six." Although there were marked differences with the other murders, such as a deep bite mark above a breast, and semen in both vagina and anus, the certainty that Wearside Jack was the Yorkshire Ripper convinced the police that this was also one of his victims. Sutcliffe would later vehemently deny this, and it would take a deathbed confession to identify the real culprit as convicted sex offender Christopher Smith. Just days after being stopped for drink-driving in 2008, Smith died from cancer, but not before writing his confession, nor before a DNA sample could be taken and analysed. It showed up as a match for DNA retrieved from the body 33 years before.

The hunt for Peter Sutcliffe is remembered as much for these mistakes, wrong turns and hoaxes that blighted the police investigation, as for the palpable relief when he was eventually apprehended:

Ripper "killed more"

SECRET PROBE SAYS BLUNDERS LEFT SUTCLIFFE FREE TO STRIKE

THE Yorkshire Ripper probably murdered and attacked many more women, a secret report discloses.

Bungling police also missed a glaring opportunity in 1977 to link Peter Sutcliffe to an earlier killing, leaving him free to carry out seven more murders.

The report into the Ripper probe by West Yorkshire police was unveiled yesterday after being kept secret since 1982. It was carried out by ex-Inspector of Constabulary Sir Lawrence Byford.

Sir Lawrence said there was an "unexplained lull" in Sutcliffe's activities between 1969 when he first came to police attention and his first recognised attack in 1975.

He said: "It is my firm conclusion that between 1969 and 1980 Sutcliffe was probably responsible for many attacks on unaccompanied women which he has not yet admitted – not only in the West Yorkshire and Manchester areas but also in other parts of the country.

"Details of a number of assaults since 1969 fall into his established pattern."

Sutcliffe, 60 today, was jailed for life in 1981 for murdering

13 women and trying to kill seven more. But police blunders left him free to kill.

Officers who interviewed him in November 1977 failed to examine his Ford Corsair whose tyres would have linked him with the murder of Irene Richardson nine months earlier.

He went on to murder seven more times before his arrest in January 1981.

An anonymous tip-off to police by Sutcliffe's friend Trevor Birdsall stayed in a filing tray. A report on a visit to police by Mr Birdsall was lost.

Sir Lawrence said: "This was a stark illustration of the decline in efficiency."

In total, Sutcliffe was questioned and freed nine times by murder police.

Sir Lawrence suggested the investigation suffered "information overload" because of massive public response to hoax letters and tapes sent by John Humble, known as Wearside Jack. In March, Humble was jailed for eight years for attempting to pervert justice.

Daily Mirror, 2nd June 2006

Trevor Birdsall had known Sutcliffe since 1966, and had been driving the night of the first assault, with the weighted sock. He was also present on another occasion, when a woman Sutcliffe had argued with in a pub disappeared later that night. Despite suspecting his friend, Birdsall wouldn't attempt to tip off the police until November 1980, which coincidentally turned out to be after the last assault. Birdsall's anonymous letter, and his subsequent visit to the police station the next day, were overlooked. The police were simply overwhelmed by the volume of information they had to sift through, although when checking their files against Sutcliffe's name, he had already been entered into their index-card system three times before.

Sutcliffe was finally arrested after being interrupted trying to have sex with a prostitute in January 1981. A routine check of the car they were in showed the number plates to be false, so he was taken in for questioning. The police also couldn't help but notice his similarity with the survivors' and witness descriptions of the Yorkshire Ripper that they had been amassing over the years. This warranted a better search of the area where they had picked him up. They found his hammer, knife and a rope, which he had quickly dumped when allowed to urinate a short distance away. They found another knife in the toilet cistern at the police station. Two days later they had a confession, and they had their Ripper. Or did they?

Conspiracy theorists are never far from a big story, and the Yorkshire Ripper case is no exception. On a few occasions witnesses had implicated a man with an Irish accent. Two blood types had been found at the crime scenes, and Sutcliffe's matched only one of them. This evidence and the police artist's impression of the mystery man convinced semi-retired businessman Noel O'Gara that a man he had known as William "Bill" Tracey was the real Yorkshire Ripper, and Sutcliffe was merely a copycat killer who hadn't carried out all the murders he confessed. Corroboration of this version of events would come from, amongst others, Sutcliffe's father.

The strong suggestion was that a deal had been agreed upon between Sutcliffe's defence team and the director of public prosecutions that would guarantee him a place in a psychiatric hospital instead of being sent to prison. In accordance with this, Sutcliffe pleaded not guilty to 13 counts of murder, but guilty of manslaughter through diminished responsibility. He claimed God had spoken from a gravestone, commanding him to kill prostitutes.

A 2006 report concluded that Sutcliffe was probably already killing between 1969 and 1975. While there are no proven incidents, some unsolved cases do match his methods. Sutcliffe has been repeatedly attacked by fellow inmates while in prison, on one occasion being blinded in his left eye by a pen. Despite a diagnosis that he was fit for release from Broadmoor high-security psychiatric hospital in 2009, the High Court rejected his 2010 appeal, and confirmed a whole life tariff.

Gordon Cummins
A.K.A. The Blackout Ripper
COUNTRY England
VICTIMS 4
METHOD strangled, stabbed
MUTILATION dismembered

An educated young airman with delusions of grandeur, George Cummins murdered four women in six days in the midst of the Second World War while billeted in London, and attempted to murder two more. He was regarded as eccentric by colleagues, speaking with an affected accent and believing he was descended from aristocracy. Cummins sexually assaulted most of his victims, mutilating the bodies of three of them by slashing them with implements such as knives and razors and, in one case, sexually mutilating his victim with a tin opener. Fingerprints found on the tin opener revealed that the murderer was left-handed.

Taking advantage of air-raid blackout conditions during the London

Blitz as a cover for his crimes, and even carrying out a murder in an air-raid shelter, Cummins became known as "The Blackout Ripper", and was described as a "savage sexual maniac" by a pathologist who examined one of the bodies. There is good reason to believe Cummins would have extended his spree into a long-running series, mainly because of the sexual mutilation of his victims, which is not common among spree killers.

Cummins was easily traced by the serial number on his gas mask, which he dropped as he fled the scene of an attempted murder after being interrupted by a delivery boy. While he was being pursued, he tried to kill one more time, but this time was successfully fought off. As the Yorkshire Ripper would do 30 years later, Cummins gave the woman five pounds for her silence, but his identity was already known and he was tried in April 1942, and hanged at London's Wandsworth Prison in June 1942, in the middle of an air raid.

Anthony John Hardy
A.K.A. The Camden Ripper
COUNTRY England
VICTIMS 11
METHOD bludgeoned
MUTILATION decapitated, dismembered, bitten

The 10-year-old boy cast his line again. It had been a slow morning. It had been the same for his two mates. No bites for them either. Regent's Canal wasn't dishing out any of the silvery treasure that slid beneath its slick surface today. It was a shame because there was plenty of fish to be caught along that Camden stretch of the Regent's Canal: bream, carp (common, leather, ghost and mirror), eels of course, but also gudgeon, perch, roach, ruffe, tench and, if you were lucky, you'd hook one of those monster pike you sometimes saw fleeting in the shadows below. No guarantee you'd land it though. They're tough buggers, but it was a buzz trying. Not today though, very slow, and they'd have to get back for their lunch soon. Time for one more go, and then they'd have to leg it.

Changing his cast angle, the boy pitched his lure closer to the reeds that grew out from the shadows beneath the rampant ivy smothering Bridge No. 28, which the Royal College Street crosses. The pikes liked the dark and lurked among the reeds waiting for smaller fish to blunder past. It was a risky strategy on the part of the fisherman. The rewards could be good – at least an eel, which he knew liked the same places – but experience had taught him that catching your hook on the reeds, or, worse, on dumped rubbish like a shopping trolley, could mean cutting the line and losing your prize lure.

At first the boy thought he had a bite. His line did that jolt thing that happens when a fish latches on. He felt it must be a heavy fish too. The strain on the line was bending his rod into a worrying arch. His pals had noticed and come over now, cheering him on, lending a hand. It took all three of them several breathless minutes to drag whatever had captured the boy's hook to the canal side and then up the wall to land in a dripping, formless bundle at their feet. Well before it had broken the surface, they knew it wasn't a dream catch, and that it wasn't even alive.

Paula Fields was a 31-year-old prostitute and crack addict, whose body had been dismembered into 10 pieces, probably with a hacksaw, the parts wrapped in bin liners, stuffed into a holdall and weighed down with bricks, before being chucked into the canal. Police found a further five holdalls, after the boys had opened their catch and had been confronted with human remains. The date was February 2001.

Three months earlier in December 2000, a man walking along the bank of the Thames at Battersea had stumbled across the floating upper half of a woman's body. An autopsy established that she had been in the water for about a fortnight and that she had probably been sliced in two with a sword. A tattoo found on her was printed in newspapers and it wasn't long before family members made contact, identifying the women as 24-year-old prostitute Zoe Louise Parker (aka Cathy Dennis).

Almost exactly two years later, in December 2002, a homeless man was foraging in bins at the rear of The College Arms on Royal College Street in Camden, for food, any scraps of pub grub, to take the edge off his hunger. What he found totally took away his appetite. Inside were bags of body parts, including two severed sections of legs, which he valiantly delivered to the local hospital. A more thorough police search discovered a further eight similar bags, one containing an upper torso. Right and left arms, and a left foot, were found in a large wheelie bin, about 100 yards away.

Pathologists could tell that the remains were of two separate women, but their identification and establishing their cause of death was not straightforward, because neither heads nor hands could be found. One was eventually identified by the serial numbers on breast and buttock implants as 29-year-old Elizabeth Selina Valad. It had been her legs in the bin. From DNA analysis, the other turned out to be 34-year-old Brigitte MacClennan, who accounted for the other body parts and torso. Both women were crack-addicted prostitutes.

Yesterday, as a special service was held at St Pancras Old Church in Camden to pray for the dead women, teams of police continued to search the area, including a stretch of the nearby Regent's Canal, for further clues.

Daily Mirror, 3rd January 2003

In January 2002, almost a year before this grisly discovery, police had been called to an altercation in a nearby block of flats, also in Royal College Street. The antagonist was Anthony Hardy, a mechanical engineering graduate and ex-psychiatric patient with a history of alleged assault. Returning to Britain from Tasmania in 1986, where he had attempted to kill his wife a few years before, Hardy was first imprisoned for breaking a restriction order trying to see his now ex-wife and children. On both occasions Hardy had sought medical help, and was prescribed medication to treat manic depression. Heavy alcohol and drug abuse exacerbated his symptoms, resulting with him becoming homeless and being imprisoned for theft in the mid-1990s. In 1998, he was arrested again, but the rape charge brought by a prostitute was dropped and he was released, despite ongoing enquiries into three other allegations of rape. He had been given the flat after causing rifts with tenants at his previous accommodation, but he had continued with his anti-social ways.

There was no question that he was weird. He would sit for hours in the communal courtyard with a can of strong lager late at night, just staring at his flat as if he was afraid to go in.

Daily Mirror, 17th January 2004

Hardy had been reported by a neighbour for scrawling obscene graffiti on a door and pouring battery acid through her letterbox, following an argument over a flooded bath. When the police arrived at the location in Royal College Street to answer the call they insisted on searching Hardy's flat. An inner door to a spare room was locked, and Hardy initially claimed not to have a key, saying that it was in the possession of a lodger who was overseas for three weeks. Shortly afterwards a key was found stitched into a secret lining of his coat, the door was opened and police discovered the corpse of 38-year-old prostitute and crack addict Sally Rose White, which had cuts to the head, bite marks on the thigh and bruising. The pathologist, Dr Freddy Patel, deemed these injuries non-fatal, offering the dubious diagnosis of death from heart attack as a result of coronary heart disease. Patel was later suspended after being found guilty of misconduct in this and a series of other high-profile autopsies.

With only criminal damage to a door held against him, Hardy was sectioned under the Mental Health Act and placed on a ward at St Luke's Hospital in Muswell to undergo a psychological evaluation; he was released from there in November 2002. By December and the discovery of the bodies in the bins nearby, Hardy was an obvious suspect, facing up to five murder charges for the deaths of Fields, Parker, White, Valad and MacClennan. But he had disappeared.

Still, armed with a warrant, the police broke down the door to his flat, and found no shortage of incriminating evidence. The flat was decorated with numerous black crosses and "odd pictures of human anatomy", with "slivers of dried skin and flesh stuck and smeared to the wallpaper". They found Valad's decomposing torso, wrapped in a bin liner, a hacksaw with human skin still attached to the blade, an electric jigsaw, piles of pornographic magazines, and paraphernalia used during Hardy's sadomasochistic sex rituals, and while posing and photographing the bodies. In some of the photographs, the victim was wearing a devil's mask, baseball cap and Mr Men 'Mr Happy' socks, with a Rampant Rabbit vibrator placed near her vagina.

Shamefully, after the acid attack and the discovery of White, the assessment panel had not been sent a psychiatrist's report that warned of Hardy's violent tendencies, and had not been informed of his police record, resulting in their assessment of him being only "low to medium risk". Consequently, he had been free to leave, return to his flat for a further month, carry out the murders of Valad and MacClennan, dismember their bodies and dispose of parts in the local bins. Retrospectively, Hardy could be seen distributing those bin bags on CCTV, but it was only after the vagrant had chanced on their contents that Hardy was finally picked up while on the run, as he was forced to approach hospitals to get his alcoholism-related diabetes prescription. He was arrested and charged with the murder of Valad, MacClennan and White. Uncooperative throughout questioning, Hardy pleaded guilty to all charges on going to trial in November 2003 and received life imprisonment. When interviewed, his neighbours mentioned their suspicions that something wasn't quite right about Hardy and his flat, specifically things like drilling and sawing noises in the middle of the night:

My Jack Russell dog always sensed there was something different about his flat.

Whenever I walked past it with her she would strain on her leash towards the door and I had to pull her away. Obviously she could smell something that I couldn't. Now it makes me shudder when I think what scent she must have been picking up.

Others in the block say they remember hearing drilling noises coming from his flat, but at the time you never suspect it's sinister.

Daily Mirror, 17th January 2004

The murder and bisection of Zoe Parker still remains a mystery, along with the violent murders of more than two dozen British prostitutes over the past two decades, a number that is probably much higher if the number of women reported missing are really dead, as it is presumed. Hardy is suspected of at least six additional murders in the Camden area, maybe more, but not the death of Paula Fields. Although they didn't know it, the police had already netted her murderer.

John Sweeney
A.K.A. The Scalp Hunter
COUNTRY England
VICTIMS 7
METHOD bludgeoned, stabbed, shot
MUTILATION decapitated, dismembered

Body in the Bags

A KILLER who dismembered a prostitute and stuffed her body parts into bags may be keeping some of her limbs as trophies, Scotland Yard said yesterday.

Police divers are still searching a London canal for remains of 31-year-old Paula Fields. They were alerted by a 10-year-old boy who found the first bag as he was fishing. He is now receiving counselling.

Det Insp Mike Smith said her body was carefully dismembered with a sharp knife or saw. He said: "There may be one or two other bags outstanding or this person may be keeping other parts as trophies [...]"

Paula's remains were found in a Pierre Cardin bag, three Hot Shot bags and two other bags.

Mum-of-two Paula, who came to London from Liverpool three years ago, was a known prostitute with a £150-per-day crack cocaine habit [...]

Det Chief Insp Norman McKinlay, who is leading the investigation, said: "This is a truly horrific murder."

Daily Mirror, 3rd March 2001

The police really wanted to find out who had killed Fields, but it didn't look like one of Hardy's murders. They were struggling for leads while dismembered bodies continued to turn up, pulled out of canals in various bags and containers:

Torso link is probed

THE dismembered body of a woman found in a suitcase dumped in a canal has "obvious similarities" with another unsolved murder, police said yesterday.

Det Supt Maureen Boyle said police would investigate any links between the remains of a black woman found on Saturday and the unsolved murder of prostitute Paula Fields who was dismembered in 2000.

Teenagers found the latest victim in Regent's Canal, North London.

The woman, aged between 18 and 30, 5ft 3in, and slim, had been dead at least two days, say police.

The cause of her death is not known.

Daily Mirror, 13th April 2004

More worrying was the fact that the pattern of murders wasn't restricted to the UK. Bodies in holdalls in canals were also showing up overseas, prompting consolidation of a cross-border agreement for collaboration between European Union police forces. It was mainly intended to cut through the red tape surrounding extradition proceedings, but it was also very useful in terms of sharing information.

In 2008, the Metropolitan Police were contacted by the Cold Case Team in Rotterdam, who were reviewing the murder and mutilation of a women whose remains had been pulled out of Rotterdam's Westersingel Canal in May 1990. Eighteen years had passed since then and advances in DNA technology enabled identification of their discovery as 33-year-old American Melissa Halstead, who had been scouted as a model when she was 17 years old, and had moved to London in 1986 to work as a photographer. Her pictures had been published in *Vogue* and she seemed to have had good prospects for a successful career until she was deported in 1988 for working without a permit.

The Dutch police had contacted their colleagues in London because they thought they recognized some similarities with the finding of Fields: the two bodies had been cruelly mutilated in the same way, both women were in their early 30s, had lived in London, and had troubled pasts. Both were known to have been in violent relationships, and to be addicted to drugs. Furthermore, both their remains had been wrapped and put in weighted holdalls and canvas bags, before being dumped in canals, apart from their heads, hands and feet, which were still missing. However, comparisons between the two cases didn't end there. Suddenly an obvious link presented itself – a culprit already in a British prison for attempted murder. Searching his cell in Gartree Prison, guards found various morbid poems and pictures, one of a headless body cut into 13 pieces.

> Dad-of-two [John] Sweeney is serving life for the attempted murder of girlfriend Delia Balmer who he maimed on her doorstep in December 1994. After the attack he went on the run and turned up at the Northampton home of estranged wife Ann Bramley. He confessed he had killed three people and "done something really bad which would make her hair stand on end".
>
> *Daily Mirror,* 5th April 2011

After travelling around Europe in 1976, Liverpool-born Sweeney had married Ann Bramley, only to divorce her a few years later and then remarry her in 1981. They had two children, but family life was unsettled. His son Michael recalls, "I remember hearing about him throwing a brick through our window, hitting our pet turtles. Then he broke into our home with a pickaxe and hid behind the door. The neighbours called the police and he was arrested."

In fact the police were called several times, and Sweeney was bound over to keep the peace in 1982 after being found by officers in Bramley's wardrobe brandishing a hammer and an axe. This was the final straw for Bramley – they divorced again, and the court order seemed enough to dissuade Sweeney from continuing his harassment, as he headed to London in 1983 instead, to continue his work as a carpenter. A few years later he met Halstead and entered a relationship with her, one he described as "love–hate".

Sharing a house in Stoke Newington with Halstead, Sweeney was arrested three times for violently assaulting her, once being overheard shouting, "Who do you think you are? I'm the one who says what you can and can't do." At some point Halstead moved to new accommodation, and Sweeney was twice fined – a paltry £5 on each occasion – once for actual bodily harm when he hit her in the face with a stool in her new Knightsbridge home, and again when he kicked her in the legs. He was again bound over to keep the peace in April 1988. About this time, Halstead told her sister, Chance O'Hara, that, "If she ever went missing, that John Sweeney would have killed her. He had threatened that he would kill her and he would make sure no one would ever find her body."

Following her deportation from Britain, Halstead travelled to Vienna, but Sweeney tracked her down, broke into her flat and tied up her flatmate. Driven by jealous rage, he searched for evidence of Halstead having any

The real Dracula
was far more
bloodthirsty.

**"The Brides
in the Bath
Murderer"** George
Joseph Smith.

"The Black Panther" Donald Neilson.

"The Acid Bath Murderer" John George Haigh.

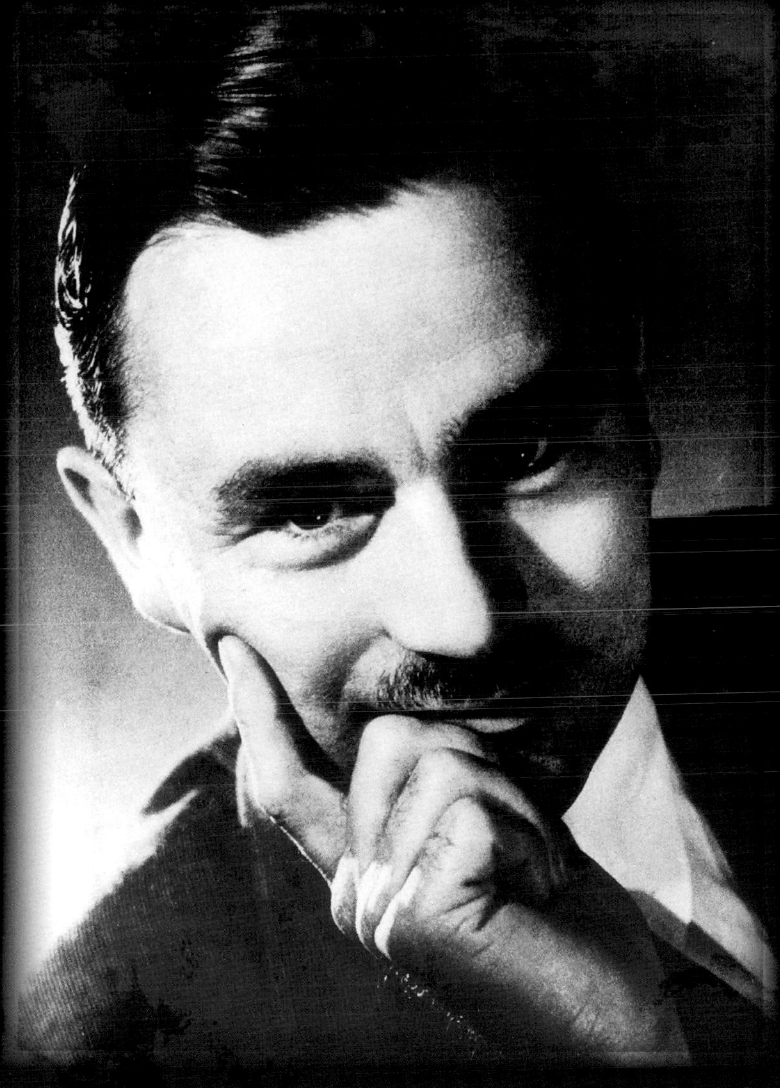

"The Crossbow Cannibal" Stephen Griffiths.

Peter Tobin.

John Bodkin Adams.

“The Teacup Poisoner” Graham Young.

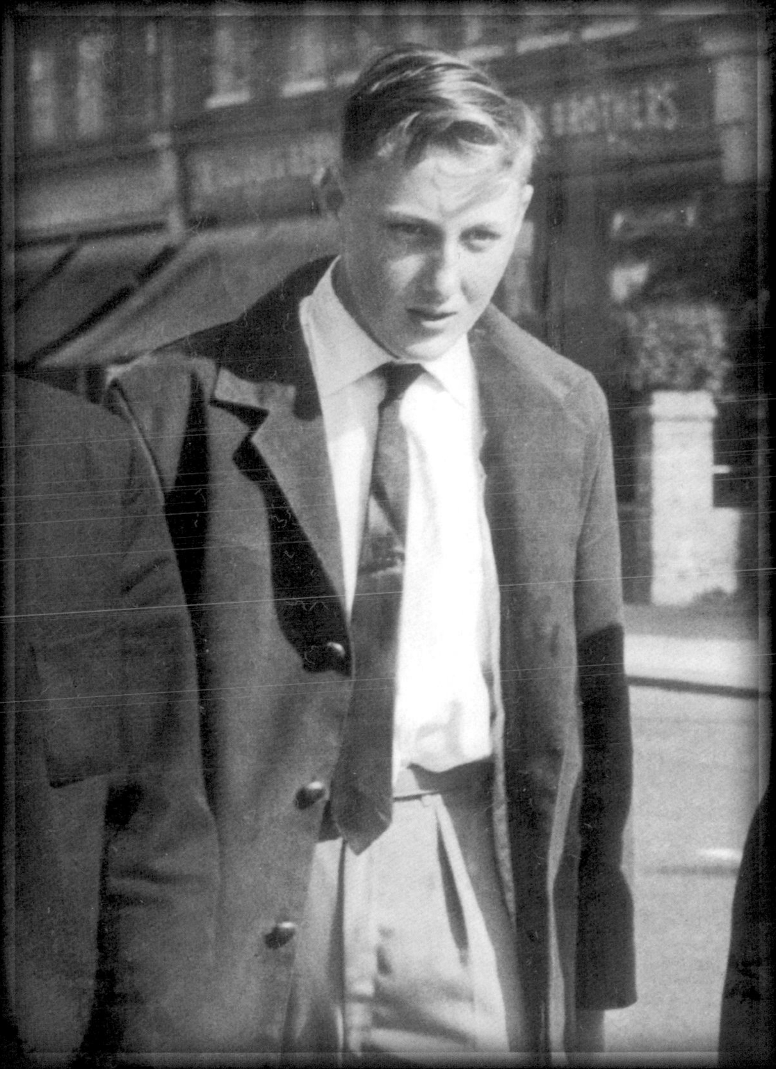

"Dr Death" Harold Shipman.

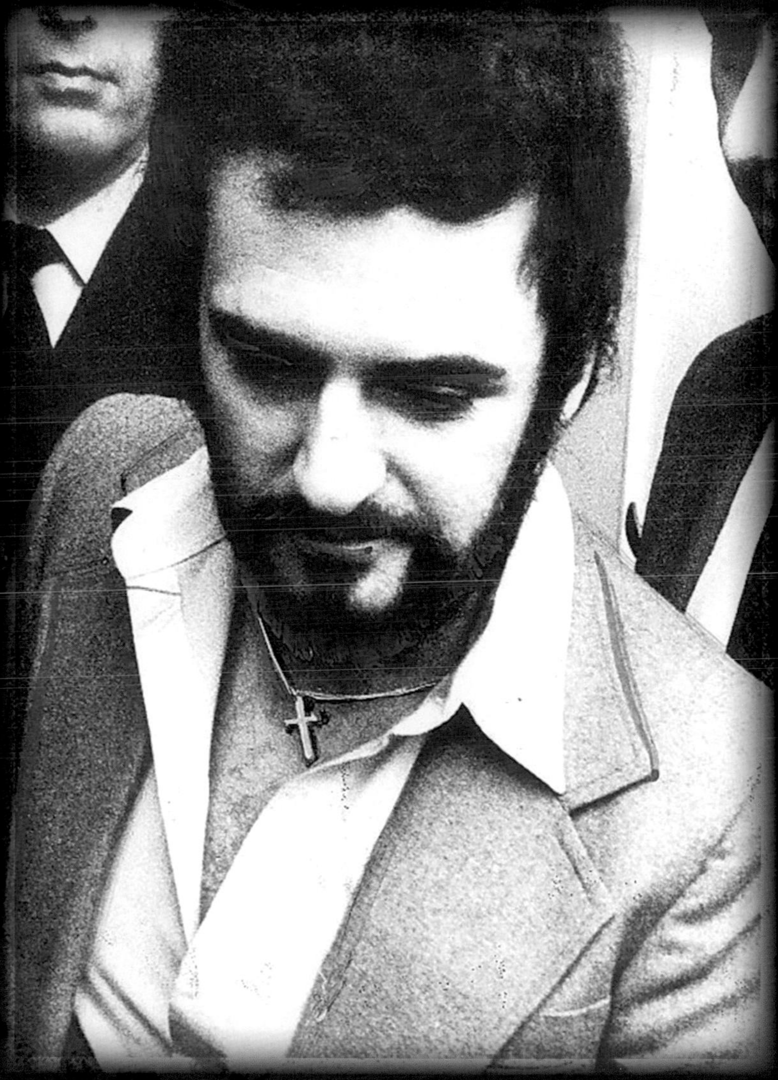

"The Yorkshire Ripper" Peter Sutcliffe.

"The Blackout Ripper" Gordon Cummins.

"The Camden Ripper" Anthony John Hardy.

"The Scalp Hunter" John Sweeney.

John Reginald Christie.

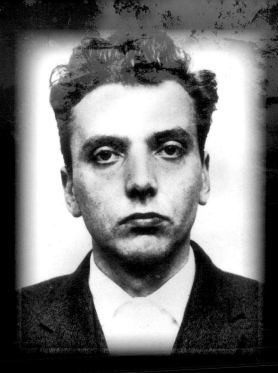

"The M1 Maniac" Robert Black.

Fred West.

Rose West.

relationships. He returned a few days later, fractured her skull with a claw hammer, and was sent to jail. During his detention, Sweeney painted two sets of hands and feet, which he described as, "That is her being the puppeteer and I am in a man trap." Six months later, in March 1989, Halstead had forgiven him and, pleading for leniency, got him released with a suspended 12-month prison sentence, and a 10-year deportation order. Reunited, they travelled to Stuttgart and then to Amsterdam. In May 1990, parts of Halstead's dismembered body were found in an Army surplus kit bag floating in the Westersingel Canal, naked, folded in half and bound with lengths of sisal rope.

Returning to London at Christmas of that year, Sweeney began a relationship with Australian nurse Delia Balmer. By November 1994 Balmer had realized her mistake and tried to dump him. Enraged, he took out a gun and held her captive for 48 hours. During that time Sweeney tortured her, and boasting about killing Halstead and two male German tourists that he had caught in bed together with her. He described cutting them up and "feeding her [Halstead] to the fish in the canal", but the next day brushed it off as a joke. Seizing an opportunity when a friend called, Balmer escaped and Sweeney was arrested.

Released immediately on bail, he ambushed Balmer in late December 1994, as she returned home from work. Trapping Balmer under her bike, Sweeney slashed at her chest and hair with an axe, "I watched one of my fingers go flying through the air. He had the axe above his head ready to finish me off. I had just curled up ready to go." Sweeney was only stopped when neighbour Jiles Allen attacked him with a baseball bat; he fled, leaving behind a green canvas rucksack containing a groundsheet, a length of rope, masking tape, surgical gloves and a saw blade.

This is when he went to Bramley's home to confess that he had "done something really bad", but, having clearly overcome his guilt 11 days after the attack, he wrote to the police calling Balmer an "evil witch", and referring to the attack as an "AXEident".

Using several aliases including Joe Carroll he then lived as a fugitive on building sites across Britain and Europe for the next six years.

Paula moved in with Sweeney and they began sleeping together. But he accused her of stealing his tobacco and using his mobile phone.

On the night of December 13, 2000 a neighbour was woken up in the early hours by a male voice screaming and shouting: "No, no, no."

Detectives now believe this may have been Sweeney's reaction after Paula discovered his true identity and he killed her two days later. When they raided his flat they found a hoard of 200 terrifying poems and pictures, a machete, a garotte, a loaded Luger pistol, two shotguns and ammo.

Daily Mirror, 5th April 2011

The precise arms he had stashed at his flat in Charteris Road were: two loaded sawn-off shotguns, a Webley & Scott .410, a Savage Arms Corporation 16-gauge, and a huge stash of bullets and cartridges. There was also a brown wig, a machete, an axe, a rounders' bat, bin liners, cable ties and a garotte made of bamboo.

In addition, the "lurid and demonic sketches" and pages of verse displaying "an obsessive and virulent hatred of women and a preoccupation with dismemberment" found in the flat provided much needed evidence to tie Sweeney to the murders. A painting called *The Scalphunter*, was of a man's bloodied midriff, axe hooked through a belt and a scalp hanging from the buckle. An inscription read, "I will live and die as I choose, I don't believe religion or the fucking law, there are no rules, my life's an open door." A bloody stump protruded from a trouser pocket, and on the back, surrounded by kisses, were the words, "inspired by and dedicated especially to Delia. May you die in pain." It was dedicated to Balmer. Yet another, entitled *One Man Band*, contained a drawing of a woman, but forensic scientists noticed that correction fluid had been applied over a small area. When ultraviolet light was shone on it, it revealed a gravestone inscribed "Melissa Halstead, born 7 November 1956. Died–."

On the back of a scratch card Sweeney had written, "Poor old Melissa / Chopped her up in bits / Food to feed the fish / Amsterdam was the pits", while another poem read, "Melissa / We met all of a sudden / Here in London / Trouble from the Law / England no more / she took my prick / All the way to Munich / Played catch me if you can / down in Milan / A bad trip in Vienna / Blood spilled / Amsterdam wasn't much better / Love killed / When I'm dead and gone / Maybe we'll be as one." Yet another went, "The trigger goes click, the dead don't talk / Thoughts of a lunatic, out for a walk / Seen the full moon, feel like dynamite / Thoughts of arrest, bridge to cross / Torture never stops, fills me with death/ It's a mental nightmare, getting a breath of fresh air."

A few weeks after Fields turned up in the canal, Sweeney was arrested while working on a building site 100 yards from the Old Bailey. Seeing the arresting officers approach, he attempted to reach his work locker while pulling out a knife concealed in his waistband, but lost the ensuing struggle and was overpowered. A loaded 9mm Luger pistol was found amongst his locker belongings. Now Sweeney was in custody, it didn't take long to make connections between the unsolved cases:

Axeman in "serial killer" quiz

DETECTIVES believe a man who tried to murder his ex-girlfriend with an axe and a knife may have killed at least twice.

John Sweeney, 43, faces life for the attack on Delia Balmer, chopping off her finger and stabbing her.

He was dragged screaming from the Old Bailey yesterday after being convicted on gun charges. He will be sentenced for all the offences on March 5.

Sweeney dated Melissa Halstead, whose torso was found in an Amsterdam canal in 1992.

Police plan to quiz him about prostitute Paula Fields, found dismembered in a London canal in 2001.

They are also probing the disappearance of two ex-girlfriends in the 90s. Det Chief Insp Norman McKinlay said Sweeney was a "truly evil man".

He added: "All the evidence points to him being responsible for the disappearance of Halstead and Fields. He could have carried out many murders."

Daily Mirror, 26th February 2002

In 2002, Sweeney received four life sentences for possessing his weapons and attempting to murder Balmer, with the possibility of parole after nine years. The subsequent investigation brought the additional charges of double murder and trying to pervert the course of justice. The second trial began in March 2011. Sweeney attempted to lie his way through the whole of the proceedings, claiming that he was on cannabis and acid at the time, and had done drugs on the day of that attack, and was therefore "out of touch with reality". He attacked the prosecution, saying statements had been exaggerated and witnesses "groomed". He even went so far as to suggest alternative killers: Fields could have been murdered by "Camden Ripper" Anthony Hardy, and Halstead by Frank Gust, the Rhine-Ruhr Ripper, who was arrested in 1998 for murdering four women in Germany. Of the incriminating poetry and artwork, Sweeney blamed two decades of abusing cannabis, heroin, speed and LSD, saying, "It's all bullshit. It's all drunken tosh. I was stoned out of my head when I did this. It is all just nonsense."

The jury were not fooled by any of Sweeney's shenanigans. He received a whole life sentence with no parole, but that is not the end of the case. While being interviewed after his arrest in 2001, he had boasted of having slept with 30 to 40 women, giving two names that subsequently turned up as missing persons.

Outside court, police appealed for information about a woman called Sue, who vanished in the 80s. A devoted churchgoer from the Derby area in her 30s, she fled North London for Switzerland, pursued by Sweeney who had become obsessed with her. Officers also want to trace a Brazilian known only as Irani, in her mid-40s. She lived in North London around 1996 and may have worked as a cleaner.

And they fear a Colombian called Maria in her late-30s, who lived around Finsbury Park and Holloway Road, from 1997 to 1998, is yet another victim.

Daily Mirror, 5th April 2011

REAPERS

Whatsoever a man soweth, that shall he also reap

Galatians 6:7

Some serial killers seem to go about their business as if harvesting humans. Even if their victim count isn't always shockingly huge, although often it is, their functional approach to their crimes reflects a mechanistic, process-oriented attitude. Get them in, have your way, get them out. As with many psychopaths, the victim is a practical object, a commodity, someone to serve their needs, no more.

Henry Howard Holmes

A.K.A. The Murder Castle Killer, Herman Mudgett
COUNTRY USA
VICTIMS 200+
METHOD suffocated, poisoned
MUTILATION dismembered, burned

She was frightened. No, more than that. Petrified. Scared half to death. She had no idea how long she'd been in there, it was pitch black and could be any hour of the day or night. She didn't even know where "there" was, other than the imposing three-storey brick building on Chicago's 63rd Street where she had made her way straight from the station. She had been excited and hadn't wanted to keep her new employer, the eminent doctor, waiting. Hurrying inside, she had only briefly noticed the false battlements, but that explained why the stranger who had given her directions had called it "the Castle".

At the time it must have only been a subconscious thought while crossing the street, why some of the upstairs wooden bay windows were covered with sheet iron. Now, it plagued her mind constantly. The walls felt and sounded like they were made of the same stuff. Her fingers were raw from clawing at them, and she could taste blood where her fingernails had ripped off, when uncontrollable panic attacks had seized her. She didn't have any energy left for those now. All she could do was gasp for every breath, sucking the last traces of life from the stale, putrid air, as she lay slumped in a corner, in a puddle of her own urine and vomit, petrified by fear, her voice spent, and out of tears.

She was not alone in the room. When she had been able to move, it had seemed as if it had taken an age to inch around its sides, despite it seeming only a few strides wide. She had tried pacing it out, to get a sense of its dimensions, only to find it best to scrape about on all fours, having bumped her head so often on the rough rivets protruding like barbs from the annoyingly low ceiling, scratching her scalp every time she managed to blunder into one, making her start and howl. The blood and sweat trickled into her eyes and burned, but her curses and shrieks made no difference. None of her screaming, banging or wailing had. She was resigned to the room being soundproof, no one could hear her and come to help, so instead she had tried exploring its perimeter, seeking a weakness. A single chink in its armour.

Crawling, straining to see as far as her nose, her upturned face had suddenly brushed past something, a tear-stained cheek comforted with a cold and clammy kiss. Instinctively reaching out to feel what it was, her fingers penetrated a crusty, charred jelly of swollen decay. Gloopiness oozed down her wrist and she recoiled in horror, her nostrils caulked with the sticky stench, and threw herself back into the corner, frozen in fright and tormented by ghostly thoughts rushing out of the blindness.

Assuming the alias Dr Henry Howard "H H" Holmes, Herman Mudgett took his serial killing seriously, making it into not so much an art, as a process. He even went as far as to build his own 162-feet long and 50-feet wide factory of death, his "Murder Castle". At ground level, the Castle was an innocuous-looking building. Just shop fronts, including that of Holmes' own average-looking pharmacy, nothing untoward, except for the concealed alarm system rigged to warn him of any movement on the upper floors.

The uppermost second floor was also mostly unremarkable, housing a couple of offices and his domestic quarters. One room, however, was more like a vault, its asbestos-lined steel walls sure to deaden any sound from within. A gaslight fitting was standard, except for additional pipes placed to enable Holmes to snuff out the light from outside. With the gas controlled from his bedroom and continuing to stream in, the prisoner could be asphyxiated at Holmes' convenience, and, as he spied through peepholes, for his pleasure. Reigniting the gas would then set the body alight.

Even so, it was the middle level and basement that housed an extraordinary maze of rooms and corridors tailored for torture and murder, and for processing cadavers. With 51 doors and 35 rooms to house guests and staff, Holmes could achieve a despicably high turnover of victims, and could keep some incarcerated for months before their execution. For example, 50 tourists who had travelled to the 1893 Chicago World's Fair, set to commemorate the 400th anniversary of Christopher Columbus's arrival in the New World, all disappeared after booking into Holmes' hotel. Other victims, often pretty young women, were attracted there by lucrative offers of work, on the condition that they took out life insurance first, which Holmes was kind enough to pay for, and mercenary enough to collect on.

In fact bigamy, insurance scams, frauds, swindles and confidence tricks – everything from faking his accomplice's death to taking out policies on persons already dead from natural causes, then disfiguring their corpses so that he could claim accidental death – filled Holmes' past and would predominate during the year between his leaving Chicago and his arrest, nominally for horse theft. More so, wherever he went a trail of murder victims, including children, was left in his wake. Cremation was a favoured form of disposal.

Even before his arrest, the police suspected Holmes of several murders, but never as many as transpired during the course of their investigation. Tracing his activities to Chicago they discovered that the custodian of the Castle had never been allowed to clean the upper floors. It took a month to explore the building and work out all of the killing mechanisms. No architect had been engaged. Instead, Holmes was entirely responsible for the design, ensuring only he knew the layout by firing any particular tradesmen after only a week, refusing pay and materials costs, and so ensuring he was able to afford to build his involved and expensive construction.

In addition to steel-lined gas chambers, the Castle had dedicated rooms with surgical and torture equipment, such as the "elasticity determinator", an elongated bed with straps installed to test how far human bodies could be stretched. Poisons and gallows were in others. The labyrinth of secret passages, low ceilings, trapdoors leading to rooms below false floors, elevators, hidden stairwells and greased chutes all had one ultimate purpose in mind, delivery of the victim's body to the two-level cellar where vats of acid and two large furnaces awaited them. Bloodied laundry and piles of bones littered this underground crypt; as the latter were stripped of flesh, it was evident that quicklime had been used to speed decomposition. The Castle factory was producing skeletons for medical school.

An inveterate liar, Holmes concocted several alibis to try to account for the inconceivable number of murder charges brought against him, not least a rash of suicides or alternative culprits. In the end he was convicted of murdering three children belonging to his accomplice, and was hanged in May 1896, still calmly pleading his innocence for all bar two of his hundreds of murders. His neck did not snap immediately, and it took 15 minutes of twitching at the end of the rope for him to die. Holmes became notorious because he was the first well-documented American serial killer, and the public were fascinated by the newspaper coverage of his trial and execution. After the Castle became a morbid tourist attraction, in 1895 there were mysterious explosions and a fire that ripped through its upper floors. Anything left standing was demolished, and a post office was eventually built on the same site.

John Wayne Gacy

A.K.A. Jolly John, The Killer Clown
COUNTRY USA
VICTIMS 33
METHOD bludgeoned, strangled, stabbed, suffocated

Chicago is renowned for its high crime rate, especially for violent, organized crime, personified by Al Capone, even though John "Mushmouth" Johnson's wholesale protection rackets and gambling predated Capone's mob by a century. Another of Chicago's many infamous killers was John Wayne Gacy, rapist and murderer of teenage boys and young men, and the ultimate souvenir hunter. His method of stashing the bodies within the confines of his own home – although probably as much for convenience and covertness, as he thus did not have to travel anywhere to dispose of his victims' corpses – could also have been a way of exerting his everlasting control. He only disposed of bodies elsewhere when his preferred morgue was full. He managed to bury 26 bodies there and, redolent of another Chicago serial killer, H H Holmes, frequently dusted them with quicklime to speed decomposition.

Despite going to great pains to please his alcoholic and violent father, Gacy was victimized and denigrated by him, and was often beaten with a belt. When protected by his mother, he would then be called a "sissy" and "Mama's boy", and told he'd "probably grow up queer". This cultivated a fear of failure in his mind, so much so that when molested by a family friend at the age of 9 he was too afraid to tell his father in case he would be blamed. His health caused him further embarrassment. Bullied at school for being unusual and unable to participate in sports due to a heart condition, he also suffered seizures and spent long periods in hospital. His father was unsympathetic, accusing Gacy of playing hooky and increasing his physical abuse.

This troubled childhood probably laid the foundations for Gacy's criminality, as did further parallels with other serial killers – such as working in a mortuary, just like Holmes. Gacy had fled to Las Vegas after a bust-up with his father, but his job there didn't last more than a few months. He was fired when it was discovered that he had been sleeping in the embalming room, alone with corpses, some of which were found partially undressed. He only admitted later that he had once climbed into a coffin and lain under the body of a boy who had died in a way that aroused him.

The template for Gacy's murders was developed early on. After graduating in 1964 from Northwestern Business College in Illinois, and working for the Nunn-Bush Shoe Company in Springfield, he took up a more lucrative offer in Waterloo, Iowa, in 1967. Publicly, Gacy fared well, receiving accolades for his fund-raising activities, and approval from his father who admitted, "Son, I was wrong about you." Privately, Gacy was cheating on his wife, the mother of his two children, attending swinging parties, visiting prostitutes, using pornography and taking drugs. He was also molesting male employees at the three Kentucky Fried Chicken restaurants that he managed and making improper advances after plying them with drink in his basement. One was blackmailed into performing oral sex on him after being encouraged to have sex with his wife. Others were paid to partake in homosexual experiments, in the name of science.

In March 1968, two boys, aged 15 and 16, went public with accusations of sexual assault. Another boy was hired to beat one of the accusers into not testifying, but was caught and confessed, putting Gacy in the dock and earning him a 10-year jail sentence for sodomy and an immediate divorce in December 1968. Eighteen months later he was freed on parole and returned to Chicago to become a cook, but not in time to see his father again, who had died on Christmas Day 1969. In February 1971, within his 12-month probation period, Gacy was again accused of the sexual assault of a teenage boy, but the charge was dropped, and his parole board was never informed. Yet another charge of sexual assault against a young man was dropped in June 1972.

In partnership with his mother and sisters, in August 1971 Gacy bought 8213 West Summerdale, a new two-bedroom 1950s ranch-style house, located in a nice, clean, family-oriented neighbourhood. This new beginning included him giving up the food service industry to start a construction business. In July 1972, his mother moved out to make way for his new wife, Carole Hoff, and her two daughters. Hoff knew of Gacy's previous conviction, but she was newly divorced and easily wooed.

Again, publicly, things appeared to be going well, while privately the marriage was breaking down. As a backdrop to community projects and parade organizing – which brought him into contact with First Lady Rosalynn

Carter, and even led to him becoming a children's party entertainer, "Pogo the Clown" – Gacy had "come out" to his wife as bisexual, and often brought teenage boys back to the garage. His use of gay pornography in the house added to their problems and they divorced in March 1976. In fact, there would have been much more serious grounds for divorce if she had known of the two murders he'd committed since buying the house.

In January 1972, rather than sleeping in a Greyhound bus terminal, 15-year-old Timothy Jack McCoy had accepted an offer to stay the night and be paid for sex at 8213 West Summerdale. Evidently, the following morning, Gacy mistook McCoy waking him, still holding a kitchen knife used while preparing breakfast, as an attack. McCoy was repeatedly stabbed in the chest, and was buried in the narrow crawl space beneath the house and covered in concrete.

In July 1975 Gacy attempted to handcuff Tony Antonucci, another 15-year-old, whom he had employed a short time before, in his own home. Antonucci was able to free himself and Gacy left peacefully. A week later, 17-year-old John Butkovitch went to Gacy's house to collect wages owed him, but instead was handcuffed, strangled and buried under the concrete floor in the garage.

Alone in the house after Hoff moved out, Gacy killed at least nine more teenage boys aged between 14 and 19 in the half-year between April and October 1976, tying or handcuffing them, before they were strangled or choked, then burying them all in the crawl space, except for one, who ended up beneath the dining room floor. Over the next two years, Gacy continued to murder young men, increasing his violence and levels of torture. The number of missing teenagers and young men in the area was striking, and Gacy was often questioned as a result of his employment and the fact he had known the individuals, but each time he either pleaded ignorance, or had a story ready, such as a disaffected youth running away from home. The list of missing now numbered 33.

Yet, the police continued to overlook several instances where parents of missing boys or others lobbied them to investigate Gacy. Two such appeals came directly from 19-year-old Robert Donnelly and 26-year-old Jeffrey Rignall, both of whom claimed to have survived abduction by Gacy. What happened was recorded in the subsequent court proceedings. In December 1977 Donnelly,

was walking in Chicago when defendant approached him in his black car (which had spotlights on both sides) and asked for identification. Thinking that defendant was a policeman, Donnelly approached the car. Defendant threatened Donnelly with a gun and told him to get into the car. Donnelly was then handcuffed

and told to lie on the floor of the car. Defendant brought
Donnelly into his home [... Gacy] shoved Donnelly on the couch,
and grabbed his hair. When Donnelly screamed, defendant
pushed his face into the couch. He then removed Donnelly's
pants and anally raped him. Donnelly passed out. When he
regained consciousness, defendant took him into the bathroom,
shoved Donnelly's head against the wall, then placed something
around Donnelly's neck and started twisting it. He told Donnelly,
"My, aren't we having fun tonight?" He then forced Donnelly's
head into the bathtub, which was filled with water, and held
it there until Donnelly passed out. When Donnelly regained
consciousness, he discovered that his clothes had been removed
and the handcuffs had been moved so that his hands were
now cuffed behind his back. Defendant held Donnelly's head
under water again until he passed out, and when he regained
consciousness he repeated this procedure once more. When
Donnelly again regained consciousness, defendant urinated all
over Donnelly. He then showed Donnelly nude magazine pictures
of girls, asked him if he liked them, and when Donnelly said
yes, told Donnelly that he was sick. Defendant then punched
Donnelly, and once again held his head in the bathtub until
he passed out. When Donnelly again regained consciousness,
defendant picked him up from the bathroom floor and brought
him back into the room with the bar. He said, "You're just in
time for the late show" and turned on a projector and showed
a "gay" pornographic film on the wall of the room. After the
movie, defendant stuck his foot in Donnelly's stomach, put a gun
to Donnelly's head, and played "Russian roulette." He pulled
the trigger between 10 and 15 times, spinning the chamber
between pulls of the trigger, until the gun finally went off. The
gun contained a blank. Defendant told Donnelly that he had
killed girls before, but that he had stopped doing this, because
he found killing "guys" to be more interesting. He then choked
Donnelly until he lost consciousness. When Donnelly regained
consciousness, his hands were cuffed behind his back, his ankles
were bound, and there was a gag in his mouth. Defendant then
inserted some sort of object into Donnelly's rectum and he
passed out. When he regained consciousness, the object that
was placed in his rectum was still there. When Donnelly regained
consciousness, defendant removed the gag from Donnelly's
mouth, and Donnelly told him that if he was going to kill him, to
just do it and get it over with. Defendant placed the gag back in

> Donnelly's mouth, and started "playing around with" the object
> which was inserted in Donnelly's rectum. Defendant then told
> Donnelly to dress, put Donnelly in his car, and told him it would
> be his last ride. He asked Donnelly "How's it feel knowing that
> you're going to die?"

However, Gacy released him, and a week later was questioned about the alleged sexual assault. He admitted to their having had consensual "slave-sex" and no charges were raised. About this time, the crawl space was now full, so Gacy resorted to disposing his victims in the Des Plaines River. In March 1978, Rignall was coaxed into Gacy's car when offered a smoke of marijuana:

> Once inside the car, defendant placed a cloth soaked in
> chloroform over Rignall's face, causing him to lose consciousness.
> Defendant carried Rignall into his house and offered him a drink.
> Defendant appeared very relaxed. Defendant then chloroformed
> him again. When Rignall regained consciousness, he found
> himself restrained on a wooden board which was suspended by
> chains. The board had holes in it where his arms went through
> and where his head was placed. Defendant, who was naked, was
> standing directly in front of Rignall masturbating. Defendant then
> grabbed Rignall's head and shoved his penis into Rignall's mouth,
> shouting: "You love it, you love it".

Again the police were leisurely in responding to allegations of abduction and sexual assault, so Rignall took matters into his own hands, staking out the exit on the northwest-bound Kennedy Expressway where he knew he had been taken, until he recognized Gacy's distinctive black Oldsmobile – a popular sedan car made by General Motors – following it to 8213 West Summerdale. Gacy was arrested for battery in July 1978 and was still awaiting trial in December when a check run on his previous police record put him under suspicion for the disappearance of 15-year-old Robert Piest.

A search of 8213 West Summerdale earlier in the year hadn't shown up anything, but putrid smells were noticeable when police returned in warmer weather. Gacy was nominally charged with marijuana possession, which allowed the police a more thorough search of the house while he was in custody. The front room, full of plants and pictures of sad-faced clowns adorning the walls, led to an office with meticulous business records and proudly displayed dedicated photographs posed with the mayor and the first lady. Hidden in the games room, they found a large, faeces-encrusted, vibrating dildo and several gay books and magazines, some specializing in older men having sex with young boys. Various wallets, male jewellery and clothes were found in the attic, garage and workshed, but still nothing seriously incriminating.

Back towards the front of the house, a trapdoor was found in a closet. It led to a dark, dirt-floored crawl space, which was flooded. A flex hung loose nearby. It was plugged in and immediately a sump pump started its rumble. A smell of sewage and decay wafted up to the forensic team waiting above. A quarter of an hour later, what they found there was horrific:

Sex fiend's toll reaches 15

JOLLY JOHN'S HOUSE OF HORRORS

CHILDREN loved pudgy-faced John Wayne Gacy when he dressed up as a clown at parties. But they shrank away in horror yesterday as the grisly details emerged of his secret life.

Groups of neighbours watched as police removed the skeletons of teenage boys from Gacy's ranch-style home on the outskirts of Chicago.

The police have so far carried the remains of FIFTEEN victims from the dark dank space under the floorboards of Jolly John's house of horror.

If his grisly boasts are true, there are eleven more to come and another six to be found at the bottom of nearby rivers. Gacy, 36, a twice-married construction worker, claims to have raped and murdered thirty-two teenage boys after luring them to his house.

Secret

None of the neighbours suspected. But they did not know his secret ... an eighteen-month jail sentence for a sexual attack on a teenage boy in Iowa before he moved to Chicago in 1972.

If they had known, they might have asked about the constant stream of young boys calling at Gacy's house.

He said that they were workers being hired and fired from his construction company.

Next-door neighbour Edward Grexa said: "The boys would vanish as soon as they would appear.

"I would ask him what happened to them and he'd say they gave him a hard time and he kicked their butts out.

"John a murderer? Don't make sense. He was always friendly and personable."

Another bewildered neighbour said: "John didn't look like a

monster and he never said a harsh word to me.

"The only weird thing I ever noticed was the number of young lads working around there."

Police say that the bodies appear to be buried in tiers under the 30-inch gap beneath the floorboards.

Two youths have shown police where Gacy got them to dig holes under the kitchen last year. He told them that the holes were for drainage.

Callers from as far as England and Australia have been anxiously asking about the identities of the bodies.

In many cases there are no easy answers. The bodies are so decomposed that identification is almost impossible.

While the grim search for bodies goes on, Gacy is being held in an isolation room in a local psychiatric hospital.

There, the medical examiner, Dr. Robert Stein, yesterday summed up the nation's revulsion. He said: "I think we are witnessing one of the most horrible crimes of the century."

Some of the bodies were lying "face up with clothing stuffed in their mouths". Dr. Stein said that three of the victims appeared to have been strangled.

Daily Mirror, 28th December 1978

Gacy was to explain that blocking off the victims' mouths was to save his floorboards getting stained with blood when they haemorrhaged. But all of his confession was delivered matter-of-factly, without any sign of remorse, and he once jibed, "The only thing they can get me for is running a funeral parlor without a license."

His aloof attitude and separation from reality was consistent with a psychological assessment carried out in Iowa – he even attempted to sue the police for "loss of reputation in the community" to the tune of £350,000. Nevertheless, within a week of his arrest for murder, he did attempt suicide by strangling himself with a prison towel. Famously ordering a last meal of fried chicken, French fries, Coke and strawberry shortcake, and offering "Kiss my ass!" as his last words as he walked past guards on the way to the execution chamber, Gacy was given a lethal injection in May 1994, after 14 years on death row at Menard Correctional Center in Chester, Illinois:

Lethal jab executes murderer

SERIAL killer John Wayne Gacy took almost 20 minutes to die yesterday when he was executed by lethal injection.

Outside the prison in Joliet, Illinois, a 1,000-strong crowd cheered as the murderer of 33 young men and boys went to the death chamber.

After being strapped to a trolley, Gacy was knocked out with anaesthetic. But a tube became blocked as the lethal dose of drugs was being administered.

Officials hastily replaced the faulty equipment and the first execution in Illinois for 30 years went ahead.

Gacy, who has been on deathrow for 14 years, was convicted of murdering rent boys and young men he had hired to work in his construction business.

He sexually tortured many of his victims before strangling them. Police found 27 bodies hidden under the killer's house.

Daily Mirror, 11th May 1994

In October 2011, Gacy's case was reopened in an effort to identify the eight unknown bodies in his crawl space. It's now understood that he may have visited Ontario, Canada, amongst other destinations during his killing years, and the question remains whether he killed while away from home, or successfully persuaded men from abroad to visit him in Chicago. Modern DNA profiles have been obtained for all eight unidentified victims and many families have come forward to offer their assistance. But, if Gacy did kill while travelling, the fear is that there could be many more unknown victims of his.

Gerald Gallego
A.K.A. The Sex Slave Murderers
COUNTRY USA
VICTIMS 10
METHOD bludgeoned, shot, strangled
MUTILATION bitten

Soon after meeting Gerald Armond Gallego at a Sacramento poker club in October 1977, two-time divorcée Charlene Adelle Williams moved in with the seven-time married, wife beater, bigamist, convicted bank robber and long-term offender. He was 31, 5" 7' and rugged-looking. She was 19, with Barbie-like blonde hair and blue eyes, cute, diminutive and innocent-looking. But looks can be deceptive. The relationship had been troubled from the outset, but as the saying goes, love is blind, and Williams was smitten and partly too afraid to leave, plus her experiences with past partners had delivered her into a vulnerable chapter of her life.

While her upper-middle-class upbringing had been comfortable, Williams did not make the best of her IQ of 160 and a prodigious talent for playing the violin; instead, from the age of 12, she chose a path of drink, drugs and promiscuity. Her first marriage to a wealthy heroin addict ended after accusations of her pressuring him to have cocaine-fuelled sex with her and female prostitutes. Her second marriage, also while still at high school, didn't bring her the excitement she desired, so again divorced she started an affair, which her lover ended when Williams solicited a threesome with his wife.

Surviving a suicide bid and meeting Gallego, Williams was attracted to an intangible quality in him that kept her loyal despite arrogation of her money earned as a supermarket clerk, dictation of her behaviour and fashion, and his problems with erectile dysfunction, which he blamed on her. Their sex was rough, with her always as the submissive. He was also open about having sex with other women, and when Gallego brought home a 16-year-old dancer in July 1978, they had a threesome, but the women were denied contact with each other. They were there solely for his pleasure.

The next day he was incensed to catch them back in bed having lesbian sex, throwing the dancer from a window and beating Williams. Her additional punishment was a stint of celibacy. That same month, Gallego celebrated his 32nd birthday by having a foursome with Williams and his 14-year-old daughter, Sally Jo, and her friend. His daughter would later report her father for eight years of incest, sodomy, oral copulation and unlawful intercourse. It was about this time that abduction was suggested as a means of coping with Gallego's impotence, "I have this fantasy, about having girls that would be there whenever I wanted them and do whatever I wanted them to. They have to be young, too, ripe for the picking [...] possibly in the woods, a cellar, or basement type place where you could keep women and use them at your disposal." Submissive to his wishes Williams agreed to act as bait. She probably also fantasized about lesbian rape and saw this as an opportunity to assume a dominant sex role.

In September 1978, Williams enticed adventure-seeking 17-year-old Rhonda Scheffler and 16-year-old Kippi Vaught into their van at the Country Club Plaza in Sacramento County, with the offer of marijuana. Instead, a .25 calibre pistol was awaiting them and they were bound and gagged at gunpoint and driven to a secluded spot. Williams was left behind as Gallego marched the captives into the undergrowth. He returned hours later with them, simply telling Williams, "Ask me no questions, I'll tell you no lies." She was instructed to visit friends in Sacramento as an alibi which she did, later admitting that, "She liked the lifestyle offered by Gallego [...] she had calmly and coldly gotten 'stoned' with a friend in Sacramento after kidnapping two teenage girls for Gerald's sexual gratification."

Picking the threesome up in their other vehicle, an Oldsmobile similar to Gacy's, Williams drove to another quiet spot, where Gallego concussed the girls with a tire iron, and shot them in the head, Vaught three times. When their bodies were found the next day in a ditch, there were bite marks on the breasts, made by a different set of teeth on each girl. Williams had been an active participant, recalling that she had been highly aroused and ecstatic. A week later Gallego was not pleased to find out that Williams was pregnant, and forced her to have an abortion. Three days after that they crossed the state line to skip his daughter's charges, and were married in Reno, but were eventually informed the marriage was null because Gallego had failed to divorce a previous wife.

On Father's Day in June 1979, Williams duped 14-year-old Brenda Judd and 13-year-old Sandra Colley into the van with an offer of leafleting work at the Washoe County Fair, Nevada. Covered by a .44 calibre pistol, they were trussed and repeatedly raped while Williams drove into the desert, then they were untied and forced to have sex with each other. The girls were then bludgeoned with a hammer and a shovel, which Williams described as, "A loud splat like a flat rock hitting mud, and the girl sank to her knees and slowly toppled over on her face." Their bodies were folded into a shallow grave.

In September 1979, Williams and Gallego returned to Sacramento as Mr and Mrs Stephen Robert Feil, an identity stolen from Williams' cousin. Gallego took bar jobs but also had multiple affairs, getting one mistress pregnant. In April 1980, Gallego commanded, "I want a girl! Get up!", and the same pattern was repeated in the abduction, rape and murder of 17-year-olds Stacey Redican and Karen Chipman Twiggs, who were taken from Sunrise Mall in Citrus Heights, California. In May, they found out Williams was pregnant again, and they remarried in June 1980, under their aliases.

A few days later, they picked up pregnant 21-year-old Linda Aguilar, whom Gallego raped then killed on a remote beach, with blows to the head with a rock. Although the pair thought she was dead, after making sure by strangling her corpse, the autopsy confirmed that she and her unborn child asphyxiated from inhalation of sand, as she panicked trying to free herself from her shallow grave. A month later in July, drunk from a long drinking session, Gallego and Williams lurked in the car park waiting for 34-year-old bartender Virginia Mochel to come out of the bar which they had just visited. Unlike the other victims, they already knew her, plus she wasn't taken into the countryside, but instead to their apartment, where she was raped while Williams watched TV. Later Williams drove Virginia and Gallego out of town, where he strangled and buried the victim.

Gallego was becoming more violent, so, in September, Williams moved out, while he went off to see an old girlfriend. They were reunited in November 1980, and went searching for sex slaves in her parent's Oldsmobile. Early in the morning Gallego, still drunk from the night before, saw and abducted 22-year-old Craig Miller and his fiancée, 21-year-old Mary Elizabeth Sowers, at gunpoint, in broad daylight. Gallego and Williams took the couple to a secluded place, where Gallego shot Miller three times in the back of the head. The boyfriend removed, Gallego once again got Williams to drive to their apartment, where he repeatedly raped his prisoner, while Williams watched TV. Three shots in a rural location at point blank range killed their final victim.

A friend of the couple had noted the car number plate when he had seen them being driven off. The car was traced and suspicions raised over Gallego's and Williams' account of their whereabouts the previous evening. Bolting, they went on the run to Reno, then got on a bus for Salt Lake City, moving onto Denver and Omaha, Nebraska. Needing more money, Williams phoned her parents to wire it through to the Western Union Office, which they did; however, they also told the FBI. The couple were arrested and, in 1984, Gallego was tried for murder in both California and Nevada.

Williams struck a plea bargain which would give her a fixed term 16-year eight-month sentence in exchange for testifying against her husband, giving evidence for the prosecution of the murders carried out between 1978 and 1980, totalling four women in Nevada, three in Sacramento, and one near the California–Oregon border. Gallego provided his own defence, giving rise to a bizarre situation when over six days he cross-examined his own wife and accomplice, turned key prosecution witness. Gallego was sentenced to death in both states.

Murderer ... like dad

KILLER Gerald Gallego is to follow his father to the gas chamber.

Gallego, 36, has been sentenced to death in San Quentin jail, California, for the sex killing of a young couple.

His father was executed 28 years ago for killing a policeman.

Daily Mirror, 26th May 1983

But Gallego was never executed, instead he died of rectal cancer in July 2002 in a Nevada prison. As part of her deal, Williams had been released five years earlier, after serving her full sentence, and passed into obscurity, but their legacy, and child, lives on. While Williams gave birth to Gallego's child in prison, in the same year as her release, methamphetamine users

James Anthony Daveggio, 41, and his girlfriend, Michelle Lyn Michaud, 43, abducted, tortured, raped and finally strangled 22-year-old Vanessa Lei Samson in Oakland. They cited the Gallegos as their role models.

David Birnie
A.K.A. The Moorhouse Murderers
COUNTRY Australia
VICTIMS 4
METHOD strangled, stabbed, bludgeoned

David Birnie was the first of six children born into a dysfunctional family living in a squalid house in a suburb of Perth, Australia. They were known for their promiscuity, alcoholism and incest, and for the mother's frequent payment of taxi fares with sexual favours. With something like that, word gets around. Perhaps unsurprisingly, Birnie developed – via an adolescence of animal abuse, attempted rape and a series of jail sentences – into an adult with unhealthy obsessions for sex, pornography and abnormal sexual interests.

Birnie and neighbour Catherine Harrison had first started going out together in their teens. He gave her the love and affection she'd never had, having been shunted between family custodians, and she repaid him with undying loyalty, but not necessarily faithfulness. They carried out 11 burglaries together, putting him in jail for nine months beginning in June 1969, but Harrison only on parole because she was pregnant, although not by Birnie.

A month later, a further eight charges of burglary added three years to his sentence and four years' probation to hers. Breaking out of jail in June 1970, Birnie reunited with Harrison to go on a rampage that would return him to jail a month later for a further two-and-a-half years, convicted of 53 counts of theft and burglary. This time Harrison was sentenced to six months and her newborn child was taken into custody until her release.

Once free, Harrison became a live-in domestic, and fell in love with Donald McLaughlan, her employer's son. They married on her 26th birthday in May 1972 and went on to have six children together. Their first, Little Donny, was run over by a car when 7 months old, a tragedy that was witnessed by Harrison. She was not a born housewife, and caring for her unemployed husband, their children, her father and uncle proved too much. The house became dirty and dilapidated and the children were soon reduced to a state of wretched deprivation and hunger. The death of her son and the couple's living conditions, plus Harrison's ongoing love of Birnie, drove her to walk out in 1985, confessing to an already two-year-long affair with her one true love.

Reunited with Birnie, who had also recently ended his own failed marriage, Harrison changed her surname to his by deed poll and became his common law wife, and the couple moved in together into 3 Moorhouse Street, Willagee, on the outskirts of Perth. They also discovered a shared fantasy of abducting sex slaves, to help meet Birnie's highly sexed needs, but also to spice up their relationship. The thrill of injecting his glans penis with analgesics and having kinky sex four or five times a day had worn off. They began to plan. Birnie convinced Harrison that she would achieve intense orgasms by watching him having sex with another woman. One that was bound and gagged.

In October 1986, 22-year-old Mary Nielson visited the breaker's yard where Birnie worked as a labourer, looking for car tyres. He offered a bargain offer if she swung by his house to pick the spares later that day. As soon as she arrived she was stripped at knifepoint, gagged, and chained to the bed, and raped by Birnie. As Harrison watched, she asked what excited him. He told her that the biggest turn-on was knowing the girl was soon going to die. They hadn't discussed that part of the plan, nonetheless, their captive was taken to nearby woodland, raped again, and strangled with nylon cord, twisted tight with a stick. Before burial, Birnie stabbed the body, saying it would speed up decomposition by letting all the gasses escape. This was something he had read in a book.

Two weeks later, 15-year-old Susannah Candy was subjected to almost exactly the same sadistic abuse, except she was abducted while walking along the street, and forced to write a letter to her family explaining that she had run away to Queensland with her friends, before being raped. This time Harrison also took part in the sex, then helped sedate the girl, and strangled her where she lay at Birnie's request, as a symbol of her devotion to him. At the start of November, they picked up stranded 31-year-old Noelene Patterson, who had run out of gas and was grateful to the couple for stopping to offer a helpful lift. The lift led to her being chained to the bed naked, and an ordeal that lasted three days. This time, Harrison felt threatened, sensing Birnie was becoming infatuated with his elegant and stylish sex slave, and insisted that he kill her. At the burial site, Harrison felt her jealousy ebbing into ecstasy with every handful of sand thrown into the dead woman's face.

Within the week, 21-year-old Denise Brown found herself chained to the bed, shortly after accepting a lift while waiting at a bus stop. In a return to the pattern of the first murder, she was raped and murdered at the burial site, this time in the Wanneroo pine plantation. The actual killing was particularly cruel. Initially, Birnie stabbed Brown in the neck while penetrating her. Providing light via a torch, Harrison found a larger knife to finish the job. While covering the body with sand in a shallow grave, Brown suddenly sat up, screaming. Birnie whacked her head with an axe. She sat up again. Birnie turned the axe around to use the sharp side and split her skull open.

Brown's brutal death had an effect on Harrison. She got off on their sex with the slaves. She didn't really mind the stabbing and strangulation. But splattering brains was a step too far. She would claim that this had marked a turning point. However, just beforehand, on the way to the plantation, they had attempted to pick up someone else, a 19-year-old woman walking along the street. She would have the opportunity to reflect on how lucky she had been:

I felt uneasy. I didn't recognise the car. There was a man driving and a woman in the front seat of the car. The man kept looking down, not looking at me and the woman was drinking a can of UDL rum and coke. I thought the fact that she was drinking at that time of day was strange. He didn't look at me the whole time. It was the woman who did all the talking. She asked me if I wanted a lift anywhere. I said, "No, I only live up the road".

They continued to sit there and I looked into the back seat where I saw a small person with short brown hair lying across the seat. I thought it must have been their son or daughter asleep in the back. The person was in a sleeping position and from the haircut, looked like a boy but for some reason I got the feeling it was a girl. I told them again I didn't want a lift because walking was good exercise. The man looked up for the first time and gazed at me before looking away again. By this time more cars had appeared and I started to walk away but they continued to sit in the car. Finally the car started and they did another U-turn and drove [...] towards the pine plantation. It wasn't until I saw a really good photo of Catherine Birnie that I realised who they were.

Only a few days later, 17-year-old Kate Moir ran half-naked into a grocery store telling a story of abduction by a couple, and repeated rape by the man, while the women watched. She had escaped through a window when the man was out of the house, and she had been left untied by the woman, who had gone to answer the door. The couple had spoken of arranging a cocaine delivery, because the man needed some to inject into his penis. Harrison would later tell police, "I think I must have come to a decision that, sooner or later, there had to be an end to the rampage. I had reached the stage when I didn't know what to do. I suppose I came to a decision that I was prepared to give her a chance."

The girl had remained alert, taking a mental note of the telephone number when she had been forced to call her parents to let them know she was okay and staying with friends. She had also managed to remember where the house was and hide her bag and cigarettes as proof she had been there.

Police took Birnie and Harrison in for questioning, not believing their explanation that the girl had willingly come to the house to smoke a marijuana bong, and sex had been consensual. Interrogation of each separately was going nowhere until a detective jokingly suggested to Birnie, "It's getting dark. Best we take the shovel and dig them up." Birnie replied, "Okay. There are four of them."

At their trial, beginning in February 1987, Harrison acted wildly, kicking and screaming and spitting until she was near Birnie. While the charges were being read out, she gently caressed the ball of his thumb. He pleaded guilty to four counts of murder and one of abduction and rape. The families of his victims were saved the agony of a long, drawn-out trial, which he said was, "The least I could do." The couple both received four consecutive sentences of life imprisonment. This was recently modified to full term with no parole. Harrison is currently being held at Bandyup Women's Prison. Birnie was moved to solitary confinement for his own protection, first at the maximum-security Fremantle Prison, then Casuarina Prison. They were only allowed to communicate by letter, of which 2,600 were exchanged over the course of 18 years, until Birnie hanged himself in October 2005, a day before he was due to appear in court for raping another inmate.

Delfina González Valenzuela
A.K.A. Las Poquianchis
COUNTRY Mexico
VICTIMS 91+
METHOD starved, bludgeoned
MUTILATION burned

María de Jesús González Valenzuela
A.K.A. Las Poquianchis
COUNTRY Mexico
VICTIMS 91+
METHOD starved, bludgeoned
MUTILATION burned

Following a long history of abuse and prostitution, four sisters, Delfina, María de Jesús, Carmen and Maria Luisa González Valenzuela, opened a chain of bars and bordellos across the central Mexican states of Guanajuato and Queretaro. For a decade and a half from the early 1950s, the sisters harvested the local remote villages for pretty young girls, who would accept offers of work as maids and waitresses, driven by the dream of bright lights and big cities. If the girl was less willing, she was abducted.

The prettiest young virgins were saved for wealthy clients. Others would be raped and tortured. All were incarcerated, forced into cocaine and heroin addiction, and allowed few freedoms. If a woman fell pregnant, she would be beaten to induce abortion. The foetus was dumped in the backyard. If one of the women was seriously ill, often from a STD, or was losing her looks as a result of her exploitation, she would be locked in a room and starved to death, or the other prostitutes would be forced to bludgeon her to death. Men arriving to the brothel carrying large amounts of money were robbed and also killed.

In January 1964, one of the working women managed to escape and fled home. She and her family reported the sisters, fortunately to one of the few police not on the local brothel payroll, and the place was raided. A dozen emaciated and filthy women were found in the building, while the bodies and skeletons of 80 women, 11 men and many foetuses were exhumed from the backyard.

The sisters had to be protected from the baying mob who wanted a lynching, but it was the dozens of prostitutes that were their real threat, testifying about the horrific conditions and treatment that they had been forced to endure. Carmen had already died of cancer in the late 1950s, but the three surviving sisters were each sentenced to 40 years in prison.

Delfina was killed in October 1968, when builders working above her cell accidently dropped a bucket of cement on her head. Maria Luisa died of natural causes in November 1984. When her body was found it had already been partly eaten by rats. María de Jesús was freed and rumoured to have married before dying in the 1990s. In 2002, excavations for a building project found a further 20 skeletons at one of the sisters' brothel sites.

KEEPERS

I love the lie and lie the love
A-Hangin' on, with push and shove
Possession is the motivation
that is hangin' up the God-damn nation
Eugene McDaniels

Many serial killers keep souvenirs of their conquests – tokens of their victims, which can literally be parts of their bodies or hair, "rendering persons into personal possessions" as someone once put it. But usually disposing of the body becomes necessary with onset of decomposition, and to get rid of the evidence. So if not a head, hand, foot or breast, then possessions like photographs, underwear, shoes and so on, or newspaper clippings of their deeds are kept. All these are thought to be a way the serial killer can attempt to recreate the ecstasy of their near-sexual experience. While ownership of such tokens is undoubtedly a symbol of control, ultimate control and possession is achieved by keeping the whole body, alive – but few serial killers ever manage that.

Leonard Lake
COUNTRY USA
VICTIMS 25
METHOD shot
MUTILATION dismembered, burned

Charles Chi-Tat Ng
COUNTRY USA
VICTIMS 25
METHOD shot
MUTILATION dismembered, burned

Leonard Lake had a long-term obsession for pornography. He had begun by taking nude pictures of his sisters, whom he also blackmailed for sexual favours. His first marriage failed after his wife caught him making and appearing in amateur porn films. Charles Ng was unmarried and a kleptomaniac, who had been expelled from a number of schools in Hong Kong and England for stealing. He lied about his nationality to get into the Marines, then stole heavy weaponry and machine guns from the armoury. On the run, he met Lake in California, and had soon moved into the Wilseyville cabin complex Lake was sharing with second wife Claralyn Balasz. Ng was recaptured and imprisoned until June 1984. Freed, he immediately returned to the remote Wilseyville homestead in the Sierra Nevada Mountains. In the meantime, Balasz had moved out, refusing to appear in any more of Lake's porn films.

Sometime in June 1985 Lake and Ng broke their bench vice, the one they used on their torture victims. If they had bought a new one fair and square like law-abiding citizens instead of trying to steal one, they might never have been caught. But they were definitely not law-abiding citizens. The San Francisco store guards challenged them and apprehended Lake, but Ng got away. When the police arrived, they thought they were responding to a routine call about a shoplifter, but suspicions soon escalated as, first, it became obvious the man the store had detained was using a false identity, then a .22 revolver with an illegal silencer, bloodstains and bullet holes were found in his car. To cap it all, Lake took two cyanide pills, which were taped to his shirt collar as in the spy films, that put him into convulsions, his eyes rolling back into his skull. He died, but only after a four-day coma.

The Vietnam War had ended in 1975, but Lake had served two tours of duty there as a radar operator in the United States Marine Corps, before being kicked out in 1971 with a medical discharge for schizophrenia. The war had dealt with one rebel nation, but there were plenty more, and their weapons were getting bigger. Even before the Vietnam War was over, India had conducted its first nuclear test, and even South Africa was developing a nuclear weapon capability. North Korea was supposed to have lost the war, and here it was carrying out plutonium separation experiments, and developing its Hwasŏng-5 ballistic missile based on the Soviet Scud-B. Paranoia was rife and faulty early warning systems had an unnerving tendency to mistakenly go off: 78 times in 1979 alone. This was not reassuring when American–Russian relations had deteriorated so much that Cold War tensions had an all-time high since the Cuban Missile Crisis two decades earlier. The USA had just renewed its commitment to large spending on military programmes, and the Soviet Union had made it quite clear that their policy was immediate nuclear response upon discovering inbound ballistic missiles. The only consolation if you were involved in a nuclear war was the aptly named MAD, Mutual Assured Destruction, complete annihilation of both sides.

Less than a year prior to Lake and Ng claiming their first victim, Cold War animosity escalated when Korean Airlines Flight 007 was shot down by Soviet jet fighters in September 1983, killing all 269 people on board, including a member of the United States Congress. Only a couple of weeks later, with memories still raw and American anti-Russian hostility very apparent, a Soviet early warning station detected five inbound intercontinental ballistic missiles, which appeared to have originated from the USA. It was an error and there were no missiles, but, quite possibly, quick thinking by the station commander prevented World War III.

Lake was convinced the world was going to end in a nuclear holocaust, and he wasn't waiting for the inevitable destruction of humanity. He had formulated a plan, loosely modelled on John Fowles' 1963 novel *The Collector*, in which art student Miranda Grey is abducted by city clerk Frederick Clegg, and held captive in the hope that she will grow to love him. The final chilling moment in the story is when Miranda dies and the spurned Clegg impassively starts planning the next abduction.

Other murderers have also been inspired by *The Collector*. Christopher Wilder abducted, raped and killed at least eight women in 1984, luring them with promises of modelling contracts. He had the novel almost completely memorized. Robert Berdella, "The Butcher of Kansas City", raped, tortured and killed at least six men between 1984 and 1987, bizarrely claiming that he was trying to help his torture victims by administering them antibiotics. He cited the novel as an early inspiration, and his deeds went on to feature in the film *Se7en*. But Lake saw the method described in *The Collector* as a messianic way to repopulate the planet. He had convinced his Marines buddy Ng that they had to start breeding.

When the police searched the Wilseyville site, they were faced with carnage. Blood was sprayed across ceilings and stained surfaces and furniture. Walls and floors were riddled with bullet holes, and a four-poster bed had been rigged for electrocution. In the outlying area, detectives discovered an incinerator and charred remains, and a bunker fitted out with a rack of blood-encrusted power tools. They also noticed a broken bench vice. The tool rack slid aside to reveal hidden rooms: a concealed cell where the captives had been incarcerated, and an adjoining area containing a double bed, a side table, books, a reading lamp and video camera equipment. In reference to Lake's favourite novel, there was a plaque on the wall that read "Operation Miranda". A search of the grounds revealed bodies of seven men, three women, two baby boys and 20 kilos of bone fragments.

After Lake's arrest at the hardware store, Ng fled to Canada, where he might have stayed hidden and anonymous if it hadn't been for another shoplifting incident. After 34 days as a fugitive, Ng's kleptomania got the better of him and he was captured after a shoot-out at a department store in Calgary. A long extradition struggle ensued, resulting in Ng being handed over to US authorities in September 1991. Ng proceeded to then use every delaying tactic available to him, studying American law in the interim leading up to his trial for 12 counts of murder in October 1998. His defence was that he had been an unwilling and therefore inculpable participant in Lake's murders. Lake's detailed diary, and hours of video footage, proved otherwise. At the end of the most costly criminal proceedings in US criminal history, nearing 20 million dollars, Ng was convicted and sentenced to death in February 1999:

Death for sex killer

A FORMER British schoolboy was sentenced to death in America yesterday for 11 sex slave murders.

Charles Ng, 38, raped and tortured six men, three women and two children in a Californian mountain lair.

Hong Kong-born Ng grew up in Preston, Lancs, and went to Bentham Grammar School, North Yorks.

He went on the run in 1985 after a torture chamber and charred bones were found.

Police think there may have been up to 25 victims.

Daily Mirror, 4th May 1999

Ng is currently being held at San Quentin State Prison, where he is appealing his sentence and soliciting pen pals. Among his prison interests, he lists origami.

I am currently the only Chinese prisoner on California's Death Row at San Quentin Prison. My case, from inception to verdict, has been both a travesty and outrage of mistreatments and miscarriage of justice. Because of these and other reasons, I constantly feel misplaced, sad and lonely – like a dolphin caught inside a tuna net. I am writing because I am interested in seeking sincere friendship through correspondence and visiting with someone I can build an enduring and meaningful companionship with – someone with whom I can share good times, bad times, life, thoughts, feelings, experiences and passions from this dark hole of humanity. Out in the free world I enjoyed such things as reading, learning new subjects, wilderness exploring, martial arts, movies, travelling, cooking, outdoor adventures such as mountain hiking / climbing, scuba diving and serving as an infantryman in the United States Marine Corps. Throughout my life I have refrained from unhealthy habits such as smoking, drinking and recreational drug uses. During my incarceration I enjoy such things as origami, spirituality, self-study, exercises, writing, reading and drawing [...] Personality wise, I am quiet, shy, open-minded, down to Earth, loyal, thoughtful, dependent and sentimental, but can be wayward, overly trusting and pessimistic at times. Life is fleeting and my fate is at best uncertain. Therefore I desire to hear from new friends and reconnect with people who had touched my life and heart in the past, but with whom I have lost touch due to circumstances beyond my control. I would be most grateful to be able to share the precious time I have left in this world with honest, open-minded and good-hearted people who understand and empathize with injustices, sufferings, my struggle, my visions and yearnings, and who may be able and willing to lend helping hands along the way [...] Thank you for your attention and I look forward to hearing from you.

Gary Heidnik
COUNTRY USA
VICTIMS 2
METHOD starved, bludgeoned, electrocuted
MUTILATION decapitated, dismembered

Gary Heidnik deserves special mention here. His case received a lot of public attention, and eventually became popularized on the "big screen", with much of Buffalo Bill in the *Silence of the Lambs* modelled on him. His notoriety wasn't so much for the number of his victims, which was relatively few at two – he only just qualified as a serial killer within the FBI downscaled categorization – but was instead in recognition for the horrifying nature of his kidnap victims' imprisonment.

Like Leonard Lake, Heidnik had received a medical discharge from the armed forces for schizophrenia. Unlike Lake, Heidnik attempted suicide more than a dozen times in the quarter century subsequent to his leaving the army, including several times after his final arrest. He also shared Lake's unhealthy obsession with sex, with a particular taste in pornography featuring African–American women. Unsurprisingly, his marriage to Betty Disto, a Filipino mail-order bride, lasted only three months, ending in January 1986 after she found him in bed with three other women, and because he raped her and repeatedly forced her to watch him having sex with other women.

By the time of his separation, Heidnik had become the equivalent of a modern-day millionaire from his various investments, including *Playboy* and a church he had founded, the United Church of the Ministers of God. Heidnik was its self-appointed bishop and his congregation were predominantly mentally handicapped. But Heidnik's delusions of grandeur weren't limited to preaching. His first captive, who was lured to his house by his show of wealth, but soon found herself half-naked and chained to a pipe in the ceiling of a cold damp basement, was told that all he ever wanted was a large family. He had already fathered four children by various women, but now he wanted to gather a harem of 10 women and impregnate them all. This one big happy family would then live in the basement of his house at 3520 North Marshall Street in Philadelphia.

Heidnik had half-achieved his ambition by January 1987. His five female captives were sexually abused, beaten and tortured, both individually and in groups. He raped each every day, and sought to control them through constant fear of punishment. If he had been out, the women were offered rewards for informing on each other's bad behaviour, and they were also forced to beat and have sex with each other. He hung them from the beams for days on end, and thought he could prevent their plotting against him by deafening them, gouging out their ears with a screwdriver. In contrast, treats might involve better treatment, installation of a portable toilet, wet wipes or even a bath, or better food. Heidnik fed them erratically and insufficiently. Some days they received only bread and water, stale hot dogs or a peanut butter sandwich.

After Sandra Lindsay died in February 1987 from the ongoing abuse and a punishment of hanging, handcuffed to a roof beam for several days, another troublemaker was discouraged from further misbehaving by being shown Lindsay's head boiling in a pot, and her ribcage roasting in the oven. Other body parts were revealed in the fridge. Later Heidnik's dog wandered into the basement with a big, obviously human, bone. About this time, Heidnik also settled on a set diet of canned dog food, which the women were forced to eat.

However, the ultimate punishments were carried out in a four-foot-deep pit, covered with weighted-down plywood, which served as an isolation chamber. On one occasion, the pit was filled with water and two of the women who had been insubordinate were forced to climb in, while Heidnik poked electric cables through holes in the plywood to make contact with their handcuffs. Deborah Dudley didn't survive. Her body was wrapped in plastic and stored in the freezer, next to where the others were chained in the basement. Another demonstration of what would happen if they disobeyed their "Master".

Heidnik's first prisoner seemed to be responding to his will and was proving to be more submissive than the others. In reality, Josefina Rivera was playing a waiting game, hoping for an opportunity to make a break. Trusting her, Heidnik allowed her to accompany him outside the house, to go shopping, and even to eat at restaurants. She also assisted him in locating a replacement for Dudley, as well as sleeping with him in his bed, a luxury afforded none of the others.

Rivera finally made her escape in March 1987, by persuading Heidnik that she would bring him yet another new "wife" if he agreed to her briefly seeing her family. Convinced of her allegiance, he dropped her off near her home, agreeing to return at midnight. As soon as he had driven off, she immediately sprinted to her apartment where her boyfriend was to be found, eventually persuading him of her story, and springing a police trap to capture Heidnik, leading to the release of the remaining women. Three of them suffered permanent hearing damage. In prison for 11 years, Heidnik was executed by lethal injection in July 1999.

Police hunt for bodies in House of Horror

MY SON MUST HANG says the father of "sex slave monster"

THE FATHER of a sex monster who tortured and murdered his women captives said yesterday his son should be hanged. He added: "I'll even pull the rope."

Police were last night still digging in the cellar of a Philadelphia House of Horror trying to find victims of wealthy self-styled evangelist Gary Heidnik, 43.

Police were led to the house by one of the victims who managed to escape.

They found three other young women half-naked and chained to a sewer pipe in the sex dungeon where they had been regularly beaten and sexually attacked.

At least two other women have been killed, and police have no idea how many bodies may be buried under the cellar floor.

Heidnik's 74-year-old father Michael, who lives in Ohio, said he had not seen his son for 26 years.

He added: "They can do what they like with him. I hope they hang him – and I'll even pull the rope."

Body

One survivor said Heidnik told her he had put parts of a body through a food processor and mixed it with dog food before feeding it to his "sex slaves."

Police said they had no other evidence of this; but confirmed they had found human bones which had been cooked and a skull in a cooking pot.

Heidnik, who also picked up his victims in the streets with one of several luxury cars he owned, sometimes forced them to climb into a pit which he covered with a board weighted down with sandbags.

One woman was killed when he filled the pit with water and ran an electric charge to handcuffs she was wearing.

After his arrest, Heidnik was beaten up by fellow prisoners horrified by details of the case. He was taken to hospital with a broken nose.

Mission

Prosecutors are to ask for the death penalty for Heidnik who claimed to be a church minister.

Neighbours said he described his house as a mission for troubled women.

Daily Mirror, 28th March 1987

Marc Dutroux
A.K.A. The Monster of Charleroi
COUNTRY Belgium
VICTIMS 5
METHOD suffocated, starved

Belgians were so stunned by the failure of their legal system to locate and contain Marc Dutroux, "The Monster of Charleroi", in their midst that the public outcry led to a parliamentary investigation. Dutroux had started a life of crime by smuggling stolen cars to Czechoslovakia and Hungary. He quickly progressed onto drug dealing and mugging, which earned him enough money to buy seven properties in and around Charleroi, a small city in the province of Hainaut, Belgium. His preferred location was Marcinelle, so he developed his house at Avenue Philippeville 128 into his home, installing a concealed dungeon, about 7-foot long, 3-foot wide and 5-foot high, in the basement.

In February 1986, Dutroux was arrested for abducting and raping five young girls. In April 1989, he was sentenced to 13½ years in prison. His accomplice and lover, Michelle Martin, received only five years. Dutroux was already a divorced father of two; Martin would bear him three more children. They married in 1989, and divorced in 2003, each time while they were both in prison. His own mother wrote a letter to the prison director because he was using his supervised leave to visit his grandmother to write an inventory of her possessions. This was understandably making his family anxious and distressed. "I have known for a long time and with good cause my eldest's temperament," she wrote. "What I do not know, and what all the people who know him fear, it's what he has in mind for the future."

Dutroux was released on parole for good behaviour and as part of a clemency programme after only three years. Now free, he was able to dupe a psychiatrist into authorizing a state pension and prescriptions for sedatives, which he would later use on his victims. Indeed, a short time after his release, young girls started to go missing near his houses. By now Dutroux was running an international child pornography and prostitution ring, selling girls into prostitution throughout Europe. But, even though he was an obvious suspect for the abductions, and the police searched his houses, there was no evidence to implicate him. The police had not searched thoroughly enough, missing the dungeon where two girls had been incarcerated at the time.

In 1993 a police informant tipped them off that Dutroux was offering payment for kidnapping girls. The going rate per girl was between $3,000 and $5,000. In 1995, that same informant now told them of the dungeon, and his own mother wrote a letter to the authorities, expressing her suspicions that her son was involved in the disappearance of the girls. The police did not act on any of this information for another year. In August 1996, while carrying out routine enquiries, a witness remembered part of a car number plate. Tracing the vehicle to Dutroux, police again raided his Marcinelle home, this time finding the dungeon, occupied by 14-year-old Laetitia Delhez and 12-year-old Sabine Dardenne. Both girls had been sexually assaulted and filmed for pornography, with Dardenne's sexual abuse lasting two-and-a-half-months. Three hundred child pornography videos were also recovered.

Police find kids' cells

COPS probing Belgium's child sex horror have found more "dungeons" used to hold captive youngsters.

Deep trenches cut in a cellar floor at Charleroi were discovered in a house used by Michel Lelièvre.

Lelièvre and rapist pal Marc Dutroux have been charged with

kidnapping and imprisoning kids.

Police freed two girls aged 14 and 12 last week. Dutroux then led them to the bodies of two girls aged eight. He has also admitted seizing two others.

Daily Mirror, 21st August 1996

According to Dardenne, she had been brainwashed into believing she would be killed by Dutroux's boss, the ruthless head of a gang, if she tried to escape. He told her that her parents did not want to pay the ransom so the gang wanted to kill her. Dutroux said that he had saved her, but had to keep her hidden. To complete the ruse, he even allowed her letters to her family, which he read but never posted. Dardenne also explained what had happened when the police had raided the house:

> *I vividly remember the moment I was rescued. First, I heard the noise of the bricks being scraped across the cellar floor, and then the clank of bottles being moved, and the low thump of plastic containers being taken down from the shelves. And then I heard his voice, exactly as it always was. "It's me. I'm coming in." The door slid open heavily, with just enough room for us to get out. Suddenly I was gripped with terror. It was him all right, standing on the little step where he always waited, but behind him and around him were many other men. At that moment, I was persuaded that, true to his word, my "saviour" had gone and got the police. I hesitated for a second or two, stupefied. Could I really leave? I even asked whether it would be all right to take the coloured pencils he'd been so "kind" as to give me. "Yes, take them," he said. Idiotically, I said: "Thank you!" And, as I had to pass him to get out, like an imbecile I reached up to give him a kiss on the cheek.*

The bodies of four young girls were exhumed in total. Nineteen-year-old An Marchal and 17-year-old Eefje Lambreks had been buried under concrete at his house in Jumet. Julie Lejeune and Melissa Russo, two 8-year-old friends, had died of starvation while Dutroux had been in prison for car theft during 1995. On his release, he had killed the incompetent accomplice who had let the girls die, and buried his body alongside theirs at another of his houses in Sars-la-Buissière. His other accomplices included Martin, Michel Lelièvre, Marleen De Cockere and her lover Jean-Michel Nihoul, whose activities included arranging orgies for government officials, police officers, and a former European commissioner. There were several other arrests in connection with the sex ring.

With such high-level dignitaries involved in a paedophile ring that had escaped detection so many times, there were inevitable allegations of a cover-up, and demands for reforms of Belgium's police and judiciary. There certainly had been, as the presiding judge put it, "much energy been spent opposing an inquiry", and even the Mafia were implicated. However, a conspiracy was ruled out in February 1998 after a 17-month parliamentary enquiry. Embarrassingly, two months later, Dutroux escaped for three hours while being transferred to a court house without handcuffs, resulting in resignations from the Minister of Justice, the Minister of the Interior and the police chief .

A psychiatric report concluded that, "The age of the victims did not seem to arouse in him [Dutroux] any given effect or play a particular role, beyond allowing him to kidnap them, to manipulate them, to confine them", which suggested more the behaviour of a psychopath than a paedophile, and probably informed the court of the ongoing danger that he posed.

The trial finally began in March 2004, with Dutroux claiming to be part of a Europe-wide paedophile ring, run with the participation of police officers, businessmen, doctors and high-level politicians. Unswayed, the jury found Dutroux, Martin and Lelièvre all guilty. Nihoul was acquitted of kidnapping, but later convicted of drug offences and sentenced to five years. Dutroux was given life imprisonment, and Martin and Lelièvre each received 30 years and 25 years, respectively. Martin successfully appealed for early release in May 2011. Between 1996 and 1998, over a third of Belgians with the surname "Dutroux" applied to have it changed.

David Parker Ray
A.K.A. The "Toy Box" Killer
COUNTRY USA
VICTIMS 60
METHOD strangled
MUTILATION dismembered

David Parker Ray and his accomplice, live-in girlfriend Cindy Hendy, would play a welcoming message for their new guests. Friends unfortunate enough to pop around, or strangers abducted from bars, would probably find themselves bound and gagged at 513 Bass Road, a trailer complex on the outskirts of Truth or Consequences, a desert town of less than 10,000 people in rural southern New Mexico. There they were first chained to a post near the bed in a sunken living room, then the 20-minute audiotape of Parker Ray's southern drawl would then let them know what was going to happen to them, in case there was any doubt.

The captives were told that they had just become a sex slave, with Parker Ray as the "Dungeon Master", and that there was going to be a lot of abuse, rape, rape with dildos, sodomy, molestation and excruciating tortures. Having their nipples stretched, that sort of thing. Oral sex on demand would be regular. Sex with animals would also be a must. In short, they had just become unwilling participants in Parker Ray's sexual fantasies, and they would be shared with an evil sex-worshipping group, the congregation of "The Church of Satan". They were also told that they were not the first, and that women who had been there before had died.

Hello there, bitch. Are you comfortable right now? I doubt it. Wrists and ankles chained. Gagged. Probably blindfolded. You are disoriented and scared, too, I would imagine. Perfectly normal, under the circumstances. For a little while, at least, you need to get your shit together and listen to this tape. It is very relevant to your situation. I'm going to tell you, in detail, why you have been kidnapped, what's going to happen to you and how long you'll be here [...] You probably think you're gonna be raped and you're fuckin' sure right about that. Our primary interest is in what you've got between your legs. You'll be raped thoroughly and repeatedly, in every hole you've got. Because, basically, you've been snatched and brought here for us to train and use as a sex slave. Sound kind of far out? Well, I suppose it is to the uninitiated, but we do it all the time. It's gonna take a lot of adjustment on your part, and you're not gonna like it a fuckin' bit. But I don't give a big rat's ass about that. It's not like you're gonna have any choice about the matter. You've been taken by force, and you're going to be kept and used by force. [...] It's no big deal. My Lady friend and I have been keeping sex slaves for years. [...] we prefer to snatch girls in the early to mid-teens, sexually developed, but still small bodied, scared shitless, easy to handle and easy to train, and they usually have tight little pussies and assholes. They make perfect slaves. [...] You're going to be kept in a hidden slaveroom. It is relatively sound proof, escape proof, and it is completely stocked with devices and equipment to satisfy our sexual fetishes and deviations. [...] You're gonna be kept chained in a variety of different positions, usually with your legs or knees forced wide apart. [...] Your pussy and asshole is gonna get a real workout. Especially your asshole, because I'm into animal sex. Also, both of those holes are going to be subjected to a lotta use with some rather large dildos, among

*other things. And it goes without sayin, that there's gonna be a
lot of oral sex. On numerous occasions, you're gonna be forced
to suck cock and eat pussy until your jaws ache and your tongue
is sore. [...] Now I'm sure that you're a great little piece of ass
and you're gonna be a lot of fun to play with, but I will get tired
of you eventually. If I killed every bitch that we kidnapped, there'd
be bodies strung all over the country. And besides, I don't like
killin' a girl, unless it is absolutely necessary. So I've devised a
safe, alternate method of disposal. I had plenty of bitches to
practice on over the years, so I've pretty well got it down pat. And
I enjoy doin' it. I get off on mind games. After we get completely
through with you, you're gonna be drugged up real heavy, with a
combination of Sodium Pentothal and Phenobarbital. They are
both hypnotic drugs that will make you extremely susceptible to
hypnosis, auto-hypnosis and hypnotic suggestion. You're gonna
be kept drugged a couple of days, while I play with your mind.
By the time I get through brainwashing you, you're not gonna
remember a fuckin' thing about this little adventure. [...] Also,
we have a couple of real close friends that we party with once
in a while. They know about our hang-ups and don't have any
problem with fuckin' a slave. You may be required to service
them occasionally. But that's an easy one, for the most part,
just fuckin' and suckin'. They don't get into the heavier stuff.
However, when we have a party, sometimes I like to put on a
little show that you won't like at all. You'll be taken into the living
room and put on the floor on your hands and knees, naked.
Your wrists, ankles, knees and hips will be strapped to a metal
frame to hold your body in that position. The frame is designed
for doggie fuckin', your ass up in the air, sex organs exposed,
your tits hangin' down on each side of a metal support bar,
knees spread about twelve inches, position similar to that of a
bitch dog in heat, right in the middle of the floor so we can sit
on the couch and in chairs, and watch. I'm going to rub canine
breeder's musk on your back, the back of your neck, and on your
sex organs. Now I have three dogs. All of 'em's male, cause I
don't need any fuckin' pups. One of 'em is a very large German
shepherd that is always horny, and he loves it when I bring him
in the house to fuck a woman. After I let him in the house,
he'll sniff around you a little bit and, within a minute, he'll be
mounting you. There's about a 50–50 chance which hole he'll
get his penis into, but it doesn't seem to bother him whether
it's the pussy or the asshole. His penis is pretty thin. It goes in*

easy, but it's about ten inches long and when he gets completely
excited, it gets a hell of a knot right in the middle of it. Now I've
had slaves tell me that it feels like they got a baseball inside
of 'em. [...] The dog knot on his penis is big and extremely
uncomfortable when he's, uh, pushing it back and forth way
up in your anus. I really enjoy watching a girl wiggle, jerk and
squirm around while he's doing it. Consequently, I give him a
little, uh, assistance getting it in the right hole. Now if you think
all of this stuff is sick and depraved, you haven't seen anything
yet. This is a different world. [...] Well, I believe I've told you
about everything that I can. I cannot predict the future. I can't
predict changes of procedure. But if this tape is being played for
you, I have to assume that it is still reasonably accurate. And I
can only give you advice. Be smart and be a survivor. Don't ever
scream. Don't talk without permission. Be very quiet. Be docile
and obedient and, by all means, show proper respect. Have a
nice day.

Then Parker Ray would start torturing and abusing his sex slaves in the main trailer, repeatedly raping and humiliating them, before advancing to a smaller trailer alongside, telling them that worse was to follow in what he called his "Playroom", "Toy Box" or "Satan's Den". This smaller trailer was 15 by 22 feet. Parker Ray had invested over $100,000 on modifications, including soundproofing to keep his activities secret. It had a sole purpose. Sexual torture. A homicide investigator would later describe it:

Inside the cargo trailer was a gynecology chair, with restraints
and electrical wires. The silver wires running across the chair
were used to cause pain and force the victim to move in various
positions. He then would attach jumper cables to the victim's
nipples and groin area. David Ray had placed a TV monitor in
the right-hand corner of the trailer so his victims, who were
secured to the chair as he tortured them, could see what he was
doing to them by looking at the monitor. He had a video camera
focused on the gynecology chair to view his "operations." On
the ceiling of the trailer were chains and pulleys directly over
the gynecology chair. The walls of the cargo trailer were lined
with shelving, photographs and drawings. On the shelves were
various instruments. Authorities collected hundreds of items that
had been used to torture victims. These included surgical tools,
various sexual devices, different size dildos, ropes, chains, a

*mechanical dildo device, straps and harnesses, electric shock
machines, First Aid supplies, anatomically correct dolls, which
had miniature chains attached through their nipples.*

There was also an isolation box that could be used to encase just the prisoner's head, or their whole person could be locked into a home-made, carpet-lined coffin. A jungle of tools and accessories hung from the walls, almost entirely covering them. Where spaces had been left, diagrams of sex positions using the body harness, and photographs of previous tortures were pinned up for easy reference. On a shelf, notably there was a copy of *American Psycho* by Brett Easton Ellis. Just as other serial killers took inspiration from their favourite literature, Parker Ray turned to this 1991 story of a highly stressed, serial-killing investment banker who finds release though sexual torture.

Treatments would involve the use of whips, and various medical and electrical implements, on different parts of the captive, who was often painfully suspended from the ceiling. Strapped so as to keep their legs open wide, cattle prods and stun guns would deliver shocks to sensitive areas of the body. Powerless, the torture victim would be forcibly penetrated with oversized dildos.

Parker Ray and Hendy were arrested in March 1999 after 21-year-old Cynthia Vigil fled their home, naked except for a metal collar and chain. Two motorists swerved to avoid her as she ran, screaming, down the road, bruised and blood-splattered. Finally, she found refuge through the open door of a mobile home, where the owner called the police. When they arrived, Vigil claimed to have been abducted from Albuquerque and held captive in Parker Ray's trailers, while subjected to three days non-stop sexual torture. Evidently, she had only managed to escape when Parker Ray had gone out, after a struggle, where she had defended herself against Hendy with an ice pick. Police had failed to follow up the story of a previous captive, who had been released after four days of torture, but Vigil had welts on her back, punctures on her breasts, cuts, bruises and a bump on her head to back up her story. She was taken to hospital and patrol cars converged on the trailer site. A car had already been called out in response to the disturbance caused by Vigil's escaping. Parker Ray and Hendy claimed that she was a prostitute they had been helping to kick an addiction to heroin, and the sex had been consensual, but the scene seemed more in line with Vigil's version of events.

A subsequent FBI-enhancement and publication in the media of a tattoo noticed on the thigh of a victim appearing in one of the videotapes led to 25-year-old childminder Kelly Van Cleave coming forward. For years she had been having bizarre nightmares about being tied to a table, and tortured, and had an irrational aversion to duct tape, but couldn't think why. In the video, Cleave is gagged using a strip. While she had known and been a friend of Parker Ray's daughter, to her knowledge she had never visited their home. It transpired that she had been held captive there for three days, drugged so that she would have no memories.

After his arrest, Parker Ray talked about the videotapes that he had made. The Toy Box's mounted video camera was used to film the torture, but very few tapes had been found, the others thought to have been buried nearby.

> It was a source of entertainment, to me, to create these tapes. That's why there was a disclaimer at the beginning of the tape stating that it was for adult entertainment only [...] My fantasies are not that unusual. There's approximately two million people in the United States that have, basically, the same fantasies there's organizations, there's clubs [...] it's in the closet, what can I say. It's not that unusual.

Indeed, when the main case went to trial in April 2001, after acquittal at an initial hearing for which the audiotape was deemed inadmissible and Cleave's testimony was called into doubt, and several subsequent delays which included Parker Ray surviving a heart attack and a judge dying from one, the defence argued that the prosecution witnesses' testimony of alleged captivity could just be "harmless fantasy". The same was claimed for Parker Ray's writing.

Parker Ray had compiled his own manual for handling sex slaves, "A woman will do anything to get loose [...] Never trust a chained captive [...] If she is worth taking, she is worth keeping." His rules incorporated 16 core techniques for brainwashing a captive, including isolation, fear, abuse and occasional treats. These were strategies shared by other abductors, such as Gary Heidnik.

Hendy pleaded guilty to accessory and kidnapping, entering into a plea bargain to commute a life sentence to 36 years imprisonment at the Women's Correctional Center in Grants, New Mexico. Her confession also incriminated Parker Ray's daughter Glenda Ray, and local man Dennis Roy Yancy.

Largely on the basis of Hendy's evidence, Parker Ray was convicted of the abduction and sexual torture of three young women. Striking a deal of his own, resulting in a more lenient sentence for his daughter, Parker Ray was sentenced to 223 years in prison, responding, "I feel raped. I got pleasure out of a woman getting pleasure. I did what they wanted me to do." Thanks to her father's plea bargain, Glenda Parker Ray received two-and-a-half years in prison, plus five years' probation for involvement in her father's activities, while Yancy received two consecutive sentences of 15 years for second-degree murder and conspiracy to commit first-degree murder. He was paroled, and returned to Truth or Consequences in 2011.

While in custody awaiting his trials, Parker Ray had boasted of 40 victims, but police believe there could have been as many as 60, including his daughter's lesbian lover and Yancy's ex-girlfriend. Hendy gave details of only 14 murders, but usefully informed police that the victims' bodies had been dumped in ravines and in the 43-mile long and 200-foot deep Elephant Butte Reservoir, eight miles to the north. Parker Ray had a large skiff sailing boat with depth-finding equipment on board with which he could have located the deepest places in that lake. Sure enough, a map was recovered from Parker Ray's trailer: it was of the lake and was covered in x's. Hendy told them that an early victim had resurfaced, so Parker Ray always slit the stomachs open after that, to make sure the bodies stayed submerged. Despite extensive searches in the desert as well as lake diving expeditions, none of the bodies have ever been found. While being transferred to Lea County Correctional Facility in 2002, Parker Ray died of another heart attack.

CANNIBALS

Whoso eateth my flesh, and drinketh my blood, hath eternal life
John 6:54

As well as keeping tokens of their victims, trinkets, souvenirs, personal possessions or pieces of person, serial killers can take their domination one stage further. Control and ownership of someone is final if, rather than being captured on the outside, that person is internalized and subsumed into the serial killer. One perverse way to regard this relationship is as the victim taking control, like a spirit entering someone's body and controlling them from within. But, to the psychopath in their egocentric universe, they cannot be overpowered. They are superior to all others, they are the survivor while others are destroyed, and here before you, in these body parts, is the dismembered proof.

Consumed and assimilated. Japanese cannibal Issei Sagawa famously killed and ate a Dutch student, inspired by an all-consuming love, "My passion is so great I want to possess her. I want to eat her. If I do she will be mine forever." Nico Claux pandered more to the French stereotype when it came to cannibal cuisine, "Sometimes I brought select meats home with me to be cooked, but my preference was to eat them raw. It tasted like tartar steak, or carpaccio. The big muscles of the thighs and back were good, but there was no good meat in the breasts, only fats." In contrast, Papua New Guineans describe the taste of human flesh, depending on how lean the meat is, as somewhere between cassowary and pork.

Andrei Romanovich Chikatilo
A.K.A. The Rostov Ripper, The Butcher of Rostov, The Red Ripper, The Forest Strip Killer
COUNTRY Russia
VICTIMS 56+
METHOD stabbed, strangled
MUTILATION dismembered, mastication

In the years preceding the outbreak of the Second World War, Russia was in Stalin's vice-like grip, in preparation for the Great Purge, a cleansing of the political system and a rebirth of the Soviet Union. The Soviet Constitution ruled over by the Communist Party was about to be adopted, while widespread famine crippled remote and poor areas such as the Ukraine, as all food was confiscated for central redistribution. Andrei Chikatilo was born into this hardship, a time when rumours abounded of desperate families being forced to resort to cannibalism, stealing the children of their neighbours. His older brother was even supposed to have disappeared in this way.

As a boy, Chikatilo shared a bed with his parents, but was badly beaten by his mother for being a chronic bed-wetter. Frailties and his avidity for reading made Chikatilo a target for bullying at school. He became more withdrawn on finding he was impotent, only experiencing ejaculation when 17 years old while wrestling with an 11-year-old friend of his younger sister. The same sister introduced him to his future wife, whom he married in 1963. Although his impotence inhibited sex, they managed to conceive a son and daughter by Chikatilo scooping his semen into his wife's vagina.

In March 1981, Chikatilo lost his job as a teacher after complaints of sexual assault of his young pupils. This might have suggested a starting point for his killing, if it had not already begun three years before, when he had attempted to rape 9-year-old girl Yelena Zakotnova in December 1978. Unable to reach tumescence, he strangled the girl, reaching orgasm as he stabbed her body. This would be the only way he could get sexual gratification from here onwards, and would be the main driving force behind his obsession. Blood stains and evidence from an eyewitness could have thwarted Chikatilo's serial killer career, but police arrested and eventually executed the wrong man, after extracting a confession through torture.

Chikatilo attempted to resist his homicidal urges. He again failed to rape 17-year-old Larisa Tkachenko in September 1981, taking out his frustration by battering and strangling her. Having no knife, he mutilated her body with a stick and his teeth. In June 1982, he stabbed and slashed 13-year-old Lyubov Biryuk.

Accepting his murderous ways, Chikatilo murdered a further six victims aged between 9 and 19 between July and December of 1982, honing his preferred technique of luring mostly vulnerable children away from bus and railway stations and taking them to nearby woods where he would sometimes bludgeon or strangle, but mainly stab and slash and disembowel them, finally gouging out their eyes, perhaps to remove the image of their killer, as laid down in Russian folklore.

By 1984, Russian police had found 23 bodies exhibiting similar wounds, many young girls and boys in the country surrounding the small town of Rostov in the federal constituency of Yaroslavl Oblast. The constituency's coat of arms includes a black bear, a halberd slung over its shoulder and a paw raised, it long claws poised ready to rip. For the proud Communist state, unused to such a long series of gruesome killings, they were in a state of denial, made more so because the killings were particularly horrendous. Investigators reported that they could see the victim's horror. All the victims had been mutilated with cut abdomens and removed breasts, and it was clear to see that many of those body parts had been chopped away by the killer, using his teeth.

A pattern in the killings was evident. For the first time in the Soviet Union a psychiatrist, Dr Aleksandr Bukhanovsky, produced a 65-page offender profile of the killer as a man aged between 45 and 50 years, of average intelligence, probably married, and an impotent sadist only reaching sexual climax through victimization. A lot of the bodies were also found near to transport hubs, suggesting the killer used the Soviet transportation system extensively, perhaps as a production worker. Chikatilo was by then indeed working as a factory clerk.

Despite a media blackout that created fear and rumour among the public, a high-profile police presence and spot checks at bus and railway stations proved successful in forcing the killer into remoter areas, where they had undercover agents keeping watch. In November 1990, a bloodied man was spotted emerging from woods onto a railway platform to wash his shoes and clean his coat. This seemed suspicious to the undercover policeman, so he asked the man to show his papers. The man was Chikatilo, by then a 54-year-old grandfather and long-term Communist Party member. Chikatilo was allowed to go, but an incident report was filed. Twenty-four hours later a body displaying the hallmark injuries of the serial killer was found in the same woods. A look back through recent records quickly came up with Chikatilo's name.

In November 1990, Chikatilo was apprehended coming out of a pub. While under surveillance, he had been observed approaching a number of children. Now he was in custody, police had to look much further back in the records, to resurrect over 30 murders they suspected him to have committed. But the evidence connecting Chikatilo was scant and they would only have the legal 10 days to make a case. What they really needed was a confession, but they were not prepared for the sadistic cruelty about to be revealed to them, particularly the most heinous crimes, which spanned a dozen years.

Chikatilo responded best to Bukhanovsky, who spoke with him matter-of-factly, positioning no guilt or wrongdoing, in contrast to the alternative, heavy-handed police interrogation. Bukhanovsky read directly from his serial killer profile. In fact, Chikatilo very much enjoyed relating his story to Bukhanovsky, and showed great enthusiasm but little emotion during the physical re-enactments that he demonstrated with dummies in the KGB gymnasium and during visits to the crime scenes. He spelt out how he had tricked his victims, disarming and tying their hands with a length of rope behind their backs, and the different ways and precise angles that he had stabbed them, and even how he had sex with them, while they were dying or already dead. He also admitted to masticating body parts.

In total, Chikatilo admitted to the known 36 murders and a further 20 that the police did not know about. All except three of the bodies have been found. Facing charges for 53 murders, Chikatilo stood trial, presenting himself as a lifelong victim of Russia's social and political environment.

Chikatilo was caged behind white bars throughout his trial, which was often reduced to a spectacle of shouting and altercation. Chikatilo seemed to have been driven insane, grimacing madly and rocking in his chair. Defending himself, he blamed Stalin and the Communist Party, his parents and the cannibalism of the famine. He also dropped his trousers, exposing himself to the court. If all this was intended to present a case of insanity and diminished responsibility, then it failed. In October 1992, the judge read out Chikatilo's sentence:

Taking into consideration the monstrous crimes that he committed, the court has no alternative but to impose the only sentence that he deserves. I therefore sentence him to death.

The courtroom erupted into spontaneous applause. Chikatilo was executed by a single shot to the back of the head, behind the right ear, in February 1994.

In a disturbing sequel, in 1997 Vladimir Anatolyevich Mukhankin pleaded guilty to murdering eight women in Rostov, one man, five women and three children during a two-month period. He called himself "the pupil of Chikatilo", but rescinded that, claiming instead, "Chikatilo was a chicken, I am cooler than he!" His death sentence was commuted to life imprisonment.

Dean Corll
A.K.A. The Candy Man, The Houston Mass Murderers
COUNTRY USA
VICTIMS 28+
METHOD bludgeoned, shot, strangled
MUTILATION dismembered, mastication

Even though North America had experienced some of the world's most horrific serial killing by the early 1970s, Dean Corll's case was so shocking, it became known as the deadliest. A minimum of 28 teenage boys, aged between 13 and 20, would turn up raped and murdered in the three short years between 1970 and 1973. The hippy dream had faded and America was being dragged through the slime of Watergate. It was post-Kemper, Manson and Mullin, and too soon for Berkowitz. The country deserved a few years of peace surely. A few years for a nation to catch its collective breath.

Nope.

When the family's candy business closed, Corll became an electrician, keeping in touch with David Brooks, whom he had befriended a few years before, when Brooks had been only 12 years old. Corll persuaded Brooks to adapt their relationship into a sexual one, paying the now 15-year-old boy to receive oral sex from him. Elmer Henley, a school friend of Brooks, and one year younger than him, then got involved with the duo, carrying out some burglaries with them. Then Corll offered the pair 200 dollars for every teenage boy that they brought him. Henley had been told the boys would be sold into a homosexual slavery ring; the truth and real extent of Corll's killing came out later in an argument.

Corll's victims were usually picked up and driven to his house, lured by the offer of a party. There, some were given drink and drugs until they passed out, while others were tricked into putting on handcuffs, or simply grabbed by force. Stripped naked, they were tied to a plywood torture board or the bed, and sexually assaulted and tortured. This could last several days, during which the victims were often forced to write or phone their parents to give an excuse for their absence. They were eventually shot with a .22 calibre pistol or strangled. To dispose of the bodies, they were first wrapped in plastic and then buried in Corll's rented boat shed, at one of two particular beaches, or in woodland near his family's log cabin.

As Brooks and Henley continued to lure victims to Corll, often lifelong school friends, Corll's bloodlust intensified. In August 1973, Henley invited 19-year-old Timothy Kerley to Corll's place for a party. By this time Brooks had married his pregnant fiancée and he wasn't there on this occasion. After several hours, Henley and Kerley went out for sandwiches, picking up 15-year-old Rhonda Williams on their way back. She had left home that evening after being beaten by her drunken father. Corll was furious a female had been introduced onto the scene, but they partied, drinking and smoking, for some hours more.

Henley woke to find himself handcuffed, and the others bound and gagged. Corll was threatening to kill him as well. He persuaded Corll to untie him so he could help out in the torture and killing, and they then both tied Kerley and Williams to opposite sides of the torture board, the boy on his front, the girl on her back. Corll then stripped and started raping and torturing Kerley, commanding Henley to rape and kill Williams. Corll's sadism was getting worse, and Henley and Brooks had shared their growing concern for their own safety. Henley realized he'd just made a narrow escape.

Corll had put his gun down, which Henley now snatched up, ordering Corll to back off. Corll goaded him that he wouldn't pull the trigger. Henley shot him in the forehead and shoulder before Corll staggered out of the room. A further three bullets were fired into his back. He slid down the wall, dead.

Kerley persuaded Henley to call the police and make a full confession of his involvement, placing Corll as the ringleader. In a twist, Brooks blamed Henley, "Henley was sadistic and liked to tie the boys down spread-eagled on a board on the floor and perform unnatural sex acts before murdering them." Brooks was sentenced to life imprisonment, and Henley received six consecutive 99-year terms, totalling 594 years.

A search of the boat shed revealed the largest number of bodies. All of the victims had been sodomized and most had been sexually tortured. Pubic hairs had been plucked out, penises chewed, objects inserted into rectums, and glass rods shoved into urethrae and smashed. Corll had also castrated some of his victims while they had still been alive.

Leonarda Cianciulli
A.K.A. The Soap-Maker of Correggio
COUNTRY Italy
VICTIMS 3
METHOD bludgeoned
MUTILATION dismembered, cannibalism

Leonarda Cianciulli, married to a registry office clerk, had 17 pregnancies during her marriage. Cianciulli miscarried thrice and 10 of her children died young. Superstitious, she would seek the advice of fortune-tellers. One told her that all of her children would die, so it is no surprise that she was overly protective of her surviving four children. When the Second World War began in 1939 and her eldest son, Giuseppe, joined the Army, desperate measures were required to protect him from harm. Cianciulli decided that human sacrifice was the only answer, and she knew a few friends who would fit the bill.

The first visitor was given drugged wine. When she was unconscious, Cianciulli killed the woman using an axe and cut the body into nine pieces.

The blood was collected in a basin:

> I threw the pieces into a pot, added seven kilos of caustic soda,
> which I had bought to make soap, and stirred the whole mixture
> until the pieces dissolved in a thick, dark mush that I poured into
> several buckets and emptied in a nearby septic tank. As for the
> blood in the basin, I waited until it had coagulated, dried it in the
> oven, ground it and mixed it with flour, sugar, chocolate, milk and
> eggs, as well as a bit of margarine, kneading all the ingredients
> together. I made lots of crunchy tea cakes and served them to the
> ladies who came to visit, though Giuseppe and I also ate them.

Over the next year, two more visitors met the same end; the final victim
was a soprano who had even sung at the opera in La Scala:

> She ended up in the pot, like the other two [...] her flesh was
> fat and white, when it had melted I added a bottle of cologne,
> and after a long time on the boil I was able to make some
> most acceptable creamy soap. I gave bars to neighbours and
> acquaintances. The cakes, too, were better: that woman was
> really sweet [...] I gave the copper ladle, which I used to skim the
> fat off the kettles, to my country, which was so badly in need of
> metal during the last days of the war.

The singer's sister-in-law knew that she was visiting Cianciulli, so when
she didn't reappear the police were alerted. In 1946, having confessed,
Cianciulli was sentenced to 30 years in prison, plus three years in an
asylum, where she died from a cerebral haemorrhage in October 1970.
Many years before, one of those fortune-tellers had told her, "In your right
hand I see prison, in your left a criminal asylum."

Pedro Rodrigues Filho
A.K.A. El Pedrinho Matador (Little Peter the Killer)
COUNTRY Brazil
VICTIMS 100+
METHOD shot, stabbed, strangled
MUTILATION cannibalism

A tally of over 100 victims is attributed to Pedro Filho, who was born
deformed because of the beating inflicted by his father on his mother
while he was still in the womb. His first attempted killing came when

he was aged only 13. His first successful killing was a year later. He murdered the vice-mayor of his local town for sacking his father.

Filho took refuge in the southeast of Brazil. The woman he was with was killed by the police, which started a long run of retribution – seven dead and 16 injured before he was 18 years old. Revenge was pivotal to Filho's life. He butchered his father for butchering his mother with a machete. He also ate part of his father's heart.

Filho was arrested in May 1973 and sentenced to 128 years in prison, for killing at least 71 people. This was soon extended to 400 years following the murder of fellow inmates, including another serial killer, The Park Maniac, Francisco de Assis Pereira. Despite this, Filho, one of the most prolific living serial killers, was released in April 2007 because Brazilian law caps all sentences at 30 years.

Shen Changping
A.K.A. The Cannibal Brothers
COUNTRY China
VICTIMS 11
METHOD strangled
MUTILATION dismembered, cannibalism, burned

Shen Changyin
A.K.A. The Cannibal Brothers
COUNTRY China
VICTIMS 12
METHOD strangled
MUTILATION dismembered, cannibalism, burned

Other than sharing first names, Shen Changping and Shen Changyin also shared a taste for human flesh. Specifically, they murdered 11 prostitutes during the course of one year between June 2003 and August 2004, and ate their livers and kidneys. They were assisted by Li Chunling, their intended second victim who instead offered to bring them more prostitutes, and three other female accomplices who were recruited in the same way. Each was forced to kill the women they lured to the men's apartment.

Bodies would be dismembered, sometimes in a mincer, and dissolved in sulphuric acid, the remains flushed down a toilet. Shen Changyin had previously murdered a man in 1999, before he had fled his hometown of Nanwu in Henan Province a year later. The Shens and Li were given the death sentence in September 2005, and their accomplices received sentences ranging from three to 20 years in prison.

Nikolai Dzhumagaliev

A.K.A. Metal Fang
COUNTRY Uzbekistan
VICTIMS 100
METHOD bludgeoned
MUTILATION dismembered, cannibalism

Nikolai Dzhumagaliev murdered and ate perhaps as many as 100 women, sharing some with his unsuspecting dinner guests. He served 10 years, then the Uzbekistan authorities granted his parole and he now moves freely around Eastern Europe and probably beyond. The only dead giveaway are his white metal teeth in the style of "Jaws" from James Bond, for which he earned the nickname "Metal Fang".

Albert Fish

A.K.A. Gray Man, Werewolf of Wysteria, suspected
Brooklyn Vampire
COUNTRY USA
VICTIMS 100+
METHOD strangled, bludgeoned
MUTILATION dismembered, vampirism, cannibalism

Albert Fish's immediate family was respectable, despite a history of mental illness and alcoholism. When he was 5 years old, Fish's father died, and his mother was unable to cope with a job and childcare, so he was sent to an orphanage where whipping was a prevalent punishment, "I saw so many boys whipped, it took root in my head." He enjoyed these sadistic beatings, both of others and of himself.

Aged 12, he fell in love with a boy who taught him about urolagnia, also known as "golden showers" and "watersports", and coprophagia, otherwise eating faeces. At the public baths he could watch boys undressing, and by the age of 20, he had become a male prostitute, and had started raping boys.

In 1898, in an apparent change of direction, Fish became a painter–decorator and entered into a marriage arranged by his mother. In reality, he continued molesting boys under 6 years of age. The marriage was to end 20 years later, when his wife deserted him for another man, leaving him to bring up all six of their children. The burden was too much for Fish and his behaviour became increasingly bizarre: he complained of auditory hallucinations and showed an interest in religion and cannibalism. Raw meat was served at the dinner table, especially on nights with a full moon.

The children never made any claims of abuse by their father, but Fish did get them and their friends to discipline him, often hitting his buttocks with a wooden paddle studded with nails. He played other masochistic games with children, getting them to hit him with sticks, and push pins up under his fingernails. It is probable that he continued such practices, and developed tastes for new sadomasochistic homosexual ones, while working as a male prostitute in Europe. He had also become convinced God was commanding him to torture and castrate children.

Back in New York, Fish answered an ad requesting employment, which was placed in a newspaper by 18-year-old Edward Budd in May 1928. Fish visited the Budd household in June, calling himself Frank Howard, and invited the boy to start work on his farm upstate. Fish was unable to take Budd with him straight away but returned bearing presents of his farm produce a few days later, all the while endearing himself to the family as a kindly old gent who generously gave small gifts of money for the children.

On seeing the younger sister, 10-year-old Gracie Budd, dressed in white silk and pearls, he produced a considerable stash of banknotes that he got her to count. Charmed, the parents allowed him to take their daughter to his niece's birthday party that very evening. She never returned. A nationwide search, with fliers detailing the girl and her disappearance led to nothing, and it wasn't until November 1933 that anything was known about her fate, when Fish wrote a letter to her mother:

My Dear Mrs. Budd.

In 1894 a friend of mine shipped as a deck hand on the Steamer Tacoma, Capt. John Davis. They sailed from San Francisco for Hong Kong China. On arriving there he and two others went ashore and got drunk. When they returned the boat was gone.

At that time there was a famine in China. Meat of any kind of was from $1–3 a pound. So great was the suffering among the very poor that all children under 12 were sold to the Butchers to be cut up and sold for food in order to keep others from starving. A boy or a girl under 14 was not safe in the street. You could go to any shop and ask for steak – chops – or stew meat. Part of the naked body of a boy or a girl would be brought out and just what you wanted cut from it. A boy or girl's behind which is the sweetest part of the body and sold as veal cutlet brought the highest price.

John staid there so long he acquired a taste for human flesh.

On his return to N.Y. he stole two boys one 7 and one 11. Took them to his home stripped them naked tied them in a closet. Then burned everything they had on. Several times every day and night he spanked them – tortured them – to make their meat good and tender.

First he killed the 11 yr old boy, because he had the fattest ass and of course the most meat on it. Every part of his body was Cooked and eaten except head, bones and guts. He was Roasted in the oven (all of his ass), boiled, broiled, fried, stewed. The little boy was next, went the same way. At that time, I was living at 409 E. 100 St. near-right side. He told me so often how good Human flesh was I made up my mind to taste it.

On Sunday June the 3, 1928 I called on you at 406 W 15 St. Brought you pot cheese, strawberries. We had lunch. Grace sat in my lap and kissed me. I made up my mind to eat her.

On the pretense of taking her to a party. You said Yes she could go. I took her to an empty house in Westchester I had already picked out. When we got there, I told her to remain outside. She picked wildflowers. I went upstairs and stripped all my clothes off. I knew if I did not I would get her blood on them.

When all was ready I went to the window and Called her. Then I hid in a closet until she was in the room. When she saw me all naked she began to cry and tried to run down stairs. I grabbed her and she said she would tell her mamma.

First I stripped her naked. How did she kick, bite and scratch. I choked her to death, then cut her in small pieces so I could take my meat to my rooms, Cook and eat it. How sweet and tender her little ass was roasted in the oven. It took me 9 days to eat her entire body. I did not fuck her tho I could of had I wished. She died a virgin. Too bad. Hugs and Kisses.

Fish had left a trail of his child-snatching, and was mostly described as the "Gray Man" or as an old, grey tramp, but police were slow to make the connection between each of the several cases. It was his abduction and murder of the Budd girl that led to his eventual capture, conviction and execution. Tracing the stationery that Fish's letter had been written on to a company nearby, the janitor there told investigators he had taken some, but left it in a rented room when he had moved out. The man who had next taken the room had already checked out, but a postal cheque was there needing to be picked up. When he arrived for the cheque, the waiting policeman had to overpower Fish, who had pulled out a razor blade in an attempt to escape.

In custody, Fish confessed to murdering the Budd girl, even though he had intended to kill the brother. As his letter had said, he had not raped her, but he admitted to twice ejaculating involuntarily. He also confessed to two earlier child abductions and killings, although the real number was estimated to exceed 100, supported by his boast of having, "had children in every state". In July 1924, 8-year-old Francis McDonnell failed to return home after playing catch with friends. He was found in woods, sexually assaulted and strangled. Three years later 4-year-old Billy Gaffney was snatched from the hallway outside his family's apartment:

I brought [Billy Gaffney] to the Riker Ave. dumps. There is a house that stands alone, not far from where I took him ... I took the boy there. Stripped him naked and tied his hands and feet and gagged him with a piece of dirty rag I picked out of the dump. Then I burned his clothes. Threw his shoes in the dump. Then I walked back and took the trolley to 59 St. at 2 A.M. and walked from there home.

Next day about 2 P.M., I took tools, a good heavy cat-of-nine tails. Home made. Short handle. Cut one of my belts in half, slit these halves in six strips about 8 inches long. I whipped his bare behind till the blood ran from his legs. I cut off his ears, nose, slit his mouth from ear to ear. Gouged out his eyes. He was dead then. I stuck the knife in his belly and held my mouth to his body and drank his blood.

I picked up four old potato sacks and gathered a pile of stones. Then I cut him up. I had a grip with me. I put his nose, ears and a few slices of his belly in the grip. Then I cut him through the middle of his body. Just below the belly button. Then through his legs about 2 inches below his behind. I put this in my grip with a lot of paper. I cut off the head, feet, arms, hands and the legs below the knee. This I put in sacks weighed with stones, tied the ends and threw them into the pools of slimy water you will see all along the road going to North Beach.

I came home with my meat. I had the front of his body I liked best. His monkey and pee wees and a nice little fat behind to roast in the oven and eat. I made a stew out of his ears, nose, pieces of his face and belly. I put onions, carrots, turnips, celery, salt and pepper. It was good.

Then I split the cheeks of his behind open, cut off his monkey and pee wees and washed them first. I put strips of bacon on each cheek of his behind and put them in the oven. Then I picked 4 onions and when the meat had roasted about 1/4 hour,

I poured about a pint of water over it for gravy and put in the onions. At frequent intervals I basted his behind with a wooden spoon. So the meat would be nice and juicy. In about 2 hours, it was nice and brown, cooked through.

I never ate any roast turkey that tasted half as good as his sweet fat little behind did. I ate every bit of the meat in about four days. His little monkey was as sweet as a nut, but his pee-wees I could not chew. Threw them in the toilet.

In March 1935, Fish was convicted of murdering Gracie Budd despite his plea of insanity, claiming his devout faith had driven him to sacrifice children, as in the bibical story of Abraham and Isaac, to seek absolution for his sins. Eating them was his equivalent to communion. He was executed in Sing Sing Prison's electric chair in January 1936, and was enthusiastic about his violent and painful end, "It will be the only thrill I have not tried." His autopsy discovered that Fish had derived sexual gratification by jabbing sewing needles into his penis and scrotum. He had started inserting them after his wife had left, and nearly two dozen of them were found in his pelvic region.

STRANGLERS

Life is not measured by the breaths you take
but by the moments that take your breath away
Anonymous

Strangulation is popular amongst serial killers as a close-contact way to kill. "It's up close and personal", one once said. With their bare hands they can fine-tune the pressure being applied to the victim's neck – it gives them the ultimate control that they seek. They can literally increase the throttle, or decrease it depending on how unconscious they have rendered their victim. Other attractive aspects are the immediacy of the methods, and the lack of dependence on preparation and equipment, but if a ligature is needed, then anything from cables to underwear will suffice.

Pedro Alonso López
A.K.A. The Monster of the Andes
COUNTRY Columbia
VICTIMS 350+
METHOD stabbed, strangled
MUTILATION dismembered

Pedro López is quite simply the most prolific serial killer alive today, and one of the most deadly of all time, and hardly anyone has ever heard of him. His own prophesy clearly hasn't come true, "I am the man of the century," he once boasted, "No one will ever forget me." No one ever should. López exacted his reign of terror for over a decade, and across three South American countries, claiming in excess of 350 victims, all young girls. What's more, it is very probable that he has been free to continue his terror for this last decade, "I will be happy to kill again. It is my mission."

In March 1980, police in Ambato, Ecuador, captured López after local market stallholders had chased him down when he had been trying to coax one of their daughters to go with him. He was restrained and the police were called. At first, he refused to divulge any information about himself, but then the police installed a local priest dressed as an inmate as an informer in his cell. López started to talk, but the horrors he revealed were too much for the priest to take and he had to be removed the next day.

However, the priest had persuaded López to start confessing his crimes, and when faced with what he had admitted so far, he happily continued in nauseating detail with Police Captain Cordova, who had also won his trust. He related to the older man as a father figure, going as far as to call him "Papa". López had never known his own father, a member of Columbia's Conservative Party killed in 1948 at the outbreak of "La Violencia", the 10-year civil war. Benilda López de Castañada was three months pregnant at the time.

By the time he was 5 years old, López had dreams of becoming a teacher, telling his mother, "Isn't it true I am good with children? One day I'm going to be a teacher." His mother claims he had a poor, but typical and loving childhood. López's version is quite different, painting his mother as an abusive, psychotic prostitute mother of 13 who would have sex in front of him. He claimed he would also witness the beatings she received from her clients, which she would then hand down to her children, "That woman was violent. It is my understanding that this woman is sick in the head, because that was not the proper way to punish your children. She would punish me with such violence."

Possibly because he got caught fondling his younger sister, López ran away from home when he was 8 years old. He was picked up by a man who offered him food and shelter, but was actually taken to a derelict house and repeatedly raped. Heading to Bogotá, the largest city in Columbia with a million people, and the newly confirmed capital, he became a street child or "gamine". These "throwaway children" as they are also known, live a life dictated by violence and revenge. The principal street drug is basuco, a cheap, impure cocaine paste, often smoked through a pipe fashioned from a can of drink, and López soon had a habit.

Emaciated and begging for food, he was taken in by a charitable American couple, who paid for him to go to a school for orphans. After two years of stability, a male teacher sexually molested him. López stole money from the school and returned to the gamines and life on the streets of Bogotá for another decade, turning to petty crime in order to survive:

I was a very alert child, very spirited with an innocent mind. The majority of my childhood, I was abandoned, and lived in filth and sleazy places. My life has been dishonest because of being abandoned ... Being a child, I lost my innocence. They dishonoured me. I was a small child, very innocent. It was something I wanted to forget. I don't deny it affected me. I have always wanted to punish those responsible.

In 1969, aged 21, López was arrested for stealing a car and sentenced to a seven-year jail term. After only two days he was gang-raped by four older convicts. The prison warden judged that killing three of them later with a home-made knife, over the course of a fortnight, had been in self-defence, and only an extra two years was added to López's existing sentence.

However, this experience of killing defined a turning point for López. Primed by pornography and resentment for his mother, he formed a hatred of women. His mother was the reason why everything had happened to him, why life had been so hard. But he didn't need to suffer any more. He was no longer a victim, no longer prey. He was the predator.

Released in 1978, he began preying on young girls amongst Peru's Indian tribes, the poorly educated, impoverished, indigenous peoples that hawk their wares on the streets. Either posing as a salesman or asking for directions, he approached girls aged between 8 and 12 years and charmed them into trusting him; he never resorted to physical abduction. Appearing helpless, he would lure them far enough away from anyone else that they would be at his mercy.

His killing in Peru only stopped when he was caught attempting to lure a 9-year-old girl. His captors, the Ayacucho tribe from northern Peru, stripped and tortured him, finally burying him up to his neck and leaving him to die. However, he was rescued by an American missionary who handed him over to the authorities. Uninterested in tribal complaints, they said that the girls were runaways, and López was deported to Ecuador.

Travelling between Ecuador and Columbia, López kept on the move, killing about three girls every week. The alarming rise in disappearances was noticed, but thought to be because of sex slavery. It was only in April 1980 that police knew a serial killer was at large, when a flash flood near Ambato unearthed the bodies of four of the missing girls. Because of the widespread shock this brought, the market traders and local townsfolk were already vigilant when López made his next attempt.

Throughout his confession, López displayed an astonishing ability for recalling names, appearance, clothing and crimes. He related in all the rape and murders of 110 girls in Ecuador, 100 in Colombia, and "many more than one hundred" in Peru. He expressed a preference for girls in Ecuador, "They are more gentle and trusting, more innocent. They are not as suspicious of strangers as Colombian girls."

> I went after my victims by walking among the markets searching
> for a girl with a certain look on her face – a look of innocence
> and beauty. She would be a good girl, working with her mother.
> I followed them sometimes for two or three days, waiting for
> when she was left alone. I would give her a trinket like a hand

*mirror, then take her to the edge of town where I would promise
a trinket for her mother.*

*I would take her to a secret hideaway where prepared graves
waited. Sometimes there were bodies of earlier victims there. I
cuddled them and then raped them at sunrise. At the first sign
of light I would get excited. I forced the girl into sex and put my
hands around her throat. When the sun rose I would strangle her.*

*It was only good if I could see her eyes, it would have been
wasted in the dark – I had to watch them by daylight. There is
a divine moment when I have my hands around a young girl's
throat. I look into her eyes and see a certain light, a spark,
suddenly go out. The moment of death is enthralling and
exciting. Only those who actually kill know what I mean.*

When I am released I will feel that moment again.

*It took the girls five to 15 minutes to die. I was very
considerate. I would spend a long time with them making sure
they were dead. I would [use the] mirror to check whether they
were still breathing. Sometimes I had to kill them all over again.*

*They never screamed because they didn't expect anything
would happen. They were innocent.*

Suddenly, it was turning out that the tragic number of missing girls had actually been murdered – by just one man. The police needed evidence to corroborate López's stories, and he was able to lead them to every one of his dumping sites, relishing the attention, re-enacting his rituals, but at no time showing any remorse, "You ask me whether I felt anything while asphyxiating certain persons. Well, no. It's strange, no? Someone who shoots another with a gun, and the other person feels the pain of the bullet. Is the shooter going to feel the same agony or the same pain?" At one point, he grabbed one of his victim's skulls and tucked it under his arm in a pose for the cameras.

The entirety of his killings and the subsequent hunt for bodies seemed, in his mind, entirely there for his immediate entertainment, and long-term immortality in the history books. This indifferent cold-heartedness made it very difficult for the authorities to accept any remorse that López did express, "I am the worst of the worst. Perhaps I took it too far because of my ignorance. The low of the low. Perhaps, even a complete animal."

Equally so, it's hard to see how López's excuse that he was assisting his victims by strangling them, "so that they would go to heaven, so that they wouldn't suffer in this world" accords with how he would arrange his *muñequitas*, or dolls, at the graveside, and act out ghoulish tea parties with them. When their inanimate play ceased to entertain him any further, he would go looking for more, "My little friends liked to have company. I often put three or four into one hole. But after a while I got bored because they couldn't move, so I looked for more girls."

Psychiatrists revealed a further dimension to López's motivation. Undoubtedly angry about his treatment and abuse over the years, he wished for revenge and notoriety that would also put him into a position of power, one where he was in control. Targeting the poor indigenous peoples throughout South America gave him an inexhaustible supply of victims for whom he felt disdain. Poor, uneducated, they were even ugly in his eyes. Revenge through ethnic cleansing was the answer López sought, "I eliminated a small group of insignificants, and allegedly took away their innocence. But, my innocence has been taken away from me."

López tried to blame all the murders on Jorge Patiño, initially introduced as a psychotic, alternate personality, but soon claimed to be someone completely individual, "I did not commit, I participated in the acts and was involved in them. He was threatening to kill me, and if I left him he would kill me." All the same, López pleaded guilty at his trial in July 1981, knowing that the sentence for one murder was the same as that for multiple murders in Ecuador, "Even if you kill one or a thousand, it's sixteen years." The inability to keep López locked up for longer has led to a call to revise the policy of limited sentences.

He was released from Ambato Prison in August 1994, two years early for good behaviour, and is reported to have spent much of his solitary incarceration smoking basuco. One hour after gaining his freedom he was back in custody, on the pretext that he had no formal documents, but really as a reason to deport him to Columbia. Police in his home country took him into custody, hoping to convict him of his murders there, and hoping that he would get the more severe life sentence possible by Columbian law. He was thus charged with a girl's murder from 20 years earlier.

López was able once more to receive a lenient sentence. He was declared insane in 1995 and placed in a prison hospital in Bogotá, but this diagnosis was reversed in February 1998, allowing him to walk free for a mere 50-dollar bail. The last time anyone ever saw him was shortly after his final release, when, 19 years since seeing her, López visited his mother, sold her furniture – a chair and bed – and disappeared. Since then, López continues to be sought, suspected of more killings.

Daniel Camargo Barbosa

COUNTRIES Columbia, Ecuador
VICTIMS 150+
METHOD strangled, stabbed
MUTILATION dismembered

Daniel Barbosa lost his mother at an early age. His father remarried, but his new stepmother was abusive, and would mock him in front of his friends, often dressing him up in girls' clothes. As a young man, he had two children by his common law wife, before falling in love with someone else. He and his new love agreed that as she was not a virgin, they would still marry, but she would have to lure and drug virgins for him to rape.

The fifth young girl to be assaulted went to the police and the couple were imprisoned in April 1964. Barbosa at first received only three years, but this sentence was overruled and extended to eight. This convinced him that murdering his victims would be necessary to cover his tracks in the future.

After being returned to Columbia from Brazil for not having official papers, it is estimated that on his release he proceeded to rape and kill over 80 young girls until he was caught in May 1974. He was sentenced to 30 years, commuted to 25, and imprisoned in the penal colony on the island of Gorgona.

Like something from a film, Barbosa escaped from the island in November 1984, on a rudimentary boat, having studied the tides. He was not eaten by sharks as suspected, but instead arrived in Ecuador, carrying out 71 rapes and murders in the municipality of Guayaquil, while living on the streets and selling biros. He would entice young, working-class girls to secluded areas by asking them directions and offering money or the possibility of work, then heading off into the woods to take a "shortcut". When alone, he would rape his victims, strangle them, then hack and slash at their bodies with a machete. Scavengers would do the rest. He was arrested in February 1986 and led the police to his killing grounds.

Barbosa gave his reason for murder as revenge for women not being the pure, chaste virgins he wanted them to be. He was convicted of the maximum 16 years for murder in Ecuador, and imprisoned alongside Pedro López in Ambato. Barbosa converted to Christianity, but even that couldn't save him. In 1994, he was murdered in jail and an ear was chopped off by a fellow inmate, who also just happened to be one of his victims' cousins.

John Reginald Christie

COUNTRY England
VICTIMS 8
METHOD strangled

A self-delusional, manipulative and dominating man, John Reginald Christie gained sexual gratification from murdering young women in the home he shared with his wife at 10 Rillington Place. Some years after claiming his first two victims, he then strangled his wife, hiding her body under the floorboards in the front room. In the three months that followed, he went on to murder and sexually assault another three women in the same house, hiding their bodies in an alcove behind the kitchen. The four bodies were discovered when the kitchen was being renovated. By then Christie was destitute and living in a homeless shelter, and was quickly captured and admitted his guilt.

His most intriguing murder was that of Beryl Evans, wife of his one-time lodger Timothy Evans. Christie, a self-assured and convincing liar, framed the simple and inadequate Evans for the murder of Beryl and their baby daughter Geraldine. Compared with the confident, self-assured Christie, who was held up as a responsible man who had a service record with the War Reserve Police, Evans was presented as unreliable, and branded a liar in court. Evans was wrongly convicted of his daughter's murder and hanged. However, once Christie admitted to all of his murders, including that of Beryl Evans, the major flaws in the police investigation were revealed. Evans' case became known as an infamous miscarriage of justice, often quoted in legal arguments against capital punishment. Christie's story was later made into an award-nominated film, named after his infamous address and starring Richard Attenborough, who spent three hours in make-up each morning having his bald pate fitted.

Ahmad Suradji

A.K.A. Datuk
COUNTRY Indonesia
VICTIMS 42
METHOD strangled

With perverse echoes of Edmund Kemper, when Ahmad Suradji buried his 42 female victims, aged from 11 to 30, amongst sugarcane near his home on the outskirts of Sumatra's largest city of Medan, he faced their heads towards his house. He believed this alignment would give him extra power. You see Suradji wasn't just a cattle farmer, he was also a self-proclaimed *dukun*, or shamanic witch doctor.

Black magic is big business in Indonesia. People are usually too poor and uneducated to buy modern medicines. When a family member falls ill, they naturally turn to the healing powers of a witch doctor. However, the belief system is so ingrained that even presidents seek *dukun* counsel, paying thousands of dollars for their services, which include everything from sinusitis to a curse on political opponents. The witch doctor is therefore a powerful influence, and Suradji needed to hone his sorcerer's skills.

Suradji's father's ghost had instructed him to ritually kill 70 women and drink their saliva, a regime which he dutifully followed for 11 years, with the help of his three wives, all sisters. There was no shortage of women coming to his door, dreaming of richer futures, more faithful husbands or simply being prettier. Many were prostitutes desperate to improve their lot.

Instead, after a fee of between 200 and 400 dollars had been extracted from them, they were buried up to their waists and strangled with electrical cable. Dead and dug out, they were undressed and reburied in the sugarcane plantation. One wife, Tumini, was tried in December 1997 as an accomplice alongside her husband.

Not believing the ghost story, the Lubuk Pakam District Court found the couple guilty, and their sentences were confirmed by the Medan High Court and Supreme Court in April 1998. Tumini received a life sentence while Suradji was sentenced to death by firing squad. He was executed in July 2008. Eighty local families came forward to report missing members, suggesting many more bodies might yet be found. However, one of his supposed victims has since turned up alive and well, working in Malaysia.

Jürgen Bartsch
COUNTRY Germany
VICTIMS 4
METHOD strangled, bludgeoned
MUTILATION dismembered, disembowelled

In 1966, 19-year-old Jürgen Bartsch was arrested after the boy he had tied up in a disused air-raid shelter, whom he had intended to torture, kill and dismember, escaped by burning through his bonds. Bartsch had thoughtfully left a lit candle while he dutifully went home, as he did every evening, to climb into bed with his parents for a TV dinner.

He had been born a bastard, and adopted by a butcher and his wife following his mother's death from tuberculosis when he was still very young. His adoptive mother suffered from obsessive–compulsive disorder, and everything had to be spotless and in its right place, with clothes folded military-style. Bartsch was forbidden to play with other children in order to keep clean. His adoptive mother also bathed him throughout his life.

Since his 16th year, Bartsch had killed four boys, aged 8, 13, 12 and 12, but had attempted over a hundred more. His ultimate goal was to slowly torture his victims to death, by skinning and butchering them alive. This is what he had intended to do to his fifth victim, who had escaped. Until then, he had taken boys to the same shelter, hitting them into submission, sexually molesting them while masturbating – but failing to achieve orgasm – then killing them by strangulation or by beating them.

Despite his loathing of butchering animals in his father's shop, he thoroughly butchered the boys' corpses, decapitating, disembowelling and dismembering their bodies. He reached an intense and sustained orgasm whilst doing so, ejaculating onto the flesh and into the body cavity.

Whether a coincidence or not, Bartsch had been told about Gilles de Rais by a Catholic priest who had sexually abused him at boarding school. Once caught, he served a decade of his life term, and even married, before requesting castration in the hope of reducing his sentence. He died during the surgery, at the hands of an incompetent anaesthetist.

Kenneth Bianchi
A.K.A. The Hillside Stranglers
COUNTRY USA
VICTIMS 12
METHOD strangled

Angelo Buono
A.K.A. The Hillside Stranglers
COUNTRY USA
VICTIMS 10
METHOD strangled

The fascinating thing about the case of the Hillside Stranglers isn't so much the crimes themselves, although torturing your victim by injecting them with the equivalent of Windolene is quite unusual. Rather, it is more about the potential victim they let go, and about the way one of the killers tried to throw his charges.

Towards the end of their killings, cousins Kenneth Bianchi and Angelo

Buono gave a lift to a woman they thought would become their next victim. However, as they got chatting, they found out the woman was Catharine Lorre, the daughter of actor Peter Lorre who was well known for playing the serial killer partly based on Fritz Haarmann, in Fritz Lang's classic film *M*. They let her go, and Lorre was none the wiser.

Shortly after his arrest in January 1979, Bianchi started a relationship with playwright, actress and serial killer groupie, Veronica Compton. He persuaded her to recreate a Hillside Strangler-style murder to make it appear as though he was innocent and the murderer was still at large. He even gave her some of his semen to be planted at the crime scene. Compton identified a suitable woman working in the bar of a motel, and set up the intended murder. But things didn't turn out as expected and she was arrested and convicted of attempted murder.

Ian Brady
A.K.A. The Moors Murderers
COUNTRY England
VICTIMS 5
METHOD strangled

Myra Hindley
A.K.A. The Moors Murderers
COUNTRY England
VICTIMS 5
METHOD strangled

There's something about the Moors Murders that strikes a chord of revulsion and dismay with the British. It's not as if serial killers in Britain compete with their North and South American counterparts for purely victim tally, but violent crime seems more shocking in the UK than elsewhere. Perhaps because of a moderate historical relationship with guns, the UK rate for homicides is about a third of that of the USA.

In the case of the Moors Murders there was a fear of the unknown, an empathy for the parents of the murdered children and a bleakness about the setting, that probably pricked the social conscience.

TWO broken-hearted mothers watched as police and helpers made a grim search in a valley in the Pennine hills yesterday.

They were the mothers of Lesley Ann Downey and John Kilbride, two missing children.

They watched as police looked for the marks of shallow graves.

For they had been told that one and possibly more bodies, victims of a mass killer, may be buried on the moors.

Mrs. Ann Downey, of Ancoats, Manchester, said: "I just had to come, though I am very afraid."

And Mrs. Sheila Kilbride, of Ashton-Under-Lyne, said: "If only I knew whether John is alive or dead ..."

John, 12, disappeared nearly two years ago.

Daily Mirror, 16th October 1965

That mass killer turned out to be, of course, the reviled team of stock clerk Ian Brady and besotted girlfriend, "the most evil woman in Britain", secretary Myra Hindley.

Within months he had convinced me that there was no God at all: He could have told me that the earth was flat, the moon was made of green cheese and the sun rose in the west, I would have believed him, such was his power of persuasion, his softly convincing means of speech which fascinated me, because I could never fully comprehend, only browse at the odd sentence here and there, believing it to be gospel truth.

Brady was indoctrinating Hindley into his world of Nazism, sex and torture, and she proved to be a willing student, reading *Mein Kampf, Crime and Punishment* and the works of the Marquis de Sade, while Brady's demands and sexual deviancy made her more adventurous and less prudish.

Two years after they had first met through their jobs in Hyde, Greater Manchester, in July 1961, Brady started talking about "committing the perfect murder", drawing on another literary source, Meyer Levin's *Compulsion*, which features the murder of a 12-year-old boy.

Shortly afterwards, Hindley enticed 16-year-old Pauline Reade into her car, asking for help to find a glove in exchange for some vinyl records. They drove to Saddleworth Moor, while Brady followed them on his motorbike, ready to rape and kill Reade. He fractured her skull with a shovel and slit her throat so deeply her spinal cord was severed and her head almost decapitated. Reade was buried in a shallow grave on the moor.

The same fate befell 12-year-old John Kilbride in November 1963. Hindley asked for help with some boxes, then drove the boy to the moor where Brady sexually assaulted him, before strangling him and burying the body. Twelve-year-old Keith Bennett was lured with the "lost glove" story in June 1964. He was sexually assaulted and strangled in a ravine. The body was never found.

Later, 10-year-old Lesley Ann Downey was abducted from a funfair in December 1964. Brady and Hindley pretended to struggle with their shopping and duped the girl into helping them carry it back to Hindley's grandmother's house. In preparation, the grandmother had been sent to relatives overnight. Inside the house Downey was gagged and bound, stripped, raped, tortured and strangled. Hindley kept a photographic record of the night's events. She also recorded the girl's cries, screams and her pleas to go home on audio tape. Downey's body was concealed in a shallow grave on Saddleworth Moor.

Brady would kill once more, to impress 17-year-old David Smith, whom Hindley's sister had married upon getting pregnant. Brady picked up Edward Evans, also 17 years old, and killed him by bludgeoning him with the flat of an axe and strangling him, in front of Hindley and Smith. A few hours later Smith phoned the police, who found Evans' body in Brady's house. During questioning, Smith mentioned that Brady had asked for the return of his "dodgy books", which he had put in a suitcase. He didn't know where the suitcase was, but Brady had a thing about railway stations.

The suitcase was found in a left-luggage locker in Manchester Central railway station. It contained Brady's library and the pornographic photographs of Downey, plus the audio recording of her torture. Brady and Hindley were clearly audible. Searching the houses, police found a large number of photographs of Saddleworth Moor and Kilbride's name scribbled in an exercise book.

Brady and Hindley were tried in April 1966 for the murders of Kilbride, Downey and Evans. Both independently pleaded their innocence and attempted to implicate Smith. Hindley claimed alibis that removed her from the actual abuse and deaths of the victims. She accused Brady of the murders, but Brady let slip that, "we all got dressed" after the Downey tape had been made, suggesting Hindley had an active role in the sexual assault and torture. In May 1966, Brady was convicted of all three murders and Hindley was found guilty of murdering Downey and Evans. They both received life sentences – the death penalty had been abolished in November 1965.

One of the UK's most notorious serial killing cases, this has continued to stir emotions. While Brady has remained recalcitrant, and adamant from the outset that he wishes to stay and die in prison, Hindley repeatedly requested parole, and assisted further enquiries in 1985 and 1987, exonerating Smith and confessing to murdering Reade and Bennett. She even revisited the moor under police protection, which eventually led to their finding Reade's skeleton. Brady was told of this and also offered to co-operate; however, his two visits to the moor were to no avail.

The police launched another search for Bennett's body in 2003.

Nothing was found despite the use of state-of-art equipment. The search was officially closed in 2009, but public donations are supporting a volunteer search project. Bennett's family independently continue to search the moor to this day.

In 1977, Lord Longford appeared on television to appeal for Hindley's release, while Spike Milligan made the case in 1996 that Hindley had only ever been an accessory to murder and should at least be moved to an open prison. Ironically, her pet name for Brady had been "Neddy", after Milligan's creation, The Goons character Neddy Seagoon.

Marcus Harvey's 1995 painting *Myra*, which showed Hindley's infamously dour mugshot recreated from thousands of children's handprints, was vandalized at the Royal Academy of Art, and caused another sensation when a film showing it was removed for causing embarrassment by its being used in advertising for the 2012 Olympics. Hindley died in Highpoint Prison in Suffolk, from bronchial pneumonia caused by heart disease, aged 60 years old, in November 2002. Twenty local undertakers refused to handle the cremation, but her ashes were scattered in due course by Patricia Cairns, a prison warden who had been Hindley's lesbian lover.

In September 1999, Brady went on hunger strike in Ashworth Hospital, Merseyside, where he was taken when diagnosed criminally insane in 1985, but he continues to be occasionally force-fed through tubes in his nose and throat. In September 2001, there was a public outcry when he was given permission to publish a book on serial killers called *The Gates of Janus*. A two-part TV adaptation called *See No Evil: The Moors Murders* received a generally positive reception, winning an award for Best Drama Serial in 2007, and *Longford*, which focussed on the campaign for Hindley's parole, won an award for Best Actor in the same year.

In September 2009, Glasgow-born Brady asked to be returned to Scotland, to be allowed to die, and in August 2010 he made a request that there should be a public decision on where he is imprisoned. In December 2011, Brady won his right for that public mental health tribunal which has been scheduled for July 2012.

Paul Bernardo
A.K.A. The Scarborough Rapist, The Ken and Barbie Killers
COUNTRY Canada
VICTIMS 3
METHOD strangled
MUTILATION dismembered

Karla Homolka

A.K.A. The Ken and Barbie Killers
COUNTRY Canada
VICTIMS 3
METHOD strangled

In 1995, Karla Homolka entered a plea bargain accusing her husband Paul Bernardo of physical abuse and forcing her to participate in the murders of three teenage girls supplied for his sexual gratification. In an attempt to appease his sexual demands, she even lured her younger sister for him, earning her the title "Canada's Most Evil Woman". Meanwhile, Bernardo accused her of the killings. Homolka received a reduced sentence of 12 years for manslaughter while Bernardo was convicted of two first-degree murders and sentenced to life in prison without parole, which he is serving at Kingston Penitentiary. Video tapes that the couple recorded of them sexually abusing and murdering their victims would later cause a public outcry in Canada, when it identified Homolka as a far more willing and active participant than she had claimed. As of October 2011, she is currently settled in Montreal, and is married, with three children.

Robert Black

A.K.A. M1 Maniac
COUNTRY Scotland
VICTIMS 16
METHOD strangled

There are Freudian hypotheses why Robert Black turned out to be a serial killer. Certainly there were plenty of clues. The broken home in Grangemouth and going to live with foster parents and then a string of children's homes around Falkirk from an early age, the taunting at school of "Smelly Robby Tulip", the fascination with other children's genitalia, and the sexual experimentation that involved forcing various objects into his anus: a wine bottle, telephone or table leg.

There was also a long history of offences for which he was only mildly punished. Black first attempted rape aged 12, with a group of other boys, but failed to penetrate the girl. When he was 15 years old he found a job as a delivery boy, which gave him an opportunity to circulate between the houses in Greenock. He would later confess that this allowed him to molest between 30 and 40 girls.

When 17 years old, he was arrested for the attempted strangulation of a 7-year-old girl, onto whom he masturbated while she was unconscious. He received a warning from the police. When 19 years old Black molested his landlord's 9-year-old granddaughter in Grangemouth – he was only evicted. He was finally sent to borstal for a year at Polmont, when it was found out that he had been sexually abusing another landlord's 7-year-old daughter in Kinlochleven.

Moving to London, Black found work as a swimming pool attendant, but used his position to spy on girls from service points under the water. At night he would break in and swim lengths, a broom handle inserted into his anus. However, his assaults reduced at this time because he had discovered child pornography. When he was accused of molesting a girl at the pool in 1976, no official complaint was raised, but he was fired, and turned to van driving instead.

While on the road, Black would use the back of his van to masturbate in while thinking of young girls, dressing in girls' clothes, especially swimming costumes, and inserting objects up his anus. Black had never forgotten the sexual release he had discovered when he had tried strangling that 7-year-old girl.

In August 1981, Black abducted 9-year-old Jennifer Cardy in Ballinderry, County Antrim in Northern Ireland as she cycled to meet a friend. Her body was found six days later. She had been sexually abused. In July 1982, he raped and strangled 11-year-old Susan Maxwell in Cornhill-on-Tweed. Her body was found 250 miles away near Uttoxeter in Staffordshire. In July 1983, 5-year-old Caroline Hogg disappeared from Portobello, a seaside suburb of Edinburgh. She had popped outside to play for a few minutes but her body turned up 10 days later in a ditch 300 miles away in Leicestershire.

By the next abduction in March 1986, the press were already calling the three previous killings the worst since the Moors Murders. Then 10-year-old Sarah Harper failed to return home from buying a loaf of bread at the corner shop in Morley, Leeds. Her body was found a month later in the River Trent near Nottingham. The pathologist reported that the girl's assailant had, "violently explored both her vagina and her anus".

In July 1990, Black was thwarted making his escape with a 6-year-old girl. The police were alerted and gave chase after his van. The girl was recovered but only after Black had bound and gagged her with tape, and stuffed her head first into a sleeping bag. She had already been sexually assaulted. In May 1994, he was convicted of three counts of murder and sentenced to a minimum life sentence of 35 years.

In October 2011 Black was further convicted of Cardy's murder and sentenced to another 25 years. He will not qualify for release until he is 89 years old. However, the list of unsolved disappearances and murders of young girls is tragically long, and there are several more deaths for which Black is under suspicion:

ROBERT Black is suspected of killing at least 12 more young girls in the UK and Europe before his capture in 1990.

He was linked to the disappearance of newspaper delivery girl Genette Tate, 13, from Aylesbeare, Devon, in 1978.

Detectives quizzed him about Genette in 2005 but he said nothing and lack of evidence meant he was not prosecuted.

Genette's father John Tate, now 69 and suffering from prostate cancer, wants a face-to-face meeting with Black to persuade him to confess.

He said: "If he told us where she was it would be a tremendous weight off my shoulders, but it would break my heart to know what she had been through."

Black is also a prime suspect in the disappearance of April Fabb, 13, from Metton, Norfolk, in 1969.

She was cycling to give her brother-in-law a birthday present. He has long been suspected of abducting Christine Markham, nine, from Scunthorpe, Lincs, in 1973 on her way to school. The case bears all the hallmarks of the four murders for which Black has already been convicted.

Among other potential victims are Suzanne Lawrence, 14, who vanished after leaving her sister's home in Harold Hill, Essex, in 1979.

The killing of Virginie Delmas, 10, whose body was found in an orchard in south-east Paris in May 1987, has been linked to Black. He may have been on holiday or working nearby at the time.

Perrine Vigneron, a seven-year-old French girl was abducted while out buying a Mother's Day card in June 1987. It is believed Black was still in the area.

Daily Mirror, 28th October 2011

Dennis Rader
A.K.A. BTK (Bind them, Torture them, Kill them)
COUNTRY USA
VICTIMS 10+
METHOD strangled, shot, stabbed

Dennis Rader held onto yearnings for bondage and torture into adulthood.

The target of his make-believe was no longer the effervescent, toothful Mouseketeer Club girls that filled his boyhood fantasies, but real girls, real women. He had acted out his intentions by torturing cats and dogs, but now he wanted to know what it was like strangling an actual person to death, and he had a new manifesto fit for purpose, "Bind them, torture them, kill them."

A young Hispanic family had moved in nearby. They would be his first targets. Before work one morning in January 1974, and at gunpoint, Rader bound the husband and wife, and their 9-year-old son and 11-year-old daughter. He killed the husband by putting a bag over his head and strangling him, but had more difficulty strangling the woman; it took two attempts before she was also dead. The boy also took longer than expected to die, in the end requiring to be strangled and smothered. His last moments were protracted enough for Rader to fetch a chair so that he could watch in comfort.

The girl also would not die while being strangled, passing out then regaining consciousness. Rader forced her into the basement where he hanged her from a sewer pipe. Rader partially stripped the suspended body and masturbated onto her bare legs. Unknown to him, three older children would return from their day at school to find their family massacred.

During infrequent bouts over the next 17 years, Rader stalked and killed a further six women, aged from 21 to 62 years. He also actively courted the newspapers, trying to generate some notoriety, and lobbying them to assign him a nickname. His preferred one was the "B.T.K. Strangler".

His last package to the press included a computer disk, from which the police were able to extract hidden digital information that led them to the church where Rader was president of the congregation council. DNA checks linked him to the semen left at his crime scenes. Rader was found guilty of 10 murders and sentenced to 10 life terms in August 2005.

Jack Unterweger
A.K.A. The Poet of Death
COUNTRIES Austria, USA, Czechoslovakia
VICTIMS 11
METHOD strangled

Unlike Dennis Rader, Jack Unterweger didn't have to go looking for fame. It found him, without him having to resort to attention-seeking pranks. While serving his sentence for murdering a prostitute by strangulation with her own brassiere, Unterweger wrote stories, plays and poems. His autobiography *Fegefeuer – eine Reise ins Zuchthaus* or *Purgatory – A Trip to Prison* was a best-seller and was made into a film.

Life imprisonment holds a maximum of 25 years in Austria, with the possibility of parole after 15. By the time he was up for parole in 1990, Unterweger's fans, including Austrian intellectuals and a future Nobel Prize winner had campaigned successfully for his release. He was lauded as an example of the prison rehabilitation programme and was soon a sought after journalist, TV host and minor celebrity.

It would later emerge that Unterweger in fact murdered six prostitutes within the first year after release, and when he was sent to Los Angeles to write articles about crime and attitudes to prostitution, he probably murdered three more. Their deaths showed the signs consistent with his other killings, where the women were beaten and sexually assaulted with tree branches, and strangled with their own brassieres.

An international chase through Europe, Canada and the USA concluded with Unterweger being arrested in Miami in February 1992. He was extradited back to Austria and charged with 11 murders, eventually found guilty of nine in June 1994, and again received a life sentence, but this time without possibility of parole. That night Unterweger hanged himself in his cell, with a noose of shoelaces and a trouser drawstring. He used the same characteristic knot with which he had strangled his victims.

Gary Leon Ridgway
A.K.A. The Green River Killer
COUNTRY USA
VICTIMS 70+
METHOD strangled, stabbed, suffocated

Gary Ridgway confessed to murdering over 70 women, mainly prostitutes, between 1982 and 1998. He preferred to strangle the women with his bare hands until the scratch wounds inflicted by his struggling victims forced him to use a cord. The naked bodies were typically dumped in woodland along the Green River in Washington State, where he would return to have sex with the corpses. The bodies were sometimes in clustered groups, and often posed. Two had small stones inserted into their vaginas.

Ridgway tried to confuse the police by moving bodies, and contaminating his own crime scenes with other people's waste such as cigarette butts, chewing gum and scribbled notes. The police sought help in their investigation from Ted Bundy, which resulted in more confessions of his own crimes but no insight into Ridgway's.

Ridgway evaded capture despite being held under suspicion of the murders on several separate occasions. DNA evidence from his semen finally led to his conviction for 48 murders and he was sentenced to life for each, plus a further 480 years were added for tampering with evidence.

Steven Gerald James Wright
A.K.A. The Ipswich Strangler, The Suffolk Strangler
COUNTRY England
VICTIMS 5
METHOD strangled

In November 2006, police in Suffolk became concerned over the disappearance of two women, 25-year-old Gemma Adams and 19-year-old Tania Nicol, both prostitutes working in the same red light area of Ipswich. By December, they knew what had happened to them:

> DIVERS yesterday found the body of a woman believed to be missing prostitute Tania Nicol in a brook where another murdered vice girl was discovered last week.
>
> Police fear the same killer may have carried out the "obviously similar" murders and may strike again.
>
> Tania, 19, went missing on October 31 while selling sex in the red light area of Ipswich near the town's Portman Road football ground. She was found in Belstead Brook at Copdock Mill.
>
> The naked body of her friend Gemma Adams, 25, was found a mile away in the same brook last Saturday.
>
> Gemma disappeared on November 15 from the same red light area. Police now believe they have found the Nike shoes she was wearing that night and are doing tests. Her clothes are missing. Since 1992 four vice girls have vanished in Suffolk and Norfolk.
>
> Two have been found strangled.
>
> *Daily Mirror*, 9th December 2006

In the following few days two more missing people were reported, 24-year-old Paula Clennell and 29-year-old Annette Nicholls, and three more bodies were found. Two of the bodies turned out to be Clennell and Nicholls; the third body was believed to be 24-year-old Anneli Alderton. Both Nicholls and Alderton had been put in crucifix poses, but none of the victims had been sexually assaulted. Within a week, two suspects were in custody. The first would be released, but the second was Wright.

> RIPPER suspect Steve Wright was a cross-dresser who wore high heels, a PVC skirt and a wig when meeting prostitutes, it was

claimed yesterday.

Forklift truck driver Wright used to run the Ferry Boat Inn in the heart of Norwich's red light area – a favourite haunt of sex workers.

But though he left in 1988, he is remembered by girls who worked the streets from 1996.

Prostitute Tina, 45, claimed Wright, 48, visited the city once or twice a week looking for sex but insisted she never got into a car with him.

She said: "He wore a wig. When he got out of the car he had a PVC skirt and high heels".

Daily Mirror, 21st December 2006

Wright stood trial in January 2008, charged with all five murders. At the centre of the case for prosecution was presentation of DNA evidence. Blood from two of the victims was found on Wright's jacket, and further victim's DNA was on a pair of gardening gloves found in his car. Fibres from clothing and car upholstery also contributed towards incriminating Wright. Additionally, there was circumstantial evidence, such as a witness to Wright washing his car in the middle of the night, and semen found on the jacket and gloves, suggestive of them having been used while moving the bodies. In contrast, the defence seemed to rely predominantly upon coincidence:

In two hours of highly-charged crossexamination, Wright's response to any question fired at him was "It would seem so yes", "It would appear so yes" or "If you say so, yes". He claims the evidence against him was pure coincidence. But Mr [Peter] Wright [QC] said: "The fact is there are no coincidences in this case, are there Mr Wright? The fact is that you murdered each of these women." He replied: "No I did not." The prosecutor continued with his barrage of questions by asking the accused: "There are a number of coincidences in this case aren't there Mr Wright?"

SW: "If you say so."

PW: "Let's consider a few shall we? You selected five women from the street of Ipswich amongst others and each of them died. Is that a coincidence?"

SW: "It would seem so, yes."

PW: "You selected five women from the streets of Ipswich and on your own account they all died very shortly after they left your company. Is that a coincidence?"

SW: "It would seem so, yes."

PW: "I am asking you, is it by coincidence or by design?"

SW: "I would say it's coincidence."

PW: "You selected five women in the order in which they died. Is that coincidence?"

SW: "It would seem so, yes."

PW: "Because you selected firstly Tania Nicol, then Gemma Adams, then Anneli Alderton, then Annette Nicholls, then Paula Clennell among others. Not only did you select the same five that met their death but you selected them in the same order in which they died. Mr Wright, is that coincidence?"

SW: "It would seem so, yes."

PW: "It would appear in so far as you pick up prostitutes in the street of Ipswich you have been singularly unfortunate."

SW: "It would seem so, yes."

Daily Mirror, 9th February 2008

In late February 2008, Wright was found guilty of all charges and given a life sentence with a whole life tariff. Wright's responses might be comical if they weren't part of a trial for serial murders. Indeed, the tastefulness of developing any entertainment from such cases is an ethical minefield.

Five Daughters, a three-part drama serial about the murders received criticism for being shown too soon, when it was broadcast in April 2010. The executive producer defended their decision to make the programme saying, "Part of the reason the families wanted to be involved was to reclaim who their daughters were and put their real personalities in the public domain. At the time they were just referred to as prostitutes, it was absolutely shocking. I think that's what this is all about", whilst a victim's family member said, "We as a family want people to know that women who work on the streets do not choose this, but are forced to do so due to crippling drug habits."

Media coverage has changed dramatically in the last decade. Rolling news and constantly broadcast news channels, updated websites and Twitter timelines all deliver around the clock. But, while modes of delivery may evolve, sensationalizing the news hasn't changed in over a century since yellow journalism was introduced, and stories about sex and perversity will always sell, however tragic the circumstances. The case of Steven Wright was no exception. How the media had portrayed the victims highlighted the ongoing attitude towards prostitutes and drug addicts. Furthermore, as early as December 2006, the media were given guidance so as not to prejudice any future trial.

The intention of making a drama that rebalances those stereotypes does not necessarily exonerate programme makers. In the USA, the Son of Sam Law, introduced following the case of David Berkowitz, protects against convicts profiting from their crimes. In the UK, the 2002 Proceeds of Crime Act covers confiscation of stolen property, but does not presently include memoirs and anecdotal accounts of crime. It is assumed that profiting from crimes by people not directly involved such as authors, screenwriters, actors, producers and so on, is not unethical or insensitive. But, if families do not opt into the process of developing that material, when can it ever be safe to make that assumption?

Subsequently, the National Theatre came under fire in January 2011 when it announced a musical was to be staged, based on interviews held with the community affected by the murders. A spokeswoman quickly went public acknowledging that billing the show as "a musical" was a bad idea, "We're not going to call it a musical in future because we recognise it gives a misleading impression; the music will do something very different by reflecting the voices of the interviewees."

Jeffrey Dahmer
COUNTRY USA
VICTIMS 17
METHOD strangled
MUTILATION dismembered, vampirism, cannibalism

Jeffrey Dahmer first killed shortly after his 18th birthday, when he picked up a hitchhiker and took him back to his father's empty house. Displaying parallels with Dennis Nilsen, Dahmer resisted his guest's attempts to leave. He didn't want to be alone, and wanted to have sex. The young man was beaten around the head and buried in the backyard.

It wasn't until nine years later that Dahmer started killing frequently, once in 1987, twice in 1988, and once in 1989. Each time, the victim would be approached in a gay bar, taken home for sex, then killed. As he was living with his grandmother at the time his opportunities were not as frequent as when he moved into his own apartment at 213, 924 North 25th Street, Milwaukee. There Dahmer murdered four times in 1990. By mid-1991, he was killing weekly.

Dahmer had a close call in May 1991 when a 14-year-old he had captured but left alone in the apartment, escaped and made his way unsteadily into the street. The boy was delirious and nonsensical, and couldn't make himself understood to two women who were trying to help. Dahmer stumbled across the trio on his way home and, alarmed to see his captive free, fabricated a cover story. The police showed up shortly afterwards, and chose to believe Dahmer's tale of a lover's tiff, despite the women's protestations, plus clear signs of injury, such as bleeding from the boy's anus.

Escorting them back to Dahmer's apartment, the police noticed a strange smell, but did not think to investigate further. The smell was Dahmer's previous victim decomposing in the bedroom. The boy soon joined him, Dahmer keeping his skull as a souvenir. It would be this penchant for keepsakes that would be his undoing.

When Dahmer made his final attempt at capture, the man managed to fight his way out of the apartment and flag down a police car. He returned with the officers and showed them the gallery of photographs of dismembered victims Dahmer had created in his bedroom. The smell of decomposition was also noxious.

Searching the apartment, the police discovered more photographs of body parts, four heads, one in the fridge along with other remains, a heart in the freezer, and various hands and penises. The smell was found to be coming from flesh dissolving in a large vat of acid. Clearly Dahmer had an interest in necrophilia and cannibalism.

In 1992, Dahmer pleaded insane, but was found sane and guilty of 15 murders. He was sentenced to 15 life terms, adding up to 957 years in prison. During his incarceration at the Columbia Correctional Institution in Portage, Wisconsin, other inmates tried to kill Dahmer on two occasions. In November 1994 they succeeded, when he died from head injuries after being bludgeoned with a broom handle.

In the year of his son's death, Dahmer's father published *A Father's Story*, donating some of the book's proceeds to the victims' families. In 2007, the investigation of the murder of a 6-year-old boy was reopened to look at new evidence implicating Dahmer. However, this was rejected and the original confession by Otis Toole was reinstated. In July 2011, the man who had so narrowly escaped death to bring about Dahmer's arrest, was himself charged with murder, and is being held in custody. His trial was originally scheduled for January 2012.

SMOTHERERS

You love me so much, you want to put me in your pocket
And I should die there smothered
D H Lawrence

Asphyxiation comes from Ancient Greek words for "without" and "heartbeat", while one form of smothering that also compresses the torso to inhibit breathing, is called "burking" after the method used by William Burke and William Hare to kill their Edinburgh victims. Smothering, whether it be by suffocation with a pillow, or forcing the victim's head under water, is a way that the more reluctant serial killer might dissociate themselves from facing their victims' final moments. On the other hand, rupturing your victim's trachea is a far more aggressive way to the same end, and equally fatal.

Dennis Andrew Nilsen
A.K.A. The Muswell Hill Murderer, The Kindly Killer,
The British Jeffrey Dahmer
COUNTRY England
VICTIMS 16
METHOD strangled, drowned
MUTILATION dismembered, cannibalism

He is so beautiful now, his skin like moonlight in water. A porcelain complexion. You must now see why I could not let him go, why he had to stay with me. I have made him beautiful, and he thanks me with his undying, no, ha! Sorry. His loyal company. He is always there for me, when I get home from work, when we sit and watch TV together, when we make love. Good sex too. We never argue. He makes me whole and will always be there for me. Well, until he starts to go off! Then I'll have to deal with him like the others. Strip down to my underpants, get horrendously pissed and set to work with my electric carving knife. It used to be my job, so I know what I'm doing.

Dennis Nilsen came from a broken home, which had been split up by his father's drinking and protracted absences. His grandfather was the closest thing he had to a father figure, and they were very close. Nilsen was therefore devastated when his grandfather died, especially as the way he found out was by his mother taking him to see the dead man's corpse. Next, it would be Nilsen's turn to be corpse-like. Aged 8, he was rescued from drowning in the sea by a boy who had been playing on the beach. Nilsen awoke to find his saviour had ejaculated onto his stomach.

In 1961, Nilsen joined the Army as a cook. Butchery skills were part of his training. His kitchen duties put a distance between him and the majority of men training for combat, so he didn't feel part of their camaraderie. Drink was his answer, and fantasizing that the naked body he saw in the mirror whilst lying on the floor so that he couldn't see his face, was actually a real corpse. This aroused him and he masturbated to the vision. He turned director and cameraman when he befriended a squaddie and got him to act out his morbid fantasies.

In 1972, Nilsen joined the police force, but left after a year, although he was fascinated by the morgue visits to see autopsies. His permanent job after that was as a civil servant in a jobcentre in London's Kentish Town. He continued to fantasize about the body in the mirror, adding make-up to create a murder victim.

In 1975, Nilsen moved to 195 Melrose Avenue in London, where he killed a dozen young men, mostly homeless and therefore hard to identify. His only company was his dog "Blip", and he was drinking a lot again. He would meet someone in his local pub, they would get talking and he would take them home. After more drink, they would go to bed and have sex. Nilsen's panic about his partner leaving and his being alone again would then put him into what he called his "killer trance". Only if he snapped out of it would that man survive. Otherwise he would be strangled with a tie or cable. This wouldn't always kill the victim, so Nilsen would finish them off by holding their head in a bucket of water, watching for the trickle of bubbles to vanish.

Nilsen would clean the bodies and place them in his bed. Sometimes he would lie under them, using their thighs to masturbate between. Other times he would straddle them and ejaculate onto their stomachs. He relished the control he had over their lifeless forms and might keep a body for sex for a week. He would also leave his current "friend" sitting in a chair, awaiting his return from work.

When he wanted to conceal a body, at first he stored it in a cupboard or beneath his floorboards. If he was lonely, he would take one out, to sit with while watching TV, dressing him for bed and kissing him "goodnight". However, he was running out of excuses about the smell to tell the neighbours. Disposing of the bodies was also a logistical problem and they were accumulating:

In the end there were two or three bodies under the floorboards. I knew that come the summer it would get hot and there would be a smell problem. [...]

I thought about what would cause it and came to the conclusion it would be the innards, the softer parts of the body, the organs.

So on a weekend, I would pull up the floorboards, I felt it terribly unpleasant and would get blindingly drunk so I could face it.

I started the dissection on the kitchen floor and would go and be sick outside in the garden.

It didn't leave a mess. If I stabbed you now with your heart pumping blood would be spurting all over the place.

But with a dead body, there is no splashing at all. The blood congeals and becomes part of the flesh. It is like a butcher's shop.

I would slit plastic bags like a bin liner, haul the body on to the sheet and cut it up.

Daily Mirror, 27th January 1993

A large pot was used to boil heads and more bin liners held body parts in cupboards and back under the floorboards. Suitcases were sometimes used, and he also secreted bags outside, in the garden shed, a hole in the ground or shoved down between two fences. When possible he would burn as many of the remains as he could without attracting too much attention from the local children playing in the streets. Ashes and bone fragments were raked into the soil. It was a job keeping track of all his stashes. When he left the house for the last time, he nearly left hands and an arm under a bush.

Nilsen moved to an attic flat at 23 Cranley Gardens in Muswell Hill in October 1981, hoping the proximity of his neighbours and being at the top of the house would limit his killing. Despite the arrangements, three more murders were carried out. His last murder was when he killed a heroin addict. He saw his actions as an act of benevolence, saving the man from further suffering. He bathed the body and placed him in bed, flanked by two mirrors. He could see their naked bodies lying in union.

With no garden at his disposal, Nilsen boiled the heads, hands and feet, and dissected the rest of the bodies into small pieces. Bones were either stored in a tea chest, put in the rubbish or dumped nearby. Fleshy bits were flushed down the toilet. It took only a few days for the drains to become blocked and Dyno Rod to be called out in February 1983. At work the next day, Nilsen joked, "If I'm not in tomorrow, I'll either be ill, dead, or in jail."

The engineer went down the manhole and found 30 or 40 pieces of flesh.

Police saw Nilsen the next day. Detective Chief Inspector Peter Jay told him: "I've come about your drains."

Nilsen replied: "Since when have police been interested in blocked drains?"

Chief Inspector Jay said the drains had become blocked with human flesh.

Nilsen exclaimed: "Oh good grief, how awful."

The officers then asked where the bodies were and Nilsen replied: "In two plastic bags in the wardrobe next door."

Nilsen agreed to "cooperate fully."

In the car on the way to the police station he was asked: "Are you talking about one body or two?"

He allegedly replied: "Sixteen. I will tell you everything."

Daily Mirror, 25th October 1983

Nilsen would be held on remand until his former residences could be forensically examined. In March 1983, Battersea Dogs Home reported that Blip had pined away and died after being separated for a month from his master. In accounting for his actions, Nilsen would later write cryptic letters, quoting from Oscar Wilde's *Ballad of Reading Gaol*, to Detective Chief Inspector Jay, which would later be read out in court:

> *I think I have sufficient principle and morality to know where the buck must come to rest. The evil was short-lived and cannot live for long outside. Now I have slain my own dragon as surely as the Press will slay me. We are all lying in the gutter – but some of us are winking at the stars. [...] I guess that I may be a creative psychopath who when in a loss of rationality situation lapses temporarily into a destructive psychopath, a condition induced by rapid and heavy ingestion of alcohol. [...] There is no disputing that I am a violent killer under certain circumstances. The victim is the dirty platter after the feast and the washing up is a clinically ordinary task.*

Nilsen was convicted of six murders and two attempted murders in November 1983, and sentenced to life imprisonment at HMP Full Sutton, later adjusted to a whole life tariff. In 2001 he was refused access to gay pornography, and in 2003 forbidden to publish his autobiography, *The History of a Drowning Boy*. He awaits an appeal decision by the European Court of Human Rights. Future parole requests were denied as of 2006.

In 2005, excerpts from Nilsen's letters to an ex-Army colleague were published, giving some insight into his prison life, when not reading or doing his job of translating books into Braille for the prison library:

> "Quite a few of us get pissed with liver crippling draughts of prison hooch, that last vestige of herbal medicine still available to cons."

But Nilsen prefers smoking drugs to boozing. He says: "The devil makes work for idle thirsts. But given the choice between booze and cannabis, I go for ganja every time." A few days ago a package containing a couple of mobile phones and some drugs was thrown over the wall here into the sports field.

The killer also mocks the authorities' attempts to shut down the illicit breweries.

> "The hooch brewers never give up," he writes. "As soon as one cache is discovered by the screws another is already on the brew.

> "As for the ganja smokers – well, apparently, there's no business like blow business."

Daily Mirror, 27th August 2005

Fritz Haarmann

A.K.A. The Butcher of Hanover, The Vampire of Hanover
COUNTRY Germany
VICTIMS 70
METHOD suffocated
MUTILATION bitten, dismembered, cannibalism

Under interrogation Fritz Haarmann confessed to killing between 50 and 70 young men between 1918 and 1924. Picking them up from Hanover's central station, he would take them home, then kill them by biting through their throats as he buggered them. Haarmann then dismembered the victims and dumped the body parts in the nearby Leine River.

Victims' possessions were either kept as souvenirs, given to his young boyfriend or sold. Victims' flesh was probably sold on the black market. Haarmann was convicted of 24 murders in December 1924, sentenced to death, and beheaded by guillotine in April 1925. The case was particularly embarrassing to the police as even though Haarmann was a known petty thief and con man with a history of mental illness, he was also a police informant and was well known to them. As with Edmund Kemper, he had been talking with policemen during the hunt for the killer.

Fritz Lang based his 1931 classic film *M* on Haarmann's story, combined with those of Peter Kürten and Carl Großmann. More directly inspired by Haarmann's crimes was the 1973 *Die Zärtlichkeit der Wölfe* or *The Tenderness of the Wolves*, while *Der Totmacher* or *The Deathmaker* focussed more on his psychology.

Serhiy Tkach
A.K.A. The Pologovsky Maniac
COUNTRY Ukraine
VICTIMS 100
METHOD suffocated

Both Edmund Kemper and Fritz Haarmann fraternized with the investigators working on their cases while they were carrying out their killings. Another embarrassing case for the police was that of Ukrainian police investigator Serhiy Tkach who, until he was stopped in 2005, suffocated his female victims, aged between 8 and 18, although the exact ages and number are unknown. Tkach confessed to murdering between 80 and 100 victims, with at least 29 over a two-year period, and committing necrophilia with each. He was sentenced to life in prison for the rape and murder of 36 women. Tkach had been so skilful applying his police knowledge in covering up his crimes that nine others had been wrongly jailed for his crimes, one having committed suicide.

Donald Henry Gaskins, Jr
A.K.A. Pee Wee, Meanest Man in America
COUNTRY USA
VICTIMS 110
METHOD suffocated, stabbed

Donald Gaskins committed his first murder in 1953 whilst in prison, by slashing the throat of a fellow inmate to impress the other prisoners. Three years were added to his original sentence of six years, which had been awarded for the attempted murder of a teenage girl with a hammer, because she had insulted him. He escaped in 1955 in the back of a rubbish truck, was rearrested, and then paroled in 1961. Two years later he was arrested again, for raping a 12-year-old girl. He again escaped custody, and again was recaptured and sentenced to eight years' imprisonment. He was released in 1968.

In September 1969, Gaskins began killing hitchhikers, on average a victim every six weeks, whom he picked up while driving around the coast roads of southern USA. He dubbed these victims "Coastal Kills", but killing wasn't his foremost priority. For fun, he tried to keep them alive for as long as possible while he tortured and mutilated them, before suffocating or stabbing them to death. He confessed to between 80 and 90 of these murders, and to eating some of his victims.

In November 1970, Gaskins moved on to what he termed his "Serious Murders". These victims were not strangers, but people he knew and had motivation to kill. This time it was personal, and he was out to avenge mockery, insults, debt, blackmail and theft. He also accepted commissions to kill.

Gaskins was arrested in November 1975 when an associate betrayed him to the police. In May 1976, he was convicted of eight murders, the number of bodies that he had led them to, and sentenced to death, which was later commuted to life in prison.

In September 1982, Gaskins again killed another inmate. He had been paid to do so by the son of the couple the convict had killed during a bungled armed robbery of their store. Unable to access his target successfully with poison, Gaskins gave the prisoner a portable radio, telling him it would work as an intercom. Making sure the prisoner was holding the radio to his ear at the arranged time Gaskins detonated the explosives it was packed with, killing him instantly. This act earned Gaskins the title, "Meanest Man in America" and the death sentence. He was executed in September 1991.

Frederick West
COUNTRY England
VICTIMS 12
METHOD suffocated
MUTILATION dismembered

Rosemary West
COUNTRY England
VICTIMS 10
METHOD suffocated

Everyone knows what happened at 25 Cromwell Street in Gloucester. It's one of those addresses burnt into our memories, along with 195 Melrose Avenue, 8213 West Summerdale Avenue, Apartment 213, 924 North 25th Street, Milwaukee and 10 Rillington Place. And now there was the Cromwell Street "House of Horror" and its "Garden of Evil":

GARDEN OF EVIL

A sheet of yellow canvas hides a terrible secret of 25 Cromwell Street

FROM the air, only a sheet of police yellow tarpaulin identifies No 25 Cromwell Street as somewhere out of the ordinary.

From the ground, a 5ft 5in policewoman is the only outward sign that something is wrong behind the varnished front door adorned with a good-luck horseshoe.

The gruesome graveyard of three murder victims could be Any Street, Anytown.

The well-kept house at No 25, near the flowering cherry-blossom trees in the heart of Gloucester looks just like the others.

It stands next to the Seventh Day Adventist church on one side and a row of identical terraces on the other.

Most of the Victorian houses have been converted into flats, or bed and breakfast accommodation.

The local population is fast changing.

But the West family had lived there more than most – 20 years.

As a mark of respect to the victims yesterday, one caring neighbour had placed a bouquet of pink carnations on the doorstep.

Others stood outside shocked in disbelief as news reached them that bodies had been found in the once-neat back garden.

One young woman, who would not give her name, had known Heather when she baby-sat for the family about 20 years ago.

The 33-year-old said: "I used to go there when I was 16 to look after the children.

"It makes me shudder now to think about it.

"Looking back there were always a lot of comings and goings late at night."

A mother of four told how one of her daughters used to play with the West's children in £38,000 house.

"She used to come home and tell me about playing in their garden and how they had a cellar with a trap door covered by a carpet," the mother said.

Shopkeeper Imtiaz Kholwadia said: "The family were regular customers – the woman used to come in with six or seven children around her.

"The boys did not play out so much and when we kicked a ball in the park they did not join in."

The brickwork of the house was recently rendered by builder

Mr West, who also built an extension in the back garden.

Police are now considering knocking it down to search through the foundations.

Neighbour Joe Hefferan, 67, said he had known the West family since they moved in. He said Mr West had a previous marriage.

"They were a lovely family," Joe said.

[...]

Daily Mirror, 2nd March 1994

Frederick Walter Stephen West was the second of six children born to a poor family of farm workers. His father welcomed incest and bestiality, saying "Do what you want, just don't get caught doing it." A motorbike accident when he was 15 years old fractured Fred's skull and produced violent mood swings in his personality. He injured his head severely again two years later. At 19 years old West narrowly escaped conviction for the sexual assault of a 13-year-old girl.

West married ex-prostitute Catherine "Rena" Costello in November 1962. She was already pregnant by another man, and Charmaine Carol was born in February 1963. In July 1964 the couple had their own child, Anne Marie. In November 1965, West accidently killed a 4-year-old boy whilst driving his ice-cream van.

The family, plus a friend of Costello's, Anne McFall, and a nanny, Isa McNeill, all shared accommodation until West's sadistic sexual demands drove away Costello and McNeill, who left for Scotland in 1966. McFall stayed, but disappeared when eight months' pregnant with West's child. In September 1967, Costello returned for a short time. When she moved out again, she left the children behind.

Rosemary Pauline West, née Letts, came from a broken home. Living with her mother until she was 15 years old, she then moved in with her father, who proceeded to sexually abuse her. She met West and moved in with him shortly afterwards, on her 16th birthday. A few months later they moved to Midland Road in Gloucester where they had their first child, Heather Ann, in October 1970.

While Fred West was serving a seven-month term in prison for theft, Rose Letts killed Charmaine in June 1971, because she never cried in pain like the other children when Letts beat her. West was told Costello had collected Charmaine and taken her back to Scotland. When Costello did turn up to collect her child in August 1971, she also disappeared. The remains of McFall and Costello would be found in a field over two decades later in 1994.

In January 1972, Fred West and Rose Letts married, even though

West was still married to Costello. In June, their second daughter, Mae, was born. Needing a larger home, they moved to 25 Cromwell Street. West converted the upstairs into bedsits, and adapted one bedroom, appointed with red light, so that it could be used by Rose for prostitution, while he watched via peepholes. West also welcomed her father's visits for sex with Rose. Out of a total of seven children, she gave birth to three of mixed race.

In December 1972, 17-year-old Caroline Roberts was taken to the house and sexually assaulted by both Fred and Rose West. Roberts had already worked for the couple as a nanny but left after rejecting their sexual advances. This time she had to comply to their rape on threat of being smothered with a pillow. Promising to return as their nanny, she actually reported them to the police, but later dropped her rape charges. The Wests were fined 50 pounds for indecent assault. In 1973, West started raping the 8-year-old Anne Marie.

Up until 1979, when Anne Marie left to escape the sexual abuse, eight young female lodgers, travelling students and abducted girls, were murdered by the Wests. The cellar was converted to house their victims, who would be kept alive for up to a week while they were needed. One victim's head was bound entirely with tape, leaving only enough room for a breathing tube. One of the students was Martin Amis' cousin. Simultaneously to the abductions, the West's children were also being sexually abused. When Anne Marie left home to escape the abuse, West turned his attentions to Heather.

There were no known murders until June 1987 when Heather complained about the ongoing abuse at school. West killed her to remove the risk of being discovered, while Rose watched. He closed Heather's eyes before he dismembered her – "If somebody's sat there looking at you, you're not going to use a knife on that person are you?" –

and would later recall that when he cut off her head, it made a "horrible noise ... like scrunching"; her legs he twisted by the feet until there was, "one almighty crack and the leg come loose".

Heather's four body parts were buried under a patio in a hole dug unwittingly by their son Stephen. Ironically, these would be the first remains found when police followed up the reports of abuse, passed on by the mother of Heather's school friend. Two other victims were found in the garden and six more buried in the cellar, by then a children's playroom.

The police also discovered a large amount of mostly violent pornography, as well as bestiality films, including *Kilroy Was Here*, "a videotape of a young woman, drugged and bound, whose captors inserted a clear plastic tube into her vagina, through which they encouraged two live mice to enter her one after the other", and other tapes showing, "women being abused by animals, including both an Alsatian dog and a boar pig". At one point during the 1980s West had seven video recorders on which he duplicated films for sale to colleagues and for under-the-counter purchases in video rental shops.

Police also found a video camera that had been used to film the victims' abuse and torture. West knew about snuff films, and it has been suggested that he would have known of their commercial potential, and would have had the opportunity, equipment and motivation to produce them.

In February 1994 the Wests were arrested and in June Fred West was charged with 11 murders, a number that was adjusted to 12 with the discovery of McFall. Rose West was charged with 10 murders. When serial killer couples are arrested, suddenly the secret bond that they shared is removed. The killing stops and their clandestine adventures are exposed for the world to judge. With this loss and the stress of interrogation, survival instincts often forces one of the partners into confession, naming their other half as the real guilty party.

In most instances, it is usually the female partner who has either ended the killing, as in the case of David Birnie and Catherine Harrison, or who has accused the man of being the murderer, as with Ian Brady and Myra Hindley, and Paul Bernardo and Karla Homolka. However, in an unusual move, Fred West initially claimed Rose's innocence during questioning, but, when spurned by her, accused his wife of killing their victims, because of "mistakes during sex romps", saying that they had agreed in a pact that he would take the blame for everything.

Before he could stand trial, West hanged himself at Birmingham's Winson Green Prison in January 1995. A couple of months later Martin Amis' novel *The Information* was published, dedicated to his murdered cousin. In October 1995 Rose West was found guilty of all 10 murders and sentenced to life imprisonment. This was later modified to be without the possibility of parole. She is only the second British woman to receive a whole life tariff. The other was Myra Hindley, whom Rose met in jail and with whom she became good friends. In October 2005, West was moved to HMP Bronzefield in Ashford but was moved again to Low Newton near Durham in October 2008, following threats from other inmates.

In October 1996, 25 Cromwell Street was demolished, but it didn't end the problems for the West family. One of the videos found in the house was thought to show John West, one of Fred West's brothers, raping his young niece, Anne Marie. It was called *Fuck My Uncle* and carried the tag line, "I always thought I'd have it off with my niece one day – I didn't think you were ready for it yet." In November 1996, John West hanged himself after being charged with multiple rape, and in December 2004, Stephen

West was jailed for sex with a minor.

In February 2011, the other West brother, Doug, announced his intention of publishing a book on the Cromwell Street murders, said to expose what really happened and finally put his brother on trial. Son of Sam Law-type rulings do not legislate against family profiting from their relatives' crimes, but there is an ongoing debate about the ethics of making dramatizations about serial killers.

Appropriate Adult, the made-for-TV film of the Wests during the interrogation and trial period, won an award in February 2012 despite accusations that it was "trampling on the graves" of the victims. A major criticism was the focus on Janet Leach, the volunteer social worker who acted as the "appropriate adult" in the film's title; she had been engaged to ensure that Fred West understood the proceedings during interrogation and trial. The police accused her of withholding evidence that had been confessed to her by West in confidence, in order to maintain an exclusivity deal with a national newspaper. In November 1995, West's confession to Leach was published. The revelation was that there might have been up to another 20 murders undiscovered, including children ritually killed in a barn.

"Fred would tell me these horrible things as if he was discussing the weather."

She said West boasted: "We had them there for days. We used to go round to children's homes for some of them, some were from the Hereford area.

"We would give them a good time and they all enjoyed the sex.

"We used to tie them up. They had tubes coming from their noses. Some suffocated, we did not mean to kill them but we did.

"Some were hung up like pigs and their throats were slit. There was blood everywhere.

"We used to hang them up and leave them there." [...]

Some of the girls were left hanging so long that they became "mummified."

All the victims had their fingertips cut off and burned ceremonially.

"One of the other men, he said liked the smell of burning finger nails," Janet recalled.

West told the voluntary worker that the girls were tortured even more brutally, and were sometimes kept alive longer, than the victims at 25 Cromwell Street.

Their bodies were slashed with knives, although The Cult were not involved in black magic.

Daily Mirror, 23rd November 1995

According to Leach, West also warned that this "Cult" were "still walking the streets and they'll kill again when all the fuss about this case has died down".

OTHERS

Yes, how many ears must one man have
Before he can hear people cry?
Yes, how many deaths will it take till he knows
That too many people have died?
Bob Dylan

There are two types of serial killer circulating in society. Those we know about but for some reason have not been locked away for their crimes, or are thought to have repaid their debt and have been released, and those who we know are out there killing, but haven't been caught yet. Here are a few for whom you should keep an eye out.

Several cases where, to date, no murderer has been identified have already been mentioned in this book. Jack the Ripper is the most renowned, and the case of the *maquiladora* murders of Ciudad Juárez is probably the most numerous, even though the murders are known not to have been perpetrated by any particular individual. However, over time, an alarming number of serial murders do happen without a killer being identified.

Some of these killers undeniably will have "got away with it". Perhaps they managed to change their ways and reform their characters. Perhaps they kept on the move, but the link has not been made between their murders in the different locations. Or perhaps the evidence is too weak, or has been lost in time, to bring about a conviction for murders at other locations, as in the case of Peter Tobin and Bible John. Alternatively, perhaps they were apprehended for other crimes, and lost the chance to kill in society.

Other possibilities include the killer themselves being killed. "The Lima Ripper" murdered seven women and dumped their body parts in landfills but the identity of the killer may always remain a mystery as the only suspect was strangled by the police psychologist during interrogation. What we are left with is a frightening number of unsolved serial murders each particular to their time and place and method. Here are just some, in roughly the chronological order that they occurred.

Thirty years after the Austin Axe Murderer, "The Axeman of New Orleans" hacked eight people to death in their beds, in a similar fashion, between May 1918 and October 1919.

During the mid-1930s, "The Cleveland Torso Murderer" killed and dismembered at least a dozen people in Ohio, maybe as many as 40. Victims were usually killed by beheading, then were dismembered, their torsos often bisected. Males were castrated. It was proposed that the similar mutilation in the high-profile "Black Dahlia" case placed Elizabeth Short as one of the victims, although this was in 1947, nine years after the last known Cleveland killing. Even with Eliot Ness, of The Untouchables fame, leading the investigation no one was ever held accountable. A recent re-examination of the case has suggested that there was more than one murderer.

In 1964 and 1965, the "London Nude Murders" or "Hammersmith Murders" were carried out by a mystery figure nicknamed "Jack the Stripper". The most likely suspect committed suicide; however, new evidence has thrown some doubt upon his guilt.

The most infamous unsolved serial killer case after Jack the Ripper is probably "The Zodiac Killer" who has claimed in the letters he wrote to have killed 37 victims in San Francisco from 1968 to 1973, although only seven are officially attributed to him. The notable aspect about the case are the cryptograms or codes the killer used in his letters to the press, which have been the focus of much interest from amateur sleuths and code-crackers. Although dismissed as a suspect, the name of Arthur Leigh Allen, who died in 1992, once again cropped up after the most recent cracking of one of the codes in 2011.

From 1968 until 1984, "The Capital City Murderer" of Madison in Wisconsin targeted long-haired women aged between 17 and 24. Eight were abducted and stabbed to death.

"The Monster of Florence" came to prominence again recently with the 2007 murder of Meredith Kercher, and the subsequent trials and 2011 acquittal of Amanda Knox and Raffaele Sollecito in Perugia. Both cases involved the same prosecuting magistrate, Giuliano Mignini, who both times tried to claim that satanic sects were to blame. Between 1968 and 1985, there were 16 murders, mostly of young couples parked in lovers' lanes in and around Florence. While four local men were convicted of the murders, doubt still surrounds the true identity of the serial killer. Several other suspects were arrested, then had to be released when the killer struck again while they were in custody. One victim was stabbed 97 times and her vagina mutilated using a grapevine. Two other women had their montes veneris or pubic areas excised using a serrated blade. Breasts were also removed, and one was even posted, along with a taunting letter, to the prosecution team.

Since 1969, at least 43 women have mysteriously disappeared along a 500-mile stretch of Highway 16 that links British Columbia's Prince

George and Prince Rupert, which has been dubbed the "Highway of Tears". Eighteen of the murders show striking similarities, suggesting they are the work of a serial killer.

"The Black Doodler" killed 14 and assaulted three gay men in San Francisco between January 1974 and September 1975. He would sketch his victims before having sex with them and then stabbing them to death.

The Australian elite are suspects in the kidnapping, torture, rape and deaths of five men, aged between 14 to 25 years, which were carried out between the late 1970s to the mid-1980s, in a series of killings called "The Family Murders". The young male victims had each been drugged then later died from massive haemorrhaging. A large blunt spike had been forced into their anuses.

Before Richard Ramirez there was "The Original Night Stalker", who killed at least 10 and raped more than 50 women in Ventura, Dana Point and Irvine, California, between 1979 and 1986. All the crimes have been linked by DNA evidence but no suspect found.

In a complicated case at Toronto's Hospital for Sick Children from June 1980 to March 1981, 43 babies were thought to have been poisoned with a medical extract of the foxglove plant. Although there were suspects and one of the nursing staff was charged with four murders, there have been no convictions. The latest episode in this story has discovered that the rubber seals in syringes used during treatment of the babies, and throughout the medical industry, have been found to contain a toxic chemical that may have caused the deaths.

In the early 1980s, six women aged between 14 and 75 were killed by "The Tynong Murderer" near Melbourne in Australia. Few clues or leads exist and the police have recently asked for any information to stop this case going cold.

"The Frankford Slasher" raped and killed seven Philadelphia women, aged between 28 and 68 years old, between 1985 and 1990. One victim's vagina had been mutilated with a three-foot piece of wood, and another had been stabbed 74 times.

"The Stoneman" dropped a heavy stone or concrete slab onto the heads of his rough-sleeping victims, crushing their skulls. The killings began in Mumbai in 1985, claiming a dozen lives, and stopped just as quickly in mid-1988, only to apparently resurface in Calcutta in mid-1989. Another 12 homeless people died in the ensuing six months. The killing stopped when the police indiscriminately arrested any suspicious-looking person out on the streets late at night, but no culprit was found. Similar killings began in Assam in February 2008.

In the first known case of serial murder in South Korea, 10 women were found bound, raped and murdered between 1986 and 1991, in the city of Hwaseong, Gyeonggi province. Despite over 3,000 suspects being interrogated, no charges have been brought.

In Mumbai, "The Beer Man" murdered seven people between October 2006 and January 2007; the only clue left in each case was an empty beer bottle.

Thirteen gay men were shot dead between February 2007 and August 2008 in Carapicuíba, a city in the state of São Paulo in Brazil. There are no suspects and the culprit is simply known as "The Rainbow Maniac" in reference to the gay pride rainbow flag.

Body parts of four people were found in December 2010, and those of six more in March and April 2011, believed to have been murdered by "The Long Island Serial Killer" or "Gilgo Killer". In the worst series of New York murders since David Berkowitz, this serial killer has possibly murdered 11 victims and dumped their body parts along Long Island's Ocean Parkway. It has been suggested that the serial killer may be a policeman because of his apparent knowledge of police procedure.

As of January 2012, Chinese police voluntarily cancelled their leave so that they could help hunt for a serial bank robber in Nanjing, the capital of China's Jiangsu province. The robber is also a serial killer, having shot six people and injured two others, even when the robbery fails and he is forced to flee empty-handed. By March 2012, 13,000 police were hunting a single suspect, Zeng Kaigui, a former armed police officer who has been on the run for eight years.

Also in January 2012, former US Marine and Iraq War veteran Itzcoatl Ocampo was arrested and charged with the stabbing to death of four homeless men and two other people in Orange County, California.

In March 2012, it was announced that Michael Gargiulo, also known as "The Hollywood Ripper", who has been in the Los Angeles County Jail since 2008 for the murder of two Californian women, is actually suspected of killing 10.

Although Rodney Alcala – known as "The New Ted Bundy" and "The Dating Game Killer" because he once appeared on the US version of *Blind Date* – was sentenced to death in 2010 for murdering a 12-year-old girl and four women in California between 1977 and 1979, even though he denied all charges, police have launched a campaign to ascertain his true victim tally. Alcala raped, asphyxiated and then resuscitated his victims, so that he could continue to rape and strangle them. He also kept a photographic record with pictures of more than 100 different women, which was published by the police in an attempt to identify 30 of his victims.

In July 2010, police arrested Lonnie David Franklin, Jr, also known as "The Grim Sleeper", for murdering a minimum of 10 Los Angeles women since 1985. The police discovered his photographic record of 160 photographs. They received about 1,000 phone calls by the end of the first day on which they had appealed for information.

The job of the investigating police officer is made a lot easier if a serial killer confesses to their crimes, and, even better, leads them to the site of their victims' remains. While this doesn't usually lead to more convictions, because a life sentence without parole is the most a killer can serve, it does help account for missing persons, and may also bring some kind of closure for the victims' families. The most recent example is that of Wesley Shermantine and accomplice Loren Herzog, known as "The Speed Freak Killers". Shermantine is awaiting execution on San Quentin State Prison's death row for the murder of four people between 1984 and 1999, so he has little to lose by admitting to more murders. In March 2012, he wrote to CBS confessing to a total of 72 murders, and even incriminated a third killer.

This list is nowhere near complete. In fact, the horrifying reality is that it hardly scratches the surface. While the FBI estimate that between 35 and 50 serial killers are currently active in the USA, others argue at least 1,000 victims are killed by serial killers working in the US medical profession each year. Worldwide there is no shortage of unsolved cases of serial murder, with alarming numbers of victims sporadically turning up, particularly in Russia and South America.

It's hard to believe that there has been a 40 per cent reduction in the homicide rate in the UK over the last decade. Hate crimes and gang warfare appear to be on the increase, as do mass murders. We seem to be caught in a spate of killing. The spree murders of Derrick Bird and Raoul Moat, both in 2010, are still recent, while the serial killings of Bellfield, Griffiths, Tobin, Shipman, Hardy and Wright have shocked and outraged the British public for their brutal cruelty and considerable waste of life. As the ink here dries, the dismembered body of actress Gemma McCluskie, who once appeared on millions of screens nationwide in the soap *EastEnders*, is being pulled out of Regent's Canal. Her brother is being charged with her murder. Already the site of one serial killer's dumped body parts, how many more victims will be pulled from its murky depths?